BREAKING THE HOUSE OF PAMUNKEY

The Final Powhatan War and the Fall of an American Indian Empire

Lars C. Adams

Published by Backintyme Publishing
Crofton, Kentucky, U.S.A.

Backintyme Publishing
1341 Grapevine Rd.
Crofton, KY 42217
270-985-8568
Website: http://backintyme.biz
Email:backintyme@mehrapublishing.com
Printed in the United States of America
September 2017
ISBN: 9780939479016
Library of Congress Control Number: 2017952582

BREAKING THE HOUSE OF PAMUNKEY

Lars C. Adams
Foreword Dr. Helen C. Rountree

Dedicated to my grandmother, Carole Carpenter, who helped give me the love of history and reading that I will always carry with me.

Also to my wife Morgan, a fellow renegade who has given me nothing but encouragement, love and support in the completion of this volume.

Foreword

The shortage of records about Virginia surviving from the 1640s has led many scholars, including me, to give the period a rather quick go-by and concentrate elsewhere. But here we have a scholarly work that has been written by someone who is fascinated by that timeframe, and who has been willing to do a tremendous amount of peripheral research in order to bring it to life. He does not just write about historical events, compelling as those are during any war. He writes about the vastly different cultures of the antagonists, to explain their motives and behavior, not only towards each other but also -- since both peoples were divided among themselves -- toward various of their own people. What emerges is a well-woven tapestry that makes a vivid story. I hope that readers will enjoy this book as much as I did.

--Dr. Helen C. Rountree

Acknowledgements

So many people have come together to help with this book's completion. First of all a special thank you to Dr. Helen Rountree who has patiently worked with me to smooth out the manuscript and offer her expert advice. Her expertise in this area has in no small way made this book far better than it would have been otherwise. Marvin Jones, my dear friend and colleague, who introduced me to this publisher, and continues to support me just as I support him, and who also reviewed this manuscript and offered excellent advice. Dr. Buck Woodard of the College of William and Mary has given invaluable input, particularly in the early chapters, and has been a great help to me on other projects over the past several years. Thank you to my exceedingly patient editor, Stacy Webb, and the other associated editors with Backintyme publishing, for continued editorial input. Thank you also to the staffs of the Waukegan, North Chicago, Wheeling and Gurnee Public Libraries who thanklessly and tirelessly engaged the interlibrary loan system that allow long distance research to me and countless scholars and students across the country. Also, the encouragement of and support of many other people such as J. Frederick Fausz, Assistant Chief Wayne Atkins, Dr. Arwin Smallwood, Doug Patterson, Mark Adams, Morgan Adams, all the members of the Chowanoke Descendants Community, my children and countless others will never be forgotten. Thank you all so very much!

Introduction

"upon Governor William Berkeley's conquest of Apechancanough it was by him and the government thought the safest way by setting all the lesser nations at Liberty from that obedience they paid to the house of Pamunkey to keep them divided and indeed the effect may be more advantageous to us for they like to warr with each other and destroy themselves more in a year than we can do it." - Thomas Ludwell, 1678

On a small Indian reservation near Richmond, Virginia, there is a sacred mound. It is inconspicuous, and without an interpretive sign a tourist might pass it by. But among the Pamunkey people, tradition holds that it contains the bones of Powhatan himself, the father of Pocahontas, as well as his lesser-known but equally important brother, Opechancano. If Opechancano is indeed buried there, his body must have been transferred to the Pamunkey as part of the peace talks that took place in 1646 following a bloody war. Opechancano, an old man who had led his people against the English tobacco plantations, had been shot in the back by a prison guard at Jamestown. Most Americans have heard of great leaders like Sitting Bull, Geronimo and Tecumseh, but it was Opechancano who came before them all. He was the first great resistance leader to fall. But his people did not.

In the summer of 2013, I had the honor of visiting the likely place Chief Opechancano was murdered in 1646. Jamestown has been under continual excavations for years. I watched as a group of interns uncovered a horse skeleton under several feet of packed dirt, meticulously picking at the earth that entombed it. Watching them work, I wondered what it must have been like for Opechancano to gaze out on the Englishmen who gawked at him a prison cell following his capture. He must have prayed for the future of his people, but I doubt he feared for his own life. At the opposite extreme, what of the colonists that captured him or the prison guard who would soon shoot Opechancano in the back? Surely both sides viewed themselves in the right. To the colonists, Opechancano had the same level of notoriety that Osama bin Laden has today. It is easy to judge the colonists as evil in hindsight, or the Indians in noble and romantic terms but that does not serve history well. The truth is that both sides were unable to see the perspective of the other, and both faced incredible hardships: Be that as it may, at the close of this war there was only one true victim. Out of the chaotic cauldron of bullets, burning and starvation came some of the most significant historical events to impact 17th century America.

Figure 1. Archaeologists uncovering a horse burial at James Fort, 2013. Photo by the author.

The Third Anglo-Powhatan War is nearly always explained within an epilogue, or perhaps more appropriately, an epitaph. It is shown either as concluding true Powhatan history, or brushed over as a largely inconsequential Indian war that was the final feeble protest of the disappearing Powhatan Indians in the face of their inevitable conquerors. Normally it is given two paragraphs, or at most, a few pages. The largest study to date has been one chapter within a history of the Virginian militia. The studies that have been devoted to this "final" Powhatan War are not altogether inaccurate, but are on the whole incomplete. In fact, most are not individual studies in and of themselves but repeat old information, usually within a broader historical work. I regard the best historical contribution on the Third Powhatan War as William Shea's *The Virginia Militia in the Seventeenth Century,* whose chapter within is based on an earlier paper of his.[1] His work does not mention some major campaigns, however, nor does it attempt to reconstruct Powhatan actions or perspective in any significant way. More recently J. Frederick Fausz, Helen Rountree, Martha McCartney, Frederick Gleach and some few others have made varying attempts at explaining different aspects of the war and Powhatan motivations during the conflict.[2] Altogether, however, the story of the Third Powhatan

[1]William L. Shea, *The Virginia Militia in the Seventeenth Century,* (Baton Rouge: Louisiana State University Press, 1983).

[2]Fausz, John Frederick, *The Powhatan Uprising of 1622: A Historical Study of Ethnocentrism and Cultural Conflict,* (PhD. Diss., College of William and Mary in Virginia, 1977) 582; Fausz, "Opechancanough, Indian Resistance Leader," in David Sweet and Gary Nash, eds., *Struggle and Survival in Colonial America,* (Berkeley and Los Angeles: University of California Press, 1981) 34; Helen Rountree, *Pocahontas's People: The Powhatan Indians of Virginia Through Four Centuries,* (Norman: University of Oklahoma Press, 1990) 83-88; Helen Rountree and E. Randolph Turner III, *Before and After Jamestown: Virginia's Powhatans and Their Predecessors,* (Gainesville, FL: University Press of Florida, 2002) 154; Martha MCartney, "Seventeenth Century Apartheid: The Suppression and Containment of Indians in Tidewater Virginia," in *Journal of Middle Atlantic Archeaology,*

War remains largely as it always has: another short story of a doomed Indian group. The following paragraphs summarize what is largely regurgitated again and again regarding the war.

> Opechancano, the Powhatans' leader and uncle of the famed Pocahontas, was reaching a very old age as he watched the English encroach further and further into his people's land. He had, in 1622, already made an attempt to destroy the English in an attack that killed 350 colonists, and by 1644, he deemed the time right to launch one final assault. On April 18, he unleashed his forces in a desperate surprise attack that killed more than previously, from four to five hundred, taking others captive. Because of the increase in English population to over 10,000, however, this did not affect them as severely as previously, when twenty-five percent of the population had been killed.
>
> His people did not continue to press in on the advantage, and withdrew following the attack, giving the English time to regroup and position themselves to retaliate. In the next two summers, relentless English attacks were extremely effective and forced the Powhatans from their towns with the construction of a series of forts and relentless patrols. In a bold move, Berkeley himself swept in to Opechancano's camp on horseback, taking him prisoner where he was later shot in prison. His successor, Necatowance, signed a treaty that transformed their sovereign

---

vol 1 (1985) 47-75; McCartney, "Cockacoeske, Queen of Pamunkey: Diplomat and Suzeraine," in *Powhatan's Mantle: Indians in the Colonial Southeast,* ed. Gregory A. Waselkov, Peter H. Wood and Tom Hatley (Lincoln: University of Nebraska Press, 1989) 243-245; Frederick W. Gleach, *Powhatan's World and Colonial Virginia: A Conflict of Cultures,* (Lincoln: University of Nebraska Press, 1997) 174-181.

chiefdom into a series of small tributary nations that would fade to insignificance.

If nothing else, I hope to change the previous narrative to reflect the fact that Virginia was far more desperate during this conflict than made out to be. Their shortages of food, clothing and supplies, along with extreme political unrest, made for the most miserable and unstable times since the beginning of the 17th century. Furthermore, while some Powhatans did withdraw, the majority did not and staged further attacks into the frontier once they realized that Virginia had run out of ammunition, creating a panic for acting governor Richard Kemp. Additionally, a mere two paragraphs, or even a whole chapter, is not enough space to capture the full details of two and a half years of war. I hope to capture as much detail and information about the individual people involved, both Powhatan and English, from what scanty records remain of the 1640s to reconstruct as vividly as possible the campaigns, battles and lives of individual families, soldiers, warriors and leaders.

Among today's Powhatan nations, the belief is that the original records from which we draw as source material are themselves biased, making a full picture of the entire story of history nearly impossible. According to the late Chief Emeritus Oliver Perry of the Nansemonds, "We were not savages, barbarians, nor heathens." The problem is that "what was written in the history books was slanted and written from the viewpoint of the so-called 'conquerors'." He also believed that the history presented in most textbooks is inaccurate, largely because it is based on the writings of English eyewitnesses, such as Smith and Strachey, who were themselves biased. They do not provide a complete picture. He, of course, was not wrong. While today's historians and anthropologists are far more culturally accepting than in decades past, it certainly presents a challenge when faced with sources that only lend to an English perspective.[3]

I do not believe I have any particular bias toward either side of this war. Although I am of native descent, I do not offer a unique native perspective from my own voice. Likewise, others of my ancestors were the Anglican colonists living in the frontier of this war. I have thus tried to understand this conflict in light of both sides, and attempt to see the war through both English and Indian eyes. It has not been easy, because the English perspective has always been the weightier one. It was they who made the records, and it is within the culture they created that I was raised. I attempt, however, to present the Powhatan perspective as much as possible. In researching the history of the war, there were few sweeping narratives to tell the complete story of the war. Except for Robert Beverley's narrative written decades after the conflict, most sources available were made in real time during the war, such as land deeds, court records and acts of the assembly.[4]

---

[3]Danielle Moretti-Langholtz, and, Sandra F. Waugaman, *We're Still Here: Contemporary Virginia Indians Tell Their Stories,* (Richmond: Palari Publishing, 2000) 11.

[4]Available land patent abstracts present information as to the extent of English plantations into Powhatan territory, Indian town positions, personal information on where colonial leaders lived, and in some instances direct references to events during the war. Fragmented court records are available for certain counties, namely York, Lower Norfolk and Northampton Counties. Of these, Lower Norfolk offers the best information on expeditions and other military action. The best real-time source by far, however, are the acts passed by the general assembly and transcribed by Hening, which tells of the battle plans, references events, gives government orders to commanders and contains the terms of the final treaty. These represent the core records, though crucial records are also available from contemporary depositions, narratives and letters, see note five. For the core records, see Nell Marion Nugent, ed., *Cavaliers and Pioneers: Abstracts of Virginia Land Patents and Grants, 1623-1800,* vol. 1 (Richmond: Press of the Dietz Printing Company, 1934); Beverley Fleet, *Virginia Colonial Abstracts, vol. 24, York County Records, 1633-1646* (Baltimore: Genealogical Publishing Company, 1961); Beverley Fleet, Virginia Colonial Abstracts, *Northampton County Records, 1645-1651,* (Baltimore: Genealogical Publishing Company, 1961); Alice Granbery Walter, *Lower Norfolk County,*

Additionally, several personal letters were preserved that were not originally intended for publications that have survived from the conflict.[5] This can be considered a good thing, for this means that while few; the surviving records bear little mark of fraudulence like John Smith's self-congradulatory writings. While having to reconstruct so much of the war from scratch is a challenge, I believe that there is also more room for native perspective than in most colonial Indian wars of the seventeenth century. Since most records were recorded in real time, in terms of financial statements, acts of the general assembly, land deeds, etc., there is less room for English-biased perspective to creep in. In addition, a unique set of documents collected from Indian elders' decades after the war gives a rare first person narrative

---

Virginia Court Records, Book "A" 1637-1646 & Book "B" 1646-1651/2, (Baltimore: Clearfield Company Inc., 2002); Conway Robinson, "Notes From the Council and General Court Records 1641-1659," in *The Virginia Magazine of History and Biography* No. 1(Jul 1900) 8:64-73; William Walker Hening, comp., *The Statutes at Large, Being a Collection of all the Laws of Virginia, from the First Session of the Legislator, in the Year 1619,* vol. 1, (New York, R. & W. & G. Bartow, 1823).

[5]Two letters from Puritan farmers in Virginia were published by a London Newspaper during the war in 1645. In 1649 a pamphlet was published by an anonymous author that gives information concerning the war, which references three letters coming from Virginia as its source material. Recently, a letter by acting governor Richard Kemp has been discovered and published, which contains excellent information. Finally, and most well-known, is Robert Beverley's history of Virginia, written in the early 18th century, that is most valuable for its information on the capture of Opechancano. Beverley knew Governor Berkeley personally and would have received this information from him, as well as Powhatans he interviewed. See Joseph Frank, "News From Virginny, 1644," in *The Virginia Magazine of History and Biography,* Vol. 65, No. 1 (Jan., 1957), pp. 84-87; Anonymous, "A Perfect Description of Virginia," [1649] in Peter Force, ed., *Tracts and Other Papers, Relating Principally to the Origin, Settlement, and Progress of the Colonies in North America, from the Discovery of the Country to the Year 1776,* Vol II (New York: Reprinted Under the Auspices of the Out-of-Print Books Committee of New York, 1947) 7-13; Richard Kemp to Sir William Berkeley, Feb. 27, 1645, in Warren M. Billings, ed., *The Papers of Sir William Berkeley, 1605-1677,* (Richmond: Library of Virginia, 2007) 61-62; Robert Beverley, *The History and Present State of Virginia,* [1705], (Chapel Hill: University of North Carolina Press, 1947).

from native sources for certain aspects of the war.[6] I also incorporate modern Mattaponi oral history whenever possible in an attempt to reconstruct the full history from both perspectives, in so much as the sources allow me.[7]

Within the text I prefer the term Powhatans to describe the native Algonquian peoples still under the chiefdom controlled by Opechancano. While specific tribal designations are often needed, such as Pamunkeys or Appamattocks, 'Powhatans' is the most commonly accepted word among today's scholars to describe any Algonquian nation that was once a part of the Powhatan Paramount Chiefdom. In the case of this book, however, there were many nations who were no longer a part of the chiefdom by 1644, and while ethnically they are today considered to be or have been Powhatans, for the sake of clarity I use the terms Rappahannocks, Accomacs and Patawomecs to describe tribal groups no longer affiliated with Opechancano by the outset of the Third Powhatan War.[8]

---

[6]Anonymous, "The Indians of Southern Virginia, 1650-1711. Depositions in the Virginia and North Carolina Boundary Case," *The Virginia Magazine of History and Biography* No. 4 (April, 1900) 7:337-338; Anonymous, "The Indians of Southern Virginia (Concluded)," *The Virginia Magazine of History and Biography* No. 1, (July 1900) 8:1-11.

[7]Dr. Linwood "Little Bear" Custalow and Angela L. "Silver Star" Daniel, *The True Story of Pocahontas: The Other Side of History,* (Golden, Fulcrum Publishing, 2007). This source is considered doubtful in historical accuracy by modern scholars, but I have chosen to include it when possible alongside historical sources for additional indigenous perspective.

[8]Rountree, *The Powhatan Indians of Virginia,* 7; Rountree, *Pocahontas's People,* 12-13.

Figure 2. A romanticized version of Pocahontas stands with arms outstretched at Jamestown Settlement, near the original site of Jamestown Fort. Popular myth often depicts indigenous Americans as noble savages, and here shows Pocahontas as welcoming the Europeans with open arms, ready for a new future. The reality is that Pocahontas was barely twelve years old and was kept captive against her will. Photo by the author.

Likewise, I use the terms tribe, nation, chiefdom, etc., interchangeably. I recognize the differing anthropological definitions in the use of such terms. For example, a tribal society is primarily a council based polity where most are regarded as equals and social rank is merit-based, a chiefdom is a socially unequal society which pays tribute to the chief, who holds power more or less absolutely, and a nation is the most complex form of government in which ideologies and governing systems are in place and able to remain intact without a particular chief in power. In this book, I use the term nation to indicate any independent polity that carries on government-to-government relations with another polity, regardless of its political development. Likewise, the term chiefdom is the most accurate term to use during this period, but it can be cumbersome, so I also use the terms tribe and nation for better flow.[9]

This war has first been termed the Third Anglo-Powhatan War by J. Frederick Fausz, who termed the 1610-1614 war the First Anglo-Powhatan War, and the 1622-1632 war the Second Anglo-Powhatan War. I have tried several different ways to change the term to something more specific and less cumbersome for the purposes of this book, but because the Third Anglo-Powhatan War is already accurate enough and widely accepted I opted not to change the name, though for easier reading I often call it simply the Third Powhatan War, or the 1644 War.[10] Additionally, I have retained the original spelling

---

[9]Robert L. Cameiro, "What Happened at the Flashpoint? Conjectures on Chiefdom Formation at the Very Moment of Conception," in Redmond, Elsa, ed., *Chiefdoms and Chieftaincy in the Americas,* (Gainesville, FL: University of Florida Press, 1998)18-42.
[10]John Frederick Fausz used these terms throughout his text, which has been adopted by all subsequent researchers. See Fausz, *The Powhatan Uprising of 1622,* 252-517.

and punctuation in the quotations from contemporary sources without alteration.

This war is significant for reasons other than that it was the war that finally broke the back of the once powerful Powhatan Chiefdom. Within this war some significant events and actions are of note that the reader should consider. As far as military action goes, this was the most successful the Virginian militia would ever be in the 17th century. Some of the first use of horses in English warfare saw action within this war as they were used as pack animals, mounts for officers and all-out cavalry raids. The longest range assault against a specific Indian target that I am aware of occurred in 1645 as over two hundred miles of river and ocean were traversed to attack a refugee Weyanoke group in an extraordinary action that would have significant historical impact in later decades. Within this war are also observable roots in later African-American slavery. What may have been the first recorded African-American uprising occurred on the Wormely Plantation and a subsequent exodus of African runaways to the Powhatans, in addition to the enslavement of many Powhatans to defray war costs.

Also, prior to this war, the Powhatan Empire completely encircled the English plantations. Opechancano largely controlled access to English goods to outside nations and restricted English relationships to outside native influences. Once the Powhatans were made tributary, the entire countryside opened up, and new interactions were possible. Sometimes the English came in peace. Other times the frontier was attacked by mysterious inland groups. New trade relationships were established and the Indian slave trade was tapped into. It was a different world before and following the 1644 war. Altogether, the Third Powhatan War clearly deserves a greater place in colonial history than has previously been allowed.

Table of Contents

Foreword ... vii
Acknowledgements ... viii
Introduction ... ix
Table of Contents ... xx
Tsenacomoco and Jamestown ... 1
- Landscape They Were Accustomed to Using ... 6
- Economy Supporting Warfare ... 9
- Population Supporting Warfare ... 10
- Calling up Fighting Men ... 12
- Ordnance ... 13
- Transport of Men and Ordinance ... 15
- Usual Strategies ... 16
- The Leaders ... 19

A Buildup of Tensions ... 29
"Fearful Flames:" The Great Assault of 1644 ... 53
"Irreconcileable enemyes:" Virginia's battle plan ... 87
Traitorous and Seditious Murmurings ... 103
"Our hopes almost spent," The Autumn and Winter of 1644 ... 127
- Powhatans During Wartime ... 127
- The Weyanoke Rebellion ... 130
- The Main Fronts ... 134

A Reversal of Fortunes ... 143
"The Southward March" ... 151
The Battle of Weyanoke Creek ... 163
"Imposibillity of further Revenge upon them" ... 177
"That great bloody Monster": The Murder of Opechancano ... 189
Tributary Nations: The Subjugation of the Powhatan ... 197
Conclusions ... 209
"We're Still Here" ... 217
Appendix I:
- Necatowance Treaty ... 231
  - Act I ... 233
  - Act II ... 233
  - Act III ... 233

Act IV 233
Act V 234
Act VI 234
Act VII 234
Act VIII 235
Act IX 235
Act X 235
Act XI 235
Act XII 236

Appendix II:
Known Engagements of the Third Anglo Powhatan War and Partially Reconstructed Roster of English and Powhatan Forces 236
Great Powhatan Assault 237
Initial Retaliatory Raids 237
Nansemond Raid 238
Weyanoke Raid 238
Pamunkey March/ Battle of Menmend 238
Chicahominy 240
Powhatan Autumn Offensive 241
English Autumn Raid 241
Autumn Raids 241
Autumn Raid 242
Frontier Patrols from Middle Plantation 242
Construction of Forts 242
Southward March 243
Bibliography 247
Index 259

Tsenacomoco and Jamestown

"They have a ... prophesie likewise amongst them, that twice they should give overthrow and dishearten the attempters, and such straungers as should invade their territories or labour to settle a plantation among them, but the third tyme they themselves should fall into their subjection, and under their conquest." -William Strachey as informed by Machumps, 1612[11]

Figure 3. A traditional Powhatan Yehawkan, made of reed mats covering a pole frame. Jamestown Settlement living history museum. Photo by the author.

[11] William Strachey, *Historie of Travaile into Virginia Britannia* (1612), (London, Printed for the Hakluyt Society, 1849) 101.

Breaking the House of Pamunkey

The cold was beginning to break in Virginia. Soon, the ground would be ready for tobacco cash crops and the Indian corn the colonists had become accustomed to eating. Hogs foraged freely in the woods, digging up any root and acorn they could find, including, too often, the crops of nearby Indian fields. It was the March of 1644, and rumblings of war were in the air. For nearly two years, Virginian colonists awaited for scraps of news from England as civil war continued to tear the country apart. Incoming merchant ships sympathized either with the King's forces or Parliament, sometimes bearing letters of marque, complicating trade. Virginia's administration remained loyal to the King, but with many pro-Parliament colonists, tensions were beginning to run high. But this was all a distraction. Watching them, sensing their unease were members of the Powhatan Paramount Chiefdom under the leadership of Paramount Chief Opechancano.

By that March, preparations had already been underway for some time. An old chief, who would bleed out on the dirt floor of a Jamestown prison in two years' time, listened carefully to his priests and councilors. Opechancano was planning an assault of massive proportions. He had done it before. In 1622, he wiped out nearly a third of the English settlers in an action that threatened to destroy the entire colony. He had participated in the first Powhatan War of 1610-1614, and was even present in the region when the Spanish opened fire in the 1570s. He was a warrior, and his was a life of war. But by 1644, he was old. He had seen so many things. He saw his niece, Pocahontas, married to colonist John Rolphe and move away to England. She never came back. He had seen his people's population and territory shrink exponentially over the decades from war, disease, and land theft. He was nearly 100 years old, an invalid, and could scarcely open his eyes. If there was one thing he could hope to accomplish before he died, it would be to restore his people's place of power over the English, and over all others. One last fight.

The Powhatan Paramount Chiefdom had once been the most powerful indigenous American polity in the Mid-Atlantic. Brought to power by Opechancano's older brother, Wahunsenaca (called Chief Powhatan by the colonists), the chiefdom comprised up to 14,000 people and over 30 towns and districts that stretched from roughly the northern to southern border of present day Virginia, from the coast inland to the piedmont. By 1607, Jamestown was founded, which marked the beginning of the end of Powhatan's "Empire." The romanticized legend of John Smith and Pocahontas distracts from the realities faced by the Powhatans. The English continued to claim more and more land for themselves, blatantly disrespecting Powhatan sovereignty. Disease spread, and war would continue to break out, killing many hundreds over the years.

The Powhatan War of 1644 was the shortest, but most conclusive, consequential, and possibly the most violent of the three major wars that Opechancano would fight against the invading colonists. The massive assault that would kill up to 500 colonists has little rival in the annals of New World history. In fact, in terms of sheer casualties, it was the most effective assault carried out by any Indigenous American group (in North or South America) against any European target. This fact alone, along with the far reaching consequences of the conflict, should elevate the historical status of this war to have far more attention paid than has previously been allowed.[12]

---

[12] The only other assault I have found that may tie with the Powhatan assault of 1644, in terms of casualties, was the Fort Mims Massacre during the Creek War of 1813, in

The Powhatan people, as a united (more or less) polity of associated chiefdoms, was a fairly new entity in the indigenous geopolitical scene by the time the English began colonization in 1607. Wahunsenaca, the chief in office at the height of Powhatan power, inherited the beginnings of his "empire" from an unknown predecessor (probably his maternal uncle or great-uncle as Powhatans trace their descent by matriline) in the mid-1500s at the heads of the James and York rivers. From there, probably starting in the 1570s, he expanded toward the coast, using diplomacy, marriage, intimidation and sometimes outright war to enlarge his realm. He was still in the process of expanding when the English interrupted his campaigns. His people were farmers, using horticulture to grow primarily corn, beans and squash, although this was only a partial reliance. Powhatans depended heavily on hunting, fishing and gathering, especially in the times of year was grain stores ran out.[13]

---

which up to 500 militia, slaves, and pro-English Indians were killed or captured. "Only" about 250 bodies remained on the battlefield, however. It appears that Opechancano's 1644 assault remains, in fact, the most destructive indigenous assault on any European colonists in North or South America ever on record.

[13] Rountree and Turner, "The Evolution of the Powhatan Paramount Chiefdom in Virginia," 265-296. Custalow and Daniel, *The True Story of Pocahontas,* 19-20;Feest, *The Powhatan Tribes,* 13, Townsend, *Pocahontas and the Powhatan Dilemma,* 43-49; Rountree, *Pocahontas's People,* 36-37; Helen Rountree, *Pocahontas, Powhatan, Opechancanough: three Indian Lives Changed by Jamestown,* (Charlottesville, University of Virginia Press, 2005) 212; Rountree, "Powhatans and the English: A Case of Multiple Conflicting Agendas," 184-190; Fausz, *The Powhatan Uprising of 1622,* 362-364; Rountree, *Pocahontas's People,*68-71.

Figure 4. The only known depiction of Opechancono, 1607. The engraving depicts John Smith grabbing his hair lock and taking the weroance prisoner. The artist was using older engravings of Virginia Indians as an example and therefore this is probably not a close approximation to Opechancano's true likeness. John Smith, Generall Historie of Virginia.

As for the English, Virginia was considered an untouched Eden, full of natural resources and most of all, space. England was overcrowded, especially in the urban centers, and commoners lucky enough to find employment were restricted to menial labor and trades with little hope of elevating themselves to higher tiers of society. In England, those who owned land attained higher societal status and greater personal freedom, but with all the land taken up and kept within families, this was nearly impossible for most. Virginia, however, was different. It was looked at as an escape. As advertised under the headright system, any incoming settlers who paid for their own passage or for others received fifty acres per head.[14] If one could not pay for their own passage they served under a master for seven years, after which they would receive their own plot. By the 1640s, they were coming in droves. But they made an analytical error. The land was not free or untouched. The Powhatans would take offense.[15]

Landscape They Were Accustomed to Using

Although some Virginians were born in America, the majority were immigrants from England. Their land was a temperate, deciduous forest (albeit largely cleared for agricultural fields for crops and grazing) that had four clearly defined seasons. Most English people who became immigrants to Virginia were from the cities, especially Bristol, and did not always have much

---

[14] Robert M. Bliss, *Revolution and Empire: English Politics and the American Colonies in the Seventeenth Century, (*New York, Manchester University Press, 1990) 29

[15] Peter Cross, *The Origins of the English Gentry,* (Cambridge: Cambridge University Press, 2005) 4-14; Marjorie Keniston McIntosh, *Poor Relief in England, 1350-1600,* (Cambridge: Cambridge University Press, 2011) 271-298

interaction with the natural environment. With a large population density and large urban centers, the demand for lumber was high, depleting the island of much of its tree cover. Consequently, much lumber had to be imported.[16]

Virginia, though also a temperate deciduous forest, was warmer than England, had sandier soil, and in the tidewater, was usually low and swampy. Much of England was also marshy, but many nevertheless expressed their surprise at Virginia's landscape and found it difficult to adjust. The Powhatans recognized five seasons and, though they sowed fields, it did not significantly alter the landscape. According to John Smith, "Their winter some call *Popanow*, the spring *Cattapeuk*, the sommer *Cohattayough*, the earing of their Corne *Nepinough*, the harvest and fall of leafe *Taquitock.* From September vntill the midst of November are the chiefe feasts & sacrifice. Then haue they plentie of fruits as well planted as naturall, as corne, green and ripe, fish, fowle, and wilde beasts exceeding fat."[17] They relied heavily on the land for naturally produced plants and animals to sustain them. Even so, Virginia was not an untouched wilderness. Powhatans would clear large swaths of undergrowth with controlled forest fires for easy traveling around their towns, as well as to encourage new plant growth which in turn would attract deer.[18]

---

[16] Oliver Rackham, *Trees and Woodland in the British Landscape: the Complete History of Britain's Trees, Woods & Hedgerows,* (London: Phoenix Press, 2001); Francis Pryor, *The Making of the British Landscape: How We Have Transformed the Land, From Prehistory to Today,* (New York: Penguin Books, 2010).

[17] Smith, *Generall Historie,* 28.

[18] Sawyer, Roy, *America's Wetland: An Environmental and Cultural History of Tidewater Virginia and North Carolina,* (Charlottesville, University of Virginia Press, 2010) 56

Figure 5. 1586 watercolor of a North Carolina Algonquian by artist John White. This rendition was used as source material for the engraving of many future Virginia Algonquians, including the preceding engraving of Opechancano.
John White, courtesy of the British Museum.

Economy Supporting Warfare

The English relied extensively on food production via agriculture, sowing specialized plowed fields of wheat, barley, oats, rye, as well as vegetables and legumes, in addition to animal proteins obtained through cultivated meat, dairy products, and fish provided by large fishing fleets. Men were the main providers. They were farmers, specialized tradesmen, merchants, sailors, soldiers, etc., with women primarily in the roles of housekeepers, providing upkeep for the home and raising children, though som in the lower classes were maids and servants. All in all, the English had an adversarial view of nature. It was to be conquered and subjugated; existing for the purpose of human benefit.[19]

Powhatans, like the English, cultivated fields of crops (maize, beans, and squash primarily) but did so on a less intensive scale. Their fields were small compared to the English, but also contained all three primary crops together in the same field. Smith again informs us: "They make a hole in the earth with a sticke, and into it they put foure graines of wheate and two of beanes These holes they make foure foote one from another; Their women and children do continually keepe it with weeding, and when it is growne middle high, they hill it about like a hop-yard… In Aprill they begin to plant, but their chiefe plantation is in May, and so they continue till the midst of Iune. What they plant in Aprill they reape in August, for May in September, for Iune in October."[20]

---

[19] Sex Roles in England. Marjorie Keniston McIntosh, *Working Women in English Society, 1300 – 1620,* (Cambridge: Cambridge University Press, 2005) 3-4.
[20] Ibid; Smith, *Generall Historie, 28;* Sawyer, Roy, *America's Wetland: An Environmental and Cultural History of Tidewater Virginia and North Carolina,* (Charlottesville, University of Virginia Press, 2010) 120-124.

These crops (planted by women with specially crafted digging sticks) were of great benefit, but were not intensively planted enough to provide the sole source of caloric intake. Besides tending the fields, women (who were not subservient to men but were autonomous individuals, in contrast with the English who considered women to be property) were the primary gatherers of wild plant foods such as tree nuts, roots and tubers such as tuckahoe, which grew in the swampy areas that the English found useless.[21] Men were responsible for animal protein, gathering a great deal of fish from reed-walled weirs, spearfishing, as well as hunting and trapping land animals such as deer, small game and fowl.[22] Both sexes contributed to the needs of the family and community, and it was this reliance on wild food found in "waste" land that made Powhatan families difficult to track down in war time. [23]

Population Supporting Warfare

Societal structure had more differences than similarities between English and Powhatan populations. The English had a very dense population, about five million people, which overpopulated the island. Furthermore, it had very rigid social

---

[21] Rountree, Helen C., "Powhatans and the English: A Case of Multiple Conflicting Agendas," in Rountree, Helen c., ed., *Powhatan Foreign Relations, 1500-1722,* (Charlottesville, University Press of Virginia, 1993) 174-175.

[22] Sawyer, Roy, *America's Wetland: An Environmental and Cultural History of Tidewater Virginia and North Carolina,* (Charlottesville, University of Virginia Press, 2010) 83-84, 86-89, 97-98; Binford, Lewis, *Cultural Diversity Among Aboriginal Cultures of Coastal Virginia and North Carolina,* (New York, Garland Publishing, 1991) 33-34; Ben C. McCary, *Indians in Seventeenth Century Virginia,* (Williamsburg, Garret and Massie, Inc., Virginia 350th Anniversery Celebration Corporation, 1957) 16-23.

[23] Sex Roles and other means of sustenance besides crops

classes stemming from inherited family connections. Gentlemen were able to obtain important positions and were not required to engage in hard labor. Commoners had to make do as farmers and tradesmen, and had to pay deference to Gentlemen. This is an over-simplification of the many layers of English society, but commoners had almost no hope of advancing to higher tiers, and overpopulation left the unemployment rate very high, with widespread poverty as a result.[24]

In Virginia, or rather Tsenacomoco as the Powhatans called it, there were about 10-15000 people in an area roughly the same size as England, giving wide expanses of natural resources between each populated place.[25] There was little to no craft specialization among the Powhatans, excepting priests, who did not have to produce their own food. All others made what they needed. Except for chiefly families, whose status was inherited, "commoners" as the English called them (in comparing them to their own society) earned their status through prowess in warfare and skill in hunting and gathering. A male Powhatan "commoner" who was particularly skilled in warfare and hunting could advance himself by becoming a war captain or advisor to the weroance, as well as amassing status symbols such as good clothing and bark covered houses (rather than poorer reed-mats). Such advancement would be impossible in England. Though chiefly families typically were dressed better and had more corn and ornamentation than the rest of the population, this

---

[24] Peter Cross, *The Origins of the English Gentry,* (Cambridge: Cambridge University Press, 2005) 4-14; Marjorie Keniston McIntosh, *Poor Relief in England, 1350-1600,* (Cambridge: Cambridge University Press, 2011) 271-298

[25] Turner,E. Randolph, "Difficulties in the Archeological Identification of Chiefdoms as Seen in the Virginia Coastal Plain during the Late Woodland and Early Historic Periods," in Custer, Jay, ed., *Late Woodland Cultures of the Middle Atlantic Region,* (Newark, University of Delaware Press, 1986) 21-22

difference was only obvious during diplomatic occasions when the English had occasion of observing them. On typical days, there was little to tell the difference between these two "classes."[26]

Calling up Fighting Men

Neither the English nor the Powhatans had a regular standing army. The English had regular officers, but foot soldiers were called up by conscription whenever the occasion required. When not at war, firearms were forbidden to the lower orders, only being permitted to the gentlemen, who were, as one might expect, normally the only ones who held officer positions. As such, whenever a large-scale maneuver was needed, a great deal of time, planning and resource gathering was necessary.[27]

Among the Powhatans, not only were weapons permitted to the "commoners," they were essentially required as hunting was done with many of the same weapons as warfare (bows and arrows, not normally clubs).[28] Every man was a fighting man among the Powhatans, and "commoners" could attain rank as a war captain through personal skill and exploits. War was normally fought as small-scale guerilla raids and ambushes, often out of personal vengeance rather than by the explicit command of the weroance.[29] When the paramount chief did command a large scale assault, such as Opechancano's 1622 and 1644 attacks, a messenger would be assigned to run to the

[26] Powhatan "classes" upward mobility, etc

[27] James Scott Wheeler, *The Making of a World Power: War and Military Revolution in Seventeenth-Century England,* (Phoenix Mill: Sutton Publishing, 1999) 22-75.

[28] Rountree, *The Powhatan Indians of Virginia,* 124

[29] Ibid, 121.

surrounding subordinate chiefdom and call them to arms. As best stated by colonist William Strachey:

> "When they intend any wars, the weroances usually advise with their priests or conjurers, their allies and best trusted chauncellors and friends; but comonly the priests have the resulting voice, and determyne therefore their resolutions. Eyther a weroance or some lusty fellowe is appointed captaine over a nation or regiment to be led forth; and when they would presse a number of soldiers to be ready by a day, an officer is dispacht awaye, who comyng into the townes, or otherwise meeting such whome he hath order to warne, to strike them over the back a sound blow with a bastinado, and bidds them to be ready to serve the great king, and tells them the rendezvous, from whence they dare not at any tyme appointed be absent. They seldome make wars for lands or goods, but for women and children, and principally for revenge, so vindicative and jealous they be to be made dirision of, and to be insulted upon by an enemy."[30]

Ordnance

Technologically, the English had the obvious advantage of firearms and steel. In England, musketeers would work from behind the protection of pikemen, who utilized long spiked poles to keep enemy cavalry at bay while the musketeers did their work. In Virginia, pikemen were done away with, adapting to the fighting style of the Powhatans somewhat by using forest patrols

[30] Strachey, *Historie of Travaile,* 100-101.

and amphibious assaults using strictly matchlock rifles and pistols, swords and torches. Horses were used to an extent, mostly by officers or as pack animals, but most attacks involved foot soldiers on the ground. Armor in England consisted of a leather buff coat, over which a chain mail suit would protect against enemy blows and reduce the impact of musket balls. Steel armor plates would be used by officers. In Virginia, chain mail was rarely used, armor being restricted to the leather buff coat, which offered some protection, but did little against Powhatan arrows and gunfire.[31]

Traditional Powhatan weaponry included the bow and arrow (which had an accurate, level range of forty yards and could pierce wooden shields), stone tomahawks, knives (stone, bone and reed, but perhaps just as commonly English knives of metal by the 1640s), as well as long, fire-hardened wooden "swords" called monahawks. The Powhatans desired firearms from the moment they first saw them demonstrated, and over the decades, especially during and after the 1620s, black market trade and theft brought a sizeable cache of matchlocks into Opechancano's arsenal. It is reported that some Virginian and North Carolinian Algonquians used armor constructed of reeds, but there is no evidence that this lasted up to the time of the Third Powhatan War. Overall, stealth and speed were favored over the need for armor, especially in the face of English firearms, and although firearms seem to be a major advantage over the bow, an arrow could be loosed many times faster than a

---

[31] Wheeler, *The Making of a World Power,* 3, 71, 76; Gaunt, Peter, *The English Civil Wars, 1642-1651,* (Oxford, Osprey Publishing, 2003) 28-29.

muzzle loader could be reloaded, and were often much more accurate.[32]

Transport of Men and Ordinance

In Virginia, the English colonists relied on waterways as the fastest and easiest mode of transportation, both for everyday purposes and for wartime assaults. Travel overland was difficult. Plantations were often interrupted by large swaths of swampland with no road system other than preexisting Indian trails, and few knew them well. In terms of transporting large groups of men and supplies for attacks, waterways made the most sense. Light foot patrols, however, were conducted during wartime by knowledgeable locals. Few had horses, but in some 1640s English assaults, horses were used as pack animals for particularly large forces. The trouble with relying for the most part on amphibious assaults, however, was that the Powhatans would often, if not usually, see the English coming and retreat before the forces arrived.[33]

The Powhatans' main highways of transport, like the English, were the ample waterways that permeated the Virginian tidewater. These were routes used to communicate between towns, trade, hunt or fish, and often engage in war. It would be a mistake to say that canoe travel was the primary mode of assault, however. Attacks were normally staged as an unexpected ambush, therefore moving undetected through the forests was

---

[32] Smith, *Generall Historie,* 31; Rountree, *The Powhatan Indians of Virginia,* 124; Rountree, *Pocahontas's People,* 31.

33 William Shea, "Virginia At War, 1644-1646", in *Military Affairs*, Vol. 41, No. 3 (Oct., 1977), 142-147;

usually deemed best. Powhatan warriors were accustomed to travelling at a jog for most of the day, if not an all-out run. Since they usually travelled light, this was easier than for the English. Normally, autumn was considered the best time for warfare, as the harvest was just stored and winter dispersals were beginning. In assaulting the English, spring was usually selected for the same reason; the winter grain stores would have run out, requiring dispersal from the towns before the next planting season. Mobility; not having to protect a nuclear town site, made it difficult for the English to locate Powhatan habitations in reprisal. [34]

Usual Strategies

In England, war was fought in the open field in massed formations of infantry, cavalry and artillery. Travel was fairly slow going, and foot soldiers were considered quite expendable, (sometimes being decimated). English colonists in Virginia would have been used to this style of fighting, but adapted to the Virginian culture and landscape by preforming small scale foot patrols and amphibious assaults without the use of traditional pikemen and cavalry. Powhatan-style warfare could not be imitated entirely by the English, but it was quickly recognized that marching mass formations of infantry in battle lines would be a futile effort.[35]

Powhatans, as opposed to the English, considered no one expendable. The goal was to eliminate as many of the enemy as

[34] Rountree, Helen, "The Powhatans and Other Woodland Indians as Travellers," in Rountree, Helen, ed., *Powhatan Foreign Relations, 1500-1722,* (Charlottesville, University Press of Virginia, 1993) 26-29, 34, 39

[35] Gaunt, *English Civil Wars,* 28-29.

possible while preserving one's own. Says Strachey, "Their chief attempts are by strategems, surprizes, and treacheries, yet the weroances, women, or children, they put not to death, but keep them captives."[36] All in all, warfare was a very personal affair to increase one's status in society by preforming brave acts. War was conducted as guerilla style ambushes, often lying in wait along well-travelled paths for the enemy to pass by, or to attack a town while the men were away, taking away the women and children to be incorporated in Powhatan society.[37] Little beyond one's weapons and a pouch of corn meal was taken into war; discomfort was taken in stride. John Smith witnessed a mock battle at the outset of colonization in which two Powhatan companies divided themselves into "Powhatans" and "Monacans," (their enemies to the west), and engaged in a staged battle. He thus was able to witness traditional Powhatan fighting tactics firsthand:

> "Having painted and disguised themselues in the fiercest manner they could devise. They divided themselues into two Companies, neare a hundred in a company. The one company called *Monacans*, the other *Powhatans*. Either army had their Captaine. These as enemies tooke their stands a musket shot one from another; ranked themselues 15 a breast, and each ranke from another 4 or 5 yards, not in fyle, but in the opening betwixt their fyles. So the Reare could shoot as conveniently as the Front... On each flanke a Serieant, and in the Reare an Officer for Lieutenant, all duly keeping their orders, yet

---

[36] Strachey, *Historie of Travaile,* 107.

[37] Frederick W. Gleach, *Powhatan's World and Colonial Virginia: A Conflict of Cultures,* (Lincoln, University of Nebraska Press, 1997) 43-45;

> leaping and singing after their accustomed tune, which they onely vse in Warres. Vpon the first flight of arrowes they gaue such horrible shouts and screeches, as so many infernall hell hounds could not haue made them more terrible. When they had spent their arrowes, they ioyned together prettily, charging and retyring, every ranke seconding other. As they got advantage they catched their enemies by the hayre of the head, and downe he came that was taken. His enemy with his wooden sword seemed to beat out his braines, and still they crept to the Reare, to maintaine the skirmish. The *Monacans* decreasing, the *Powhatans* charged them in the forme of a halfe Moone; they vnwilling to be inclosed, fled all in a troope to their *Ambuscadoes*, on whom they led them very cunningly. The *Monacans* disperse themselues among the fresh men, wherevpon the *Powhatans* retired, with all speed to their seconds; which the *Monacans* seeing took that advantage to retire againe to their owne battell, and so each returned to their owne quarter. All their actions, voyces, and gestures, both in charging and retiring were so strained to the height of their qualitie and nature, that the strangenesse thereof made it seeme very delightfull."[38]

Intertribal warfare often also took on the nature of the startling assaults later carried out against the English. For example, in the early 1600s, Chief Wahunsenaca (Powhatan) had reason to mistrust or otherwise have enmity with the small Piankatank nation on the coast of the Chesapeake Bay. A large

---

[38] Smith, *Generall Historie,* 33.

contingent of warriors entered the town, pretending that Wahunsenaca wanted them to come along for a communal hunt, but when their guard was let down, they instantly produced their weapons and killed most of the men, taking the women and children as captives. A similar scenario may have befallen the Kekoughtans.[39] In another incident among culturally similar Algonquians in North Carolina, the Coree and Matchapunga nations had been in enmity for a very long time, but had concluded a peace. The Coree came, seemingly unarmed, to a great feast where they celebrated with their new "friends" until some signal was given, and each grabbed a hidden tomahawk from under their robe and killed a great deal of the Matchapunga men.[40] In the 1622 attack on the English, familiar Powhatans came and ate with the English, worked alongside them and traded them until the appointed time, when they grabbed the closest bludgeon at hand and clubbed the nearest Englishman. At that point a larger contingent of warriors hidden in the woods charged and helped to finish them off.[41]

The Leaders

Opechancano, the younger brother of Wahunsenaca, was the paramount chief of the Powhatans by the 1640s. Little is known about Opechancano's early life, though some have

---

[39]Gleach, *Powhatan's World,* 26, 43-45, 54. Rountree, *The Powhatan Indians of Virginia,* 118-19.

[40]Lawson, *A New Voyage to Carolina ..., (Books London, 1709) 200.*

[41]Fausz, *The Powhatan Uprising of 1622,* 363-364; Gleach, *Powhatan's World and Colonial Virginia,* 146-163.

speculated he was in contact with the Spanish during the 1570s.[42] Under Wahunsenaca's leadership, he was *weroance* of the Youghtanunds and then the Pamunkeys during the earliest encounters with the English. It was he who captured John Smith and brought him before his brother (where Smith reported that Pocahontas saved his life).[43] Smith would later capture Opechancano, grabbing him by the hair and holding a pistol to his chest, demanding food from the Pamunkeys in exchange for Opechancano's life.[44] Unfortunately for the memory of Opechancano, his life was much more poorly recorded than his older brother. Though his exploits in war were written down, none of his oratory, hardly any personal interactions with his own people, or anything to describe his personal character, survives. As observed by Rountree:

> "…the very few eyewitness account we do have of Opechancanough show him not as a generous though wily host but as an able leader who had been put on the defensive. This is a pity, for reading between the lines, among his own people Opechancanough was at least as able a politician and diplomat as his brother had been… [John Smith] wrote so voluminously about his time in Virginia that the people he had the most dealings

---

[42] Barbour, Philip L., *Pocahontas and Her World,* (Boston, Houghton Mifflin Company, 1970) 4-5; Lewis, Clifford M., and Loomie, Albert J., *The Spanish Jesuit Mission in Virginia, 1570-1572,* (Chapel Hill, University of North Carolina Press, 1953) 17-18

[43] Barbour, Philip L., *Pocahontas and Her World,* (Boston, Houghton Mifflin Company, 1970) 18-22

[44] Fausz, J. Frederick, "Opechancanough, Indian Resistance Leader," in David Sweet and Gary Nash, eds., *Struggle and Survival in Colonial America,* (Berkeley and Los Angeles, University of California Press, 1981) 24-26; Barbour, Philip L., *Pocahontas and Her World,* (Boston, Houghton Mifflin Company, 1970) 52-66; Townsend, Camilla, *Pocahontas and the Powhatan Dilemma,* (New York, Hill and Wang, 2004) 43-49;

with – Powhatan, among the native people – come alive. Opechancanough had no such scribe."[45]

Opechancano's involvement in the first Powhatan War of 1610-14 is little known, though he almost certainly played a role as one of the war's leaders. Wahunsenaca died in 1618, leaving leadership to another brother, Opitchapam, but he was little respected by the Powhatans, with Opechancano commanding the loyalty of the people.[46] According to later colonist Robert Beverly, Opechancano was "a Man of large Stature, noble Presence, and extraordinary Parts. Tho' he had no Advantage of Literature. . . he was perfectly skilled in the Art of Governing his… Country-men. He caused all the Indians far and near to dread his Name, and had them all entirely in Subjection."[47]

---

[45] Rountree, *Pocahontas, Powhatan,Opechancanough,*190

[46] Ibid, 163; Townsend, Camilla, *Pocahontas and the Powhatan Dilemma,* (New York, Hill and Wang, 2004) 161-162; Rountree, Helen C., "Powhatans and the English: A Case of Multiple Conflicting Agendas," in Rountree, Helen c., ed., *Powhatan Foreign Relations, 1500-1722,* (Charlottesville, University Press of Virginia, 1993) 184-190

[47]Beverley, *The History and Present State of Virginia,* 61.

Figure 6. Wahunsenaca, the Powhatan leader at English contact, expanded from the western James and Pamunkey Rivers eastward to the coast to include smaller chiefdoms from James River north to the Rappahannock River by 1607. Map by the author.

Figure 7. Coastal dunes near the spot where Jamestown founders first landed in 1607. They were immediately attacked by local natives, likely Nansemonds, who ambushed the landing party from behind these dunes. First Landing State Park. Photo by the author.

Plans for a major war against the English began shortly after Wahunsenaca's death, and in 1622, Opechancano and Opitchapam lead the most aggressive assault on the English up to that point, killing over 350 settlers in a blitz that wiped out up to a third of the colony's population. Apparently this victory was thought to be enough reduce the English to subservience, but Virginia soon received reinforcements, counter-attacking aggressively. Tensions were high among the Powhatans, and between Opitchapam and Opechancano. Apparently Opitchapam at one point sent word to the English that he was willing to betray his brother, though this may also have been a ploy to lure them into an ambush. It was Opechancano that would sue for peace, saying "blud inough had already been shed on both sides, that many of his People were starved, by our taking Away theire Corne and burning theire howses."[48] But during the negotiations (where several hundred Powhatan leaders and warriors were present) poisoned wine was distributed, causing the Powhatans, including Opechancano, to fall to the ground in convulsions. The English opened fire, killing more, ultimately putting about 250 Powhatans to death.[49] Opechancano would escape and recover, and the war continued for years as low-grade guerilla conflict, raids and amphibious assaults. Eventually, after ten years, peace was concluded in 1632, with no clear victor. Land was contiuously taken up by yet more colonists, and the uneasy truce that was concluded would soon become strained.[50]

In the English camp, Sir William Berkeley was the royally appointed governor. Born in 1605 to a noble family, he had a priviledged upbringing and was trained as a lawyer. Fiercely loyal to the crown, (though he apparently had personal doubts about Charles I) Berkeley was a low-level courtier in Charles I's court. A lover of poetry and oratory, Berkeley was a playwright as well as an army officer and investor. "Aloof but accessible," according to his biographer, "Berkeley was an

---

[48] Fausz, John Frederick, *The Powhatan Uprising of 1622: A Historical Study of Ethnocentrism and Cultural Conflict,* (PhD. Diss., College of William and Mary in Virginia, 1977) 495

[49] Fausz, John Frederick, *The Powhatan Uprising of 1622: A Historical Study of Ethnocentrism and Cultural Conflict,* (PhD. Diss., College of William and Mary in Virginia, 1977) 497-498; Frederick W. Gleach, *Powhatan's World and Colonial Virginia: A Conflict of Cultures,* (Lincoln, University of Nebraska Press, 1997) 161

[50] Rountree, Helen C., "Powhatans and the English: A Case of Multiple Conflicting Agendas," in Rountree, Helen c., ed., *Powhatan Foreign Relations, 1500-1722,* (Charlottesville, University Press of Virginia, 1993) 192-193

urbane, witty man. Elegant etiquette complemented a keen ear for smartly coined sentences." During the Bishops Wars, he disgraced himself by apparently passing along faulty information, but still maintained a relationship with King Charles. Unable to satisfy his ambitions in Charles' court, he sought out an appointment as ambassador to Constantinople, but inexplicably changed his mind at the last moment, deciding instead to gain King Charles' approval to become governor of Virginia. This made some sense as his father was an investor in the Virginia Company and he had contact with many people associated with Virginia growing up, but it is unknown why exactly why King Charles assented, removing the currently appointed governor and installing Berkeley in his place.[51]

As a fierce loyalist, Berkeley was maligned toward the fairly large Puritan population of southern Virginia. Puritans tended to be anti-crown during a time of great schism between the King and Parliament. Viewing them as traitors, Berkeley cracked down, administering an oath of allegiance to the King, and according to one report, those who refused to take it were in danger of being ransacked by his henchmen. Berkeley had no experience with Indigenous Americans, and strictly upheld England's social hierarchy within Virginian society. Land patents would continue to be issued, often enveloping whole native corn fields and towns, inundating many Powhatans (who had no concept of permanent ownership of land) with a steady influx of colonists.[52]

Also of note was interim governor Richard Kemp, particularly since he would handle the brunt of the war in

[51] Warren M. Billings, *Sir William Berkeley and the Forging of Colonial Virginia,* (Baton Rouge, Louisiana State University Press, 2004) 1-31

[52] Ibid.

Berkeley's lengthy absence. Having previously met and travelled with Berkeley from England to Virginia, Kemp had already established a good relationship with him. Originally from Norfolk, England, Kemp immigrated to Virginia in the early 1630s and became Councilor and Secretary of the Colony in 1634. Loyal to Governor Harvey throughout his controversial administration, he clashed with a local minister who publicly ridiculed him, a sour relationship that continued even when Kemp returned to England, making the return trip for him and Berkeley difficult as litigation against them at the Reverend's behest threatened to block Berkeley's appointment as governor altogether. On his return to England during Wyatt's administration, he had allegedly stolen away Colonial record books, souring his relationship with other government officials. His meeting with Berkeley was therefore fortuitous in reestablishing his place of power and influence within Virginian politics. In fact, one wonders if Kemp had something to do with Berkeley changing his mind about being ambassador to Constantinople and pursuing gubernatorial ambitions instead.[53]

---

[53]McCartney, *Virginia Immigrants and Adventurers,* 439-440; Billings, *Sir William Berkeley,* 31-36.

Figure 8. 17th century engraving depicting the Indian uprising of 1622. John Smith, Generall Historie of Virginia.

A Buildup of Tensions

Opechancano saw the seemingly unstoppable wave of colonial advancement, and did not remain inactive. He carried on the affairs of his nation with dignity and reserve. According to the writings of Robert Beverly in the early 18th century, even in his old age he "caused all the Indians far and near to dread his Name, and had them all entirely in Subjection." He was now elderly, but his entire life had been devoted to aggressive resistance to outside forces and had built up a remarkable reputation throughout the whole region. This would be no exception, and he continued to hold a psychological grip on English minds as even at the end of the coming war, Governor Berkeley was under the assumption that Opechancano "could call into the Field Ten times more Indians than Sir William Berkeley had English in his whole Government," which was untrue, but a testament to Opechancano's ability to use psychological tactics to give the Virginians pause.[54]

Some activity of his to the southward of Virginia into modern-day North Carolina has been recorded. According to Nottoway chief Chounterounte in 1650, he was carrying on trade with the powerful Tuscarora people, who ambushed and killed some of his traders. In response, he sent a large contingent to retaliate. During this raid, a personal spat developed between the *weroance* of Powhatan town and the *weroance* of the Chowanokes, a large Algonquian nation of North Carolina. The Chowanoke *weroance* had previously launched raids into Powhatan country and captured the wife of the Powhite town's leader. During the Tuscarora raid, the Powhite *weroance* feigned

[54]Beverly, *The History and Present State of Virginia,* 62.

friendship and forgiveness, luring the Chowanoke *weroance* away from his towns only to strangle him with a bowstring.[55]

Figure 9. William Claiborne, born 1587. Veteran of the 1622 war, he led seemingly successful campaigns against the Powhatan in 1644 and is known for instigating armed conflict with Maryland. Courtesy of the Library of Virginia.

[55]Edward Bland, "The Discovery of New Brittaine…[1651]" in *Narratives of Early Carolina*, ed, Alexander Salley, (New York: Charles Scribner's Sons, 1911), 9.

Also in 1650, an English exploratory group came across the Meherrin people, who had entertained them with dancing and feasting, commenting that they did the same "to their late emporer Appechancano." This is fascinating because the Meherrins are an Iroquoian group, speaking an entirely different language than the Powhatans and having a somewhat differing culture. Apparently Opechancano was personally travelling south to the Iroquoians to establish influence over them, perhaps in an attempt to bring them into his fold. The Meherrins do not seem to have been involved in the 1644 attack as far as the records show, however, so their allegiance to Opechancano probably only went so far. The point remains, however, that while the English were expanding into Powhatan territory, Opechancano was also making efforts to strengthen himself and expand as well and seems to have had some success to the southward as he travelled to strengthen and establish relationships.[56]

1637 and onward, land was swallowed up at a startling rate. Many took advantage of the increased acreage offerings by Interim Governor West and increased holdings on the south side of York River.[57] Elsewhere in English America, tensions rose in New England resulting in the Pequot War in Massachusetts. These New England Puritans were in close contact with the Puritans of Virginia and word possibly spread to Opechancano through both English and Native contacts. Hundreds were killed and hundreds more shipped off into slavery as the entire Pequot

---

[56]Ibid., 10-11.

[57]Governor John West made a proclamation rewarding extra land to those willing to hazard settlement near to Opechancano in July 1636. The following two years saw a significant influx of settlers. See Nell Marion, ed., *Cavaliers and Pioneers: Abstracts of Virginia Land Patents and Grants, 1623-1800,* vol. 1 (Richmond, Press of the Dietz Printing Company, 1934) 44-91.

polity collapsed. Opechancano seems to have had little trade relations to the north so it is difficult to say what he knew of it, but likely he knew at least something of more English colonies cropping up all along the Atlantic seaboard besides Virginia and Maryland.[58]

By 1638 More Powhatan towns were swallowed up by tobacco factory-farms. The Nansemond town referred to in earlier deeds near the mouth of the river is never heard of again. It seems to have been abandoned as the chiefdom retreated into two principal towns in the upper waters of the western and main branch of the river.[59] Other plantations butted against the Chickahominy town of Oraniock (Anglicized in English records as "Warrany")[60] while more land was taken up "E. upon Great Weyanoke Town."[61] The Appomatocks by this point saw their entire territory taken up as English plantations took their river all

---

[58]For the Pequot War see Alfred A. Cave, *The Pequot War,* (Boston: University of Massachusetts Press, 1996). It is unknown for certain if Opechancano knew specifically of the Pequot War, particularly since it has been demonstrated that most of his trade relationships were with nations further west and south, not north where the war took place. He was, however, active in attempting to gain support from the Rappahannock and Patawomec tribes prior to the Third Anglo-Powhatan War, who in turn had more extensive northern contacts, raising the possibility, perhaps probability, that Opechancano knew something of these northern events. For Powhatan trade relationships with the northern Algonquians, see Rountree, Helen C. and Clark, Wayne E., "The Powhatans and the Maryland Mainland," in Rountree, Helen, ed., *Powhatan Foreign Relations, 1500-1722,* (Charlottesville, University Press of Virginia, 1993) 112-135.

[59]Rountree, *Pocahontas's People,* 84, 105-108; for specific references in land records see Nugent, *Cavaliers and Pioneers*, 56, 153, 92.

[60]Ibid., 83, 98, 102, 107, 108, 124, 125.

[61]Ibid., 68, 86, 88, 98.

the way to the falls, leaving little room for them except on Swift Creek.[62]

There can be little doubt that this disrupted the Powhatans' ability to produce food for themselves in their accustomed locations, but what's more, they were still expected to produce surplus corn for the use of the Virginia settlers, who could conceive of little else than to grow their cash crop.[63] Opechancano was able to keep the peace for the most part. He was respected by the united Powhatan nations as *mamanatowick* and he was obeyed without question. Most still did not want to get drawn into another ten year war in any case, but more and more frustrated warriors were itching for retribution, and were getting harder to control.

Maryland was having difficulties with Indians of their own in 1638. Apparently one group of Wiccocomicos, who had once been a marginal part of the Powhatan "Empire" above the Rappahannock River, engaged in some form of hostility toward Maryland planters toward the latter end of the year. Lord Baltimore suspected Virginian Indian involvement in the incident and sent inquiry to the Virginian government. Immediately an investigation was carried out and messengers were dispatched to the "Chickohoming Indians and the Pamonkey Indians" to ascertain their involvement. Opechancano denied any knowledge of it, saying that "they know nothing thereof... if they did, they would ffreely admit being Enemyes at prsent to those Wicocomicoes." Opechancano had either totally severed ties with the Rappahannock nations or was lying to produce a friendly image. Secretary Richard Kemp sent a letter back to

[62]Ibid., 117, 122, 134.

[63]Rountree, *Pocahontas's People,* 81.

Lord Baltimore that the Powhatans had nothing to do with it, and Virginia stood ready to militarily assist Maryland in case of an Indian war.[64]

Meanwhile, in the upper waters of the Nansemond River, there may have been two factions forming within the Nansemond Chiefdom. Two main towns seem to have remained, one on the western branch, in Isle of Wight County, and the other in the main branch, in Upper Norfolk County.[65] Interestingly, in 1638 the "King of the Nansemonds" gave his daughter in marriage to a Virginian man named John Bass, son of Captain Nathaniel Bass who had exchanged prisoners with the Nansemonds in the previous war and lost a son in the 1622 attack. She received Christian baptism and the Christian name of Elizabeth. As written elsewhere, marriages such as this one, especially from a *weroance's* daughter, were often a way of establishing kinship ties with another people, something like a peace treaty. Not to say that it was wholly political; they may have truly been in love. Still, this clearly shows a friendly relationship with at least some Nansemond, and this was therefore most likely the point at which a split in the tribe began to manifest itself, with the pro-English faction forming a relationship with the Basse family.[66]

---

[64]Richard Kemp to Lord Baltimore, February 4, 1638, in *The Calvert Papers,* vol. 1, Fund Publication, No. 28, (Baltimore, Maryland Historical Society, 1889) 156-157.

[65] During the 1640s, there is no concrete evidence that there was more than one Nansemond town. The split in the tribe only becomes obvious after the war. However, Lieutenant Upton of Isle of Wight County (approximately where a Nansemond town would later be recorded) requested assistance in dealing with local natives, which was a distance from where the Basse marriage took place (see below). Also, during the 1644 assault, the Nansemond attack was held in check at at least one location when the colonists received warning, probably from the pro-English Nansemonds. It is therefore probable, though uncertain, that there were indeed two different town locations prior to the 1644 assault.

[66]Ibid., 84-85, 105-108.

Tidewater Virginia Alqonquin and Probably Leaders-1644			
Chiefdom	**Warriors (est.)**	**Tot. Pop.**	**Weroance**
Powhatan Chiefdoms			
Pamunkey	90	360	Opechancanough*
Chickahominy	80	32	Herquapink?
Weyanoke	30	120	Ascomowett
Powhite	15	60	?
Appamattock	65	260	?
Nansemond	90	360	?
Mataponi	25	625	?
Chiskiack	60	240	Ossakican
Total	**455**	**180**	
Chiefdoms Above Rappanannock River			
Cuttatawomen	30	120	?
Moraghtacund	55	220	Matchamap?
Rappahanock	50	200	Accopatough?
Nandanghtacund	65	260	Attamahune?
Secacawon	15	60	Machywap?
Wiccocomicos	75	300	Pekwem?
Portobacco	40	160	?**
Machadoc	?	?	Pertatoan?
Patawomek	120	460	Wahaganoche?
Total	**450-500**	**1800-2000**	
Eastern Shore Chiefdoms below Maryland			
Occohannock	30	120	Wackawamp
Accomac/Gingaskin	60	240	?**

* Necatowance and Totopotomoi would also have been lesser Weroances

** These Portobaccos may have been a group newly formed after the war.

*** Wackawamp was leader of both the Accomac and Occohannock

Figure 10. Population estimates for Virginian Tidewater Algonquians at 1644. Because of poor records these numbers are approximate. Indian leaders with question marks are known leaders from records in the decade following the war, but it is not wholly known that they were leading weroances at the time of the war. Chart by the author.

In Isle of Wight, however, Lieutenant Upton, the local militia commander, became leery of local natives, likely the western branch Nansemonds, and borrowed fifty pounds of gunpowder from Fort Comfort "in case of distress and danger doubted from the neighboring Indians to the inhabitants of Isle of Wight where the said Upton is the present commander." Apparently many settlers on the south side of James River, perhaps to include Appamattocks, changed their place of habitation to the York River area, home of Opechancano's Pamunkeys, to be among "more friendly Indians." It may be that Opechancano had greater difficulty in controlling the chiefdoms on the south side of James, but was very good at keeping the Pamunkey, Chickahominy and their neighbors convincingly friendly.[67] Nor was Lower Norfolk, where the Basse marriage took place, immune to conflict, for in 1639, several colonists complained of harassment by the Nansemond. Captain Adam Thoroughgood accordingly led fifteen of his men in a reprisal attack, though the details and results of the expedition are not known.[68]

In an interesting side note, 1638 was also the year that a young Thomas Rolfe, the son of John Rolfe and Pocahontas, came to Virginia from his upbringing in England. As the first recorded multi-ethnic person in the colony, he may have found discomfort in feeling out of place. Searching for his roots, he gained permission from the governor to seek out and meet his uncle, Opechancano, as well as other Powhatan relatives of his. While the meeting probably occurred, the outcome is not known,

---

[67]John Bennett Boddie, *Seventeenth Century Isle of Wight County Virginia,* (Chicago, Chicago Law Printing Company, 1938) 95-96.

[68]Shea, *The Virginia Militia,* 52-53.

though he continued to live in and serve English Virginia afterward.[69]

Virginia and Maryland were having internal problems of their own. By this point, Governor Harvey, who had been deposed and shipped back to England, still found favor with the King, who promptly sent him back to Virginia to the horror of the counsel and assembly. He very quickly went to work on his revenge by arresting and shipping to England all the council members who had betrayed him. He even went so far as to fine and arrest a local minister who had spoken against him, forbidding him to preach. He then continued in office until 1640, though he would by then accumulate many personal debts and his political clout steadily faded to nothing as the original council members returned to their positions.[70]

Schism was itself growing between the Anglicans and Puritans of the colony as well. This was widespread throughout the English world as the King (the head of the Anglican Church) became increasingly estranged from Parliament (mostly Puritans). Sectarian hatred and even violence between Puritans, Anglicans and Catholics became increasingly common, though thus far in Virginia this was kept at a minimum as most Puritans were below James River and most Anglicans were above it. The governor's council itself was made of a combination of Puritan parliament supporters like Richard Bennett and William

---

[69]Conway Robinson, "Notes from the Council and General Court Records of Virginia, 1641-1682," *Virginia Magazine of History and Biography 13* (1905-1906) 394-395.

[70]Morton, *Colonial Virginia,* 140-143; Robert M. Bliss, *Revolution and Empire,* 29; McCartney, *Virginia Immigrants and Adventurers,* 371-373.

Claiborne along with Anglican royalists as well and apparently managed to work well enough together at this point.[71]

1640 brought some changes to the Chesapeake. Over-exportation, competition with Maryland, and other factors flooded the market with more tobacco than it could handle, and the bubble finally burst.[72] Tobacco prices plummeted and debt cases in Virginian courts soared. Not to say that the tobacco culture ended, far from it. Tobacco remained the standard form of currency and the chief export in the Chesapeake, but the level of prosperity previously enjoyed was never again realized. In addition, Governor Harvey's administration came to an end and Governor Francis Wyatt took the reins. This change of leadership and the tobacco collapse may have provided a brief sort of respite for the Powhatan people, however. This year only fifty-two land patents were issued, as opposed to the previous year of 197 patents. 1638 itself had ninety-seven patents in a single month.

While the Maryland Indian nations were becoming increasingly hostile to that colony, Opechancano seems to have been making extra efforts to win Virginia's trust. As stated, the residents on the James River's south side seem to have found friendlier native relations nearer to the Pamunkey on York River. From a law passed within a few years, it is learned that many Powhatans developed amicable relations with the settlers who

---

[71]Enmity between Anglicans and Puritans, particularly during the English Civil War, is well known and studied. For examples from Virginia see Morton, *Colonial Virginia,* 150-153; Bliss, *Revolution and Empire,* 76. Puritan letters that were published in the English newspaper Mercurius Civicus probably provide the best specific records from firsthand accounts of such conflict. See Frank, Joseph, "News From Virginny, 1644," The Virginia Magazine of History and Biography, Vol. 65, No. 1 (Jan., 1957) 84-87.
[72]Land, *Colonial Maryland,* 28.

lent them firearms, powder and ammunition as hired hunters for the colonists. Illicit trade outside of government sanction seems to have been taking place as well. It seems from later records that the Powhatans took advantage of this to begin stockpiling weapons and ammunition.

One particularly touchy incident threatened to throw the Virginian tidewater into premature war. John Burton, an English farmer, was living on the frontier and frequently came in contact with Powhatans, many of whom would hunt for him. One day, he discovered that some of his property was stolen, he assumed by a particular Indian. Enraged, he picked up his rifle and murdered the next Powhatan he saw in cold blood, who was of course the wrong man. Catching wind of this, government officials panicked, rightly fearing revenge attacks by Opechancano's warriors. Hastily hoping to appease them, they arrested Burton and put him on trial, sending word to Opechancano that justice would be served and Burton would be forced to supply monetary compensation to the slain Indian's relations. This was in compliance with Powhatan culture. Opechancano met with his advisors and counseled for measures that would ensure peace would remain in place until the proper time. Some of these councilors travelled to Burton's trial to inform the court of Opechancano's word on the matter. To everyone's amazement, Opechancano stated that he understood that Burton had killed the man by honest mistake, and that no compensation was required. All was forgiven. Burton was accordingly released, but not wanting to repeat the incident, a law was passed the following year requiring all similar conflicts to be reported to the local militia commander, who would personally resolve the matter with nonviolent means.[73]

1641 went by with even less patents taken out, numbering only thirty-two for the entire year, and these mostly only in territory already held by Virginia.[74] In 1642, however, this brief period of respite came to an end when a new Governor was appointed to Virginia. Governor Francis Wyatt was dismissed in favor of Sir William Berkeley, a fierce royalist loyal to the King, who needed as many allies as possible. The same year Berkeley became governor, the English world "turned upside down" as open war finally exploded in England's streets and countryside, and the whole empire was in a state of civil war.[75] Robert Beverly later wrote in 1705 that Berkeley undid many wrongful patents that were taken out by John Harvey, and made attempts to right these wrongs in the sight of the Powhatan people. Beverley had known Berkeley personally and had fought for him during Bacon's Rebellion, making this accounting rather biased.[76]

In fact, the opposite seems to have been true. The patents taking up Powhatan territory do not seem to have gotten out of control until Harvey was temporarily deposed and leadership was taken up in the interim by John West. [77] Later, when Francis

---

[73]Rountree, *Pocahontas's People,* 83-84; H.R. McIlwaine, ed., *Minutes of the Council and General Court of Virginia, 1622-1632, 1670-1676,* (Richmond: Virginia State Library, 1979 [1924]) 478;

[74]Nugent, *Cavaliers and Pioneers,* 118-131.

[75]Gaunt, *The English Civil Wars,* 11, 34-35.

[76]Beverley, *The History and Present State of Virginia,* 61.

[77]During the early years of John Harvey's administration, relatively few patents were taken out. At the close of the Second Powhatan War only an average of ten patents were taken out per *year* between 1632 and 1634. After he was temporarily ousted in 1635 the

Wyatt took over from 1640-1642 patents were at the lowest level they had been in nearly ten years.[78] It is only when Berkeley took over in 1642 that they once again reached levels intolerable to the Powhatans, even though a new peace treaty was established that very same year. When Berkeley took over the patenting process in May, a sudden wave of new territory was taken up, not only in the Powhatan core area, but further north of York River. For the first time, the Piankatank River began colonization, as well as the shore of Mobjack Bay, and the Rappahannock River as they approached the border between Virginia and Maryland.[79]

The Chiskiacs, who had moved to the Piankatank River, did not take this well. Plantations made north of the York River were authorized only if a rent was paid to Opechancano in baskets of corn.[80] The Chiskiacs do not seem to have gotten that

---

administration fell to John West, who made a proclamation awarding more acreage to those willing to live near the Pamunkeys. In June, 1635 through the end of the year, there was an average of twenty-one land patents per *month.* Though the average fell the following year with an average of fourteen patents per month, just one month was more than an entire year of patents under Harvey's administration. When Harvey returned, the land grab was in full swing, and he could do little to stop it, or was unwilling. When he returned in 1637 patents averaged nineteen per month with the peak in August with records reflecting seventy-one patents. In 1638 patents averaged seventeen per month and sixteen in 1639. Harvey's gubernatorial career ended the following year. See Nugent, *Cavaliers and Pioneers,* 17-118.

[78]Sir Francis Wyatt took the reins of government in 1640, and a marked decrease in land patents is to be noted. This may, perhaps, have less to do with Wyatt and more to do with the tobacco bubble finally bursting, the entire industry imploding and prices plummeting. This, naturally, meant less people taking out more tobacco land. During these years, Wyatt's main focus was on price-regulating and trying to resuscitate to tobacco market. In 1640 patents averaged four per month and in 1641 they averaged three. Sir William Berkeley became governor the following year. See Nugent, *Cavaliers and Pioneers,* 118-145.

[79]Nugent, *Cavaliers and Pioneers,* 131-133, 135-144.

[80]McCartney, "Seventeenth Century Apartheid," 52.

memo. That September and early October, the settlers who cut down their trees and built cabins on their land were apparently subject to a lengthy list of "outrages committed by [the Chiskiac] Indians." Though specifics are not mentioned in the brief excerpts of the records that survive, "outrages" normally meant destruction of property at least and possibly acts of physical violence. In fact, one planter was "drawn off his plantation," resulting from the Chiskiacs' actions. While Berkeley and his council decided on a course of action in this matter, no mention of what they actually did in response survives. All that is known is that the area continued to be planted and that the fragile peace continued for the time being.[81]

In the same council meeting as the discussion of the Chiskiac problem, word was again received from Leonard Calvert of the problems he was having with the Maryland Indians. The Susquehannas, who he previously attacked, had been making incursions on the western frontier areas of the colony, and he had little way to counter them with limited resources and manpower. After several failed attempts to fund and equip an expedition, one finally was readied under the command of Captain Cornwalyes. After the establishment of a small blockhouse at the south of Susquehanna River, Cornwalyes led fifty men to the main Susquehanna town, a palisaded village on high ground sixty miles upriver on Conestoga Creek. He secretly set up two cannon to make a surprise attack on the town walls to be followed by a charge, but the Susquehannas knew he was coming and had circled behind him with 250 warriors. In a viscous melee, Cornwalyes was driven from the field to his boats, his two cannon being captured and displayed in the Susquehanna town. News of the battle spread among Indian

[81]Robinson, "Notes From the Council and General Court Records" 64-73.

people. The Eastern Shore Nanticokes resumed hostilities against Maryland, and this may have been further encouragement for the Powhatans. As the Susquehanna War escalated in favor of the Indians, Berkeley sent a strong force to assist; the Nanticokes finally agreed to peace.[82]

The brief episodes of conflict stemming from the Chiskiak incident and problems on the Nansemond River suggests that Opechancano may have been having trouble keeping his subject chiefdoms on the fringe of his territory peaceful. It is easy to see why. This outer fringe was the most affected by English expansion and furthest away from the core area of Powhatan influence. War in Maryland, signs of violent intent south of the James River and actual violence by the Chiskiacs show that there were rumblings in Indian Country. Warriors were of age now that hadn't been a part of the last war and were probably eager to take revenge. Opechancano knew it wasn't yet the right time, however. They were too few and the English too many. The last time he attacked them, the English crumbled before him at the outset, but were resupplied and reinforced from the seemingly infinite resources of England. A game changer needed to come to light to eliminate that factor to make any chance of victory a success. Until that time came, he played nice, but also made the English believe he was stronger than he was.[83]

---

[82]Riordan, *The Plundering Time,* 110-115.

[83]While no violence occurred that has been recorded from the Pamunkey heartland, the earlier mentioned incidents with the Chiskiacs and Nansemonds further away from Opechancano show that frustrated warriors toward the fringe of his territory were difficult to keep in line. Robert Beverley demonstrates how Opechancano made Berkeley think he was stronger than he was, for even at the end of the war when Opechancano was captured Berkeley was under the impression that Opechancano could

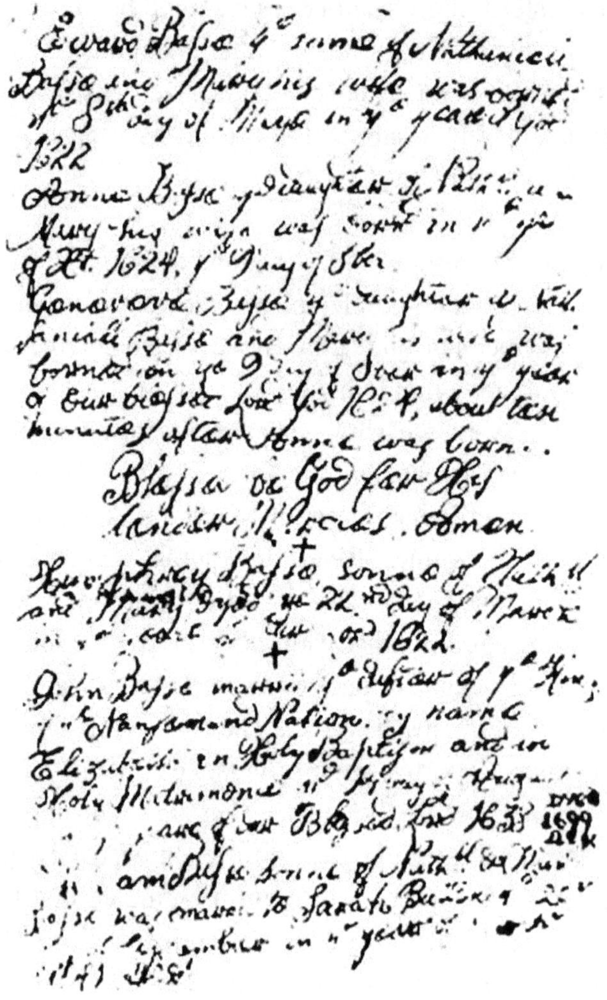

Figure 11. A 17th century prayer book record showing a marriage between John Bass, an English Settler whose younger brother was killed in the 1622 war, and Elizabeth, of whom we know nothing other than that she was the daughter of the weroance. This was the first recorded inter-racial marriage excepting Pocahontas and John Rolfe. Bass Family Prayer Book. Courtesy of the Library of Virginia.

---

gather more warriors than there were English in the whole colony. See Beverley, *The History and Present State of Virginia,* 62.

A Buildup of Tensions

The opening Opechancano needed was soon in coming. Armies raised by both King Charles and Parliament began to circle each other in England and by early autumn engaged in several skirmishes and open battles, none of it decisive, but made clear that a prolonged conflict was inevitable.[84] News of the war reached Virginia, and dissentions between Puritans and Anglicans, in addition to a few Catholics who everyone hated, began to reach the boiling point. Fiercely Royalist, Berkeley would remain loyal to the King, and used his power to bring the Puritans to subjection, which antagonized them greatly. Colonists factionalized over religious and political issues to the point that they were obvious to the observant Powhatans. The relationships that Opechancano had been forging by allowing his hunters to be hired by settlers produced fruit when his English informants gave him news that that "all was under the Sword in England, in their Native Countrey, and such divisions in our Land."[85]

Opechancano faced a tough choice, but the right course was obvious. If the problem with attacking the English was resupply and reinforcement from England, then his main problem could be over, for if England was in a state of war and confusion, they were unlikely to be able to adequately resupply the colony. It would be a gamble, but he was a bent old man now, by several accounts nearly a hundred years old. His people would never be stronger. He saw the downward trend in population over the years and no doubt knew it would likely continue. He had excited warriors ready to do it. It was now or never. [86] As Robert Beverley aptly stated years later after

---

[84]Gaunt, *The English Civil Wars, 1642-1651,* 11, 34-35.

[85]Morton, *Colonial Virginia,* 150-153; Joseph, "News From Virginny," 84-86.

[86]I believe Opechancano's age had a significant impact on the decision to attack, since he knew he would not live much longer. But I also believe that he would have still

interviews with several Powhatans, "The subtle Indians, who took all Advantages, resented the Incroachments upon them by his [land] Grants. They see the English uneasie and disunited among themselves, and by the Direction of Oppechancanough their King, laid the Ground-work of another Massacre."[87]

He needed time to plan, and needed to make sure his plans were approved by his priests, who would be able to more clearly discern the approval of Okeus, their god who was most concerned in human affairs. They needed a sign. In the meantime, he made plans differing somewhat from his last attack in 1622. Many historians have concluded that the 1644 attack was desperate and hopeless.[88] One claim has been that the English had overstepped their physical and cultural bounds and this attack was merely an attempt to correct this misbehavior so they would go back to their old bounds.[89] This is not so. I believe Opechancano and his council of priests and advisors truly planned to eliminate the English and retake their entire original territory. They expected to win.

---

refrained from attacking if the situation between England and Virginia was not deemed advantageous. The factors of the English Civil War, internal Virginia disputes and Opechancano's age all worked together to influence his and his priests decision.

[87]Beverley, *The History and Present State of Virginia,* 60.

[88]Fausz, *The Powhatan Uprising of 1622,* 582; Gleach, *Powhatan's World,* 174-175; Helen Rountree, *Pocahontas, Powhatan, Opechancanough: three Indian Lives Changed by Jamestown,* (Charlottesville, University of Virginia Press, 2005) 235; Shea, *The Virginia Militia in the Seventeenth Century,* 69.

[89]Gleach, *Powhatan' World*, 175.

Figure 12. The only known engraving of a Virginia Algonquian during the 1640s. This 23 year old male probably came from an area friendly to Europeans, such as the eastern shore or further north in Maryland. It may also be possible that he was one of the prisoners captured shortly after the 1644 attack.
Courtesy of the Library of Virginia.

The assault of 1622 involved a single calamitous attack that decimated 25-30% of the English population, but offered no follow up attack as it was apparently assumed that they would leave the country in fear afterwards, or at least respect the Powhatan as the true masters of the land. This time Opechancano knew better, and knowing his numbers were fewer than the English, correctly concluded that the only way to defeat them was not militarily in open battle but by a slow siege. An initial shocking attack similar to the one in 1622 was planned. This was to make them quit their fields, cattle, and hogs and retreat to the interior. Once this was done, night raids and guerilla attacks would destroy their livestock and grain, in the same way that the English cut their corn in previous wars in an attempt to starve the Powhatans. Without aid from England, they would defeat the English in the same way one would eat an elephant: one bite at a time. [90]

These plans were spread throughout the Powhatan chiefdoms as is observable in the coordination of the later attack. 1643 may have been spent in an increased display of friendship

[90]Anthropological and historical analysis of the first assault of 1622 has been very thorough, concluding in near unanimity that Opechancano assumed that the English would quit Virginia altogether following the attack, or else give deference to the Powhatan as a superior power. In such a scenario no follow-up attack would be necessary to the "shock-and-awe" assault. Because the 1644 assault has every appearance of mimicking the 1622 attack, it is often concluded that Opechancano did not learn his lesson from the first war and repeated his mistake. I disagree. Not only will it be seen from Richard Kemp's newly available letter that Powhatan attacks continued following the attack, but in my opinion not enough weight has been given to the anonymously written *Perfect Description of Virginia.* This account, written in 1649, clearly references three letters received from Virginia in reference to the account of the Third Powhatan War, saying that they had learned directly from the Powhatan people as to the plan Opechancano fomented prior to the attack. While a third-hand account of what the Powhatan said, this is the closest reference available to the events of the time.

as they secretly made preparations of attack. It is probable that they were continuing to stockpile firearms during this time. In January 1643 the governor's council found it necessary to give orders against certain people who were trading with Powhatans. Not long afterwards in March, the Assembly passed official acts against both trade and entertaining Indians as well as lending them guns for hunting because, "it is informed that divers psons do entertain Indians to Kill Deare or other game, And do furnish the said Indians with peeces, powder & Shott, by which great abuse not onely the Indians (to the great indangering of the Collony) are instructed in ye use of [sd] Arms."[91] While most residents who entertained these Powhatans were likely new immigrants and did not experience the last war (and were therefore more trusting), the governor's council and other experienced planters in the Assembly were less so, and therefore resolved that "what pson or psons soever shall sell or barter with any Indian or Indians for Peese Powder & Shott being thereof lawfully convicted, Shall forfeit his whole Estate, the one halfe to ye Informer the other halfe to the pson of the County where such ffact shall be Committed And if any pson shall barter or trade with ye Indians for any other Comodities Such pson shall suffer imprisonment at ye discresion of the Governor & Counsell." As for Powhatans found armed with English guns, "It shall be lawfull for any person meeting with any such Indian So furnished, to take away either Peece Powder or Shot, So as such pson taking away either Peece powder or Shott do Carrie the same to ye Comander or the County, & aquaint him therewith."[92]

---

[91] Act 23, March 1642/43, Acts of the Assembly, in Hening, *The Statutes at Large...*, 255-256.

[92] Ibid.

Figure 13. William Berkeley, born 1606. Fiercely loyal to the crown, he is known for heavy handed attitudes and policies toward non-Anglicans, but also for skillful handling of the government. Courtesy of the Library of Virginia.

A Buildup of Tensions

All the while Opechancano was planning the attack, divisions and confusion continued to worsen among the English. Maryland continued to have problems with their bordering Indians and in 1643 launched another attack against the Susquahannas, again with Virginia's assistance in men and supplies.[93] The friction between Anglicans and Puritans, Royalists and Parliamentarians, got progressively worse, and often complicated shipping. Captains of Parliament ships (called Londoners) often had trouble finding a cargo of tobacco among Royalist planters who refused them business, and Bristol captains (loyal to the King) often found themselves in conflict with these Londoners. At least in one instance a screaming match over politics escalated to a violent incident when in late February, 1642, Captain Richard Ingle "of the London merchant ship Reformation was trading off the coast of Accomack, and was entertaining twenty Virginians on board when he drew his sword on several Virginian leaders and weighed anchor, carrying away the colonists to Maryland.[94] Not long afterward, a full-fledged naval battle between a Bristol and London ship was waged on James River, in full view of observing colonists and Powhatans. This observable show of civil war would give Opechancano the impression that no support could be ad from England if attacked.

[93]Land, *Colonial Maryland,* 42-45.

[94]Riordan, *The Plundering Time,* 95-97, 130-149.

Fearful Flames:" The Great Assault of 1644

1644 dawned with increasing conflict in both England and America. As Opechancano looked for the right opportunity to reclaim Tsenacomoco, news of the battles between the King's army and Parliament forces trickled into Virginia, and dissensions between factions over issues of politics and religion were quickly reaching the boiling point. Puritans who more often than not supported Parliament were thought treasonous by Sir William Berkeley, and he may have feared a rebellion of his own. Robert Beverley, a historian of the next generation who fought for Berkeley during Bacon's Rebellion, gives the impression that Berkeley was loved by all the people during this time and corrected all the shortcomings brought by former governor Harvey. However, Puritan letters and narratives written to their brethren in New England and London discredits this notion and reveals that Berkeley antagonized the Puritans and used intimidation tactics to force submission.[95]

Besides the issues surrounding the English Civil War and religious factions, rumblings of Indian war were beginning to increase along the seaboard. Besides Maryland's ongoing troubles with the Susquahannocks, the Algonquian-speakers surrounding the Dutch colony of New Amsterdam at today's Manhattan Island were having increased friction with the

---

[95]Beverley states that Berkeley undid the "unjust" land grants of Harvey in the sight of the Indians and English and was well loved by the people. Those Puritans who were set in his crosshairs, however, said differently, in that they were subject to their homes being sacked by government gangs if they did not take an oath of allegiance to the king. See Beverley, *The History and Present State of Virginia,* 61; and Frank, "News From Virginny," 84-87

government there by late 1643. Unfortunately for them, Governor Keift was completely without understanding or common sense, ordering the murder of over one hundred Indian men, women and children as they slept. David DeVries, then resident of New Amsterdam and friend of the Indians captured every detail:

> "The soldiers... massacred eighty Indians... murdering so many in their sleep, where infants were torn from their mother's breasts and hacked to pieces in the presence of their parents and the pieces thrown into the fire and into the water, and other sucklings who were swathed and bound to small boards were then cut, struck and pierced, and miserably massacred in a manner to move a heart of stone. Some papooses so wrapped and bound were thrown into the river, and when the father and mother endeavored to save them, the soldiers would not let them come on land, but made both parents and child drown... when it was morning, [some] came out to beg a piece of bread and to be permitted to warm themselves, but then were murdered in cold blood and tossed into the water. Some came... with their hands cut off, some with their legs cut off and some holding their entrails in their arms..."[96]

This shocking action galvanized the Native people to unprecedented unification against the Dutch. DeVries tried to make peace, but it was too late, and war exploded. With a heavy heart, he quit the colony altogether as warfare spread, coming south to Virginia. This new Dutch war, as well as Maryland's

---

[96]Parr, *The Voyages of David DeVries,* 224-225.

ongoing Susquahanna War, was probably something Opechancano soon became apprised of himself, and joining this momentum was one more reason to strike at Virginia.[97]

Regardless of what Opechancano knew or didn't know about goings on to the north, he certainly retained a vigilant watch over Virginia's activities at his immediate borders. For one thing, these borders were porous, with intrusive English settlements surrounding and intertwining amongst established Powhatan towns. Interaction was inevitable, despite decrees from the governor's council discouraging such social contact. The colonists, who usually did not grow enough corn for themselves (preferring their tobacco cash crop), would hire Powhatan hunters to bring in fresh game to supplement their food stores. They would go so far as to "loan" firearms and ammunition for this purpose, from which Opechancano was able to siphon off an increasing arsenal of deadly weapons. This black market trade allowed him to keep his finger on the pulse of Virginia affairs. It would appear that Opechancano was employing a similar intelligence gathering method as his brother Wahunsenaca, as William Strachey recorded in 1612:

> "Watchfull he [Wahunsenaca] is over us, and keeps good espyall upon our proceedings, concerning which he hatch his sentinels that at what time soever any of our boats, pinacies, or shippes, come in, fall downe, or make up the river, give the alarm, and take it quickly on from the other, until it reach and come even to the court or hunting howse, wheresoever he and his eronoccocs, that is, his councellors, and priests, and then he… gives out direccions what is to be

[97]Ibid., 222-232.

> done, as more fearing then harmed, at any tyme, with the danger and mischief which he saith we intend unto him, by taking awaye his land from him and conspiring to surprize him..."[98]

In March, a group of Parliamentary commissioners arrived in Jamestown's harbor. Lord Robert Rich, the Earl of Warwick and Lord Admiral of Parliament's naval forces, sent a panel of commissioners to represent Parliament. Sir Richard had a long history with Virginia, being a member of the old Virginia Company, and owning the Richneck plantation in Warwick County in what is now Newport News. Berkeley, the staunch royalist that he was, hated him. He had good reason to. The commissioners made an enticing offer to the people of Virginia to ensure their loyalties to Parliament. Reading their proclamation, Parliament desired to "free them from all former taxations and occasions, and gave them liberty to choose their own governor; and sent command to all English ships there (which were then to the number of sixteen, most of them great ships) to assist them if need were." No taxes and they could choose their own executive leader. Such a prospect was obviously an attractive offer.[99]

Berkeley, of course, chafed at this. The people, however, through the burgesses and governor's council, could possibly overrule him and accept the commissioners' offer, and thus he was vexed. Fortunately for him, however, King Charles caught wind of the commissioners and sent a countermand of his own, which arrived at about the same time as Parliament's representatives. Having this royal backing, Berkeley "withstood parliament's commissioners, and drew most of the other

---

[98] Strachey, *Historie of Travaile,* 50.

[99] Winthrop, *History of New England,* 163.

magistrates to take oath upon sacrament to maintain the king's authority, etc., so that the whole country was like to rise in parties, some for the king and others for the parliament," and factionalize they would.[100]

Later that March, Governor Berkeley and his council (who included some Puritans, to his credit) took an oath of allegiance to the King of England.[101] Perhaps he hoped that by the example of the Puritan council members taking such an oath it would be an example emulated by the rest of the populace. Accordingly, Berkeley required all the people to take the same oath. It did not go over well. One Puritan man recounted that there was a "great mischief that was growing among us by Sir William Barclay's courses, for divers of the most religious and honest inhabitants, were mark'd out to be plundered and imprisoned for the refusal of an Oath that was imposed upon the people, in reference to the King of England." Going from house to house, Berkeley's men tendered the oath, but, "the people murmured, and most refused to take it: Those few that tooke it did it more for feare than affection."[102] Thus with government thugs ransacking and imprisoning those who refused, the Puritans were near the point of taking up arms themselves against Berkeley. As Robert Beverley later admitted, "the whole Colony was in Confusion."[103]

All sources agree that Opechancano was well apprised of these dissensions and could see that the English were segregating themselves into confused factions. He already knew of the war in

---

[100]Ibid.

[101]Robinson, *Notes From the Council and General Court Records*, 64-65.

[102]Frank, "News FromVirginny," 85-86; Bliss, *Revolution and Empire,* 50n11.

[103]Beverley, *The History and Present State of Virginia,* 60

England from English informants the last year or the year before, and knew that procuring reinforcements and supplies would be difficult (he hoped, impossible) to obtain. His network of loyal Powhatans, many of whom spoke English and even worked on plantations, were able to give fairly consistent and speedy intelligence as to the inner workings of the Virginia colony. Secret preparations for the greatest assault yet had been made for some time now, but the indication he needed to confirm that the time was right occurred when the war in England reached the shores of Virginia. David DeVries, who had arrived in Virginia from war-torn New Amsterdam, observed:

> "Two large, strange ships sailed up the river with the flood and came along one on each side of the Bristol ship [loyal to the King], breaking out their ensign of Parliament, firing broadsides at the royalist and attempting to grapple for boarding. Their fire brought down some spars and blocks, but the surprised royalist captain managed to cut his cable. With the aid of the current, he worked his craft out of reach, and by poling and rowing he pushed well up into the shallow creek beyond Blanck Point, where the deeper draft of the attackers prevented their reaching him. Lying there out of musket range, the royalist plied a gun so smartly that his foes could not launch their small boats to board him, nor avail themselves of further broadsides. Both parties kept up a desultory fire by single cannons which, however, did considerable damage to all three, and caused many casualties. At dusk the London ships, realizing that their surprise attack had failed and that the countryside was now

> aroused, dropped far into the river, where they anchored."[104]

DeVries boarded both ships the next day to investigate, and found that the Parliament vessels had attacked in desperation, not being able to find a cargo among the royalist plantations and needed a way to compensate their loss. He also found that a Virginian man, trading on the Bristol ship, was among the dead, the only recorded Virginian casualty as a direct result of the English Civil War. DeVries was already on his way out of Virginia, leaving that very day for Holland. This was fortunate, for what DeVries didn't know was that among the "aroused" countryside that had gathered to watch the battle were several wide-eyed Powhatans, either trading, spying, or working on a plantation, who reported everything, they saw to the delight of Opechancano. This was exactly the sign he was looking for. Now, with the Colonists at each other's throats, it was time for his preparations to move toward a specific date for immediate strike in what he knew would be the last war he would ever fight. To determine this, he required immediate counsel meetings to consult with his trusted advisors and especially his priests who would have divined the approval and exact date from the Okeus deities. It was finally happening. Opechancano was going to war one last time.[105]

---

[104]Parr, *The Voyages of David DeVries,* 252-253.

[105]The anonymous authors of the Puritan letters published in Mercurius Civicus do not specifically state that Opechancano was apprised of English disunity and factions, but made clear the attack did occur at a time of great social strife, speculating that if he had waited a month longer, he may have succeeded in his plans. Beverley gives Opechancano full credit for being apprised of the internal conflicts of Virginia as the chief reason behind the timing of the attack, while an anonymous author in 1649 writes that he not only knew about the internal struggles of Virginia, but of the Civil War in

Because of the comparatively small body of documentation that has survived concerning the Powhatan attack of 1644, little scholarship has gone into analyzing it. As earlier stated, many histories mention this conflict but most list the entire war as a paragraph or two of information that is largely similar to each other in content.[106] The few that have put any effort into understanding this conflict were including it as a part of a larger historical scope and therefore weren't able to dedicate a great deal of space to it. The biggest question about this second assault is, why? Did Opechancano truly believe he was going to be successful? Were the factors stacked against him not as obvious then as they appear to us now? Anthropologist Frederick Gleach suggests that Opechancano was tired of being considered an inferior power and that these encroachments on his people's land were a violation of their sovereignty. The attack and following war, therefore, would be an attempt to punish the Virginians for their wrongs and reclaim some Powhatan territory, but was not an attempt to completely eradicate the English since

---

England as well. This is confirmed further by John Winthrop, who reported that a Powhatan prisoner confirmed knowing about the Civil War and observing the naval battle. See Ibid., Frank, "News From Virginny," 84-87; Beverley, *The History and Present State of Virginia,* 60; Anonymous, *A Perfect Description...,* 11; and Winthrop, *History of New England,* 2:167-68.

[106]Many histories make brief mention of the 1644 assault and subsequent war, though do little to describe it. Others, like Helen Rountree and Martha McCartney, have described more detail to the events of the conflict but still give little insight into Opechancano's motivations. Some of the authors that mention the war are McCartney, "Cockacoeske, Queen of Pamunkey: Diplomat and Suzeraine" in Powhatan's Mantle, 243-266, McCartney, "Seventeenth Century Apartheid", 47-75, Rountree, *Powhatan's People*, 84-85; Rountree and Davidson, *Eastern Shore Indians of Virginia and Maryland*, 58-59, Fausz, "Opechancanough: Indian Resistance Leader" 34, Camilla Townsend, *Pocahontas and the Powhatan Dilemma*, 174 and Feest, *The Powhatan Tribes*, 54, among others.

they were valued for trade goods.[107] Dr. Helen Rountree confirms that Opechancano's major motivation was the land loss that was cutting out whole swaths of territory without compensation or permission. [108]While Gleach compared this attack as being similar to the first coup of 1622, historian J. Frederick Fausz admitted that Opechancano tried to take advantage of the English Civil War but also stated:

> "The Indian rebellion of 1644 cannot truly be equated with that of 1622. The 1644 attack was a desperate, futile effort against only a few English settlements; it was an outburst of frustration, not a potentially successful cultural war of annihilation. The Powhatans had silently and gradually become a remnant culture even before they attacked in 1644. The strength of the tribes, the confidence of victory, and the startling fear instilled in the English—all had made Mangopeesomon's [Opechancano's] 1622 uprising unique and different in intent and effect. In 1622, the Powhatans had launched a revolution for cultural sovereignty; in 1644, they carried out raids for cultural survival. The earlier uprising had attempted to give the Indians back their Virginia; the later attack tried to give a little of Virginia back to the Indians."[109]

Both have good points, and are true in some respects, but it is not true to say that Opechancano only wanted to partially reclaim territory or that it was an "outburst of frustration." While they were certainly frustrated, this second attack was carefully

---

[107]Frederick W. Gleach, *Powhatan's World and Colonial Virginia: A Conflict of Cultures,* (Lincoln, University of Nebraska Press, 1997) 158, 174-175.

[108] Rountree, *Pocahontas, Powhatan, Opechancanough,* 231-232.

[109]Fausz, John Frederick, *The Powhatan Uprising of 1622: A Historical Study of Ethnocentrism and Cultural Conflict,* (PhD. Diss., College of William and Mary in Virginia, 1977) 582.

planned and executed with the expectation of victory. It was the most devastating and well organized assault ever carried out by any Indigenous American group against any European target, requiring several years of preparation. Outbursts of frustration do not include such careful planning. Modern Mattaponi oral history states that Opechancano, in this attack and following war, was attempting to eliminate all the English from Virginia, in essence stating that "We are going to have to push them out before they kill us all," and that the motivation was the same in both conflicts.[110] What has survived of historical documentation confirms this. During the war Indigenous prisoners were interviewed and told the Virginians what Opechancano had planned, why he planned it and what he hoped to accomplish. Letters describing these interviews made their way to England and were referred to in the anonymous author's *A Perfect Description of Virginia* in 1649. Thus a rare glimpse into Powhatan motivations and intentions can be inquired of 17th-century Powhatan people themselves. According to one description of these Powhatan prisoners of war:

> "... some of them confessed, That their great King was by some of the English informed, that all was under the Sword in England, in their Native Countrey, and such divisions in our Land; That now was the time or never, to *roote out all the English* [italics mine]; For those that they could not surprise and kill under the feigned masque of Friendship and feasting, and the rest would be by wants; and having no supplies from their own Countrey which could not help them, be

[110]Dr. Linwood "Little Bear" Custalow and Angela L. Daniel "Silver Star," *The True Story of Pocahontas: The Other Side of History,* (Golden, Fulcrum Publishing, 2007) 93.

> suddenly Consumed and Famished. The Indians Allaruming them night and day, and killing all their Cattell, as with ease they might doe, and by destroying in the night, all their Corne Fields, which the English could not defend."[111]

Another reference to a Powhatan prisoner, probably among the same ones, was made by New England leader John Winthrop, who had heard of Virginia's troubles and wrote about it in his journal:

> "A ship coming from Virginia certifies us of a great massacre lately committed by the natives upon the English there… and that an Indian whom they had since taken confessed, that they did it because they saw the English took up all their lands from them, and would drive them out of the country, and they took this season for they understood that they were at war in England, and began to go to war among themselves, for they had seen a fight in the river between a London ship which was for parliament and a Bristol ship which was for the king. He confessed further that all the Indians within 600 miles were confederate together to *root all strangers out of the country* [italics mine]."[112]

In other words, both 17th century Powhatan people and oral history of modern Powhatan people confirms that this was a war that they expected to win. And it was a good plan. It is obvious that Opechancano was truly attempting to reclaim the

---

[111]Anonymous, *A Perfect Description…,* 11.

[112]Winthrop, *History of New England,* 2:167-168.

whole of Virginia. It is true that he was outnumbered three to one, but not being able to go among the English plantations as they used to do in the past, he probably didn't realize the extent of the English population. Even if he had known, however, it is doubtful that he would have changed his plans. His tactics are clear. The only way a small and less powerful people can bring down the emerging giant of Virginia was to cut off their resources and let them starve. As open battle was impossible, it was the only way. Since they perceived the Virginia colony to be cut off from its motherland, all Opechancano had to do was attack in such a way as to force the colonists to group together, take control of their cattle and hogs in the confusion, and slash their corn fields at night. The dissensions among them now would surely continue when they were in close quarters with each other, and they might continue to fight amongst themselves as well. This differed from the attack of 1622, in which no follow-up was attempted after the initial attack. Opechancano had learned his lesson, and Virginia was about to be under siege.[113]

As has been seen with other conflicts with the Algonquians of the Middle Atlantic, droughts, comets, eclipses and other natural signs were seen by the Indians (and the English, for that matter) as premonitions of grave incidents to come. They were always disrupting and negative. The Algonquians surrounding the North Carolina Roanoke Colony observed a giant comet and eclipse just before violent conflict and devastating epidemics altered their way of life forever. The

[113]In 1622 Opechancano and Virginia fought back and forth ferociously for the first two years of the war before collapsing into a "war of attrition" for the remainder, but it is plain that all was quiet immediately following the main strike, allowing the English ample time to regroup. This was a lesson Opechancano would not forget, but a lesson difficult to enforce among his people.

worst droughts in decades always seemed to prevail at the very time a new colony would come (i.e. the Spanish Jesuit Mission, Roanoke and Jamestown). Strange animal migrations and another giant comet were taken as ominous signs just before the violence of Bacon's rebellion of 1676.[114]

Knowing this broad spectrum of consistent interpretation of natural signs as premonition of things to come, it would be surprising if the same did not happen in the case of the Third Anglo-Powhatan War as well. Although documentation is incomplete, that is nonetheless exactly what is found. Such signs were likely taken as confirmation by Powhatan priests that the time was right and that they would be successful, whereas similar signs were taken by Virginian colonists (especially Puritans) as a divine warning of coming disaster.[115]Just two and a half weeks before the assault would occur; one unnamed Puritan man wrote that "Gods goodnesse hath beene lately very eminent in delivering me and my family from the Indian massacre." On the morning of April first:

---

[114]Webb, *1676*, 19. Kupperman, *The Abandoned Colony,* 62; Horn, *A Kingdom Strange,* 97; Oberg, *Nugent's Hand*, 59; Lee Miller, *Roanoke,* 101; Thomas Mathews, "The Beginning, Progress and Conclusion of Bacon's Rebellion in Virginia in the Years 1675 and 1676", in Charles McLean Andrews, ed., *Narratives of the Insurrections, 1676-1690,vol. 16* (New York, Charles Scribner's Sons, 1915), 15-16.

[115]Both the Powhatans and the English alike perceived natural signs as messages of divine nature. While this is not surprising regarding the Powhatan, considering they lived in a state far more connected with the natural world than the English, modern readers may find this surprising regarding the English. A fair wind, for example, may indicate God's approval of a voyage about to be undertaken, or in the case of the Third Powhatan War, an Indian massacre was considered a judgment for sin. See Edward L. Bond, *Damned Souls in a Tobacco Colony: Religion in Seventeenth Century Virginia,* (Macon, GA: Mercer University Press, 2000).

> "my wife was washing a bucke[t] of clothes, and of a sudden her clothes were all besprinkled with blood from the first beginning to the rincing [sic] of them at last in such abundance as if a hand should invisibly take handfuls of gore blood and throw it upon the linen. When it lay all in a heape in the washing-tub, she sent for me in, and I tooke up one gobbet of blodd as big as my finger and, stirring it in my hand it did not stain my fingers or the linen: Upon this miraculous premonition and warning from God having some kind of intimation of some designe of the Indians (though nothing appeared till that day) I provided for defense…"[116]

This was apparently not a singular occurrence, for stories about such signs persisted among Virginian colonists for decades. From narratives surrounding Bacon's Rebellion decades later, it was recorded that there were three signs in particular that troubled the Virginians, and probably the Powhatans as well. It was recorded by colonist Thomas Mathew that:

> "the one was a large comet, every evening for a week or more, at south-west, thirty-five degrees high, streaming like a horse's taile, westwards, until it reach'd (almost) the horrison, and setting toward the northwest. Another was, flights of pidgeons, in breadth nigh a quarter of the midhemisphere, and of their length there was no visible end; whose weight brake down the limbs of large trees whereon these rested at night, of which the ffowlers shot abundance and eat 'em; *this sight put the old planters under the more*

[116]Frank, "News From Virginny," 86-87;

> *portentous apprehensions, because like was seen as they said in 1640* [1644] *when th' Indians committed the last massacre,* [italics mine] but not after, until that present year 1675."[117]

More premonitions than what has been recorded were likely perceived by both the English and the Powhatans, but there also was more to planning the attack than just the signs. Practically speaking, the early spring was a time of dispersal for the Powhatans, as Rountree states:

> "The worst of the winter would be over, to make travelling a bit less rigorous. The summer, with its heat and foreign epidemics, would not yet have begun. A more cogent reason was that the season of cattapeuk [spring] was a time when the enemy could not retaliate against the warriors' loved ones. Powhatan families dispersed out of the towns in the early spring to take advantage of fish runs and to forage for other wild foods. They made visits back to plant crops and, at intervals, to weed them, but that was all… What safer time, for women and children, to attempt a general attack and escape angry survivors with ease?"[118]

While the detailed narratives that were written concerning the first attack of 1622 are not available for the assault of 1644, several accounts survive to give an outline of the actions and effects of the Powhatans. Robert Beverley's brief comments, along with several anonymous authors, have been well known for years. However, two additional narratives from

---

[117]Mathews, "The Beginning, Progress and Conclusion of Bacon's Rebellion," 15-16.

[118]Rountree "Pocahontas, Powhatan, Opechancanough," 212.

Puritan leaders in New England give excellent detail not found elsewhere and have inexplicably been virtually ignored in the historical narrative thus far. In addition, records from the June, 1644 Virginia Grand Assembly meeting provides additional details, so that a basic reconstruction is possible. Enough of the tactics and warfare from Powhatan culture have been demonstrated to show that the strike largely took on the same strategy as the first one, which was a traditional attack used by the Indians of this region. Phase one is to gain the enemy's trust and intermingle with them. Phase two is a sudden, startling, simultaneous attack, completely taking the enemy by surprise. Examples of this are seen from, of course, the attack of 1622, but also in intertribal conflicts observed by the English, as noted above.

In April 1644, the situation was somewhat different than in 1622, in that "the Indians were not so frequently suffer'd to come among the inner Habitations of the English,"[119] and the most important government centers were wholly off-limits as the eastern half of the Lower Peninsula was blocked off by a stockade. Also, Opechancano may have had trouble gaining enough support from the increasingly independent nations under his influence. It seems that the nations most effected by land encroachment readily joined him, but others that were relatively unaffected or enjoyed a good trade relationship, such as the Rappahannocks and Accomacs, abstained, probably to Opechancano's frustration.[120]

---

[119]Beverley, *The History and Present State of Virginia,* 61.

[120]While specific interactions were not recorded, it can be inferred that Opechancano failed in garnering support from the Rappahannocks and Patawomeks by reason of later events in the war. While it was argued that the Rappahannocks should be attacked by some in the Council, William Claiborne argued successfully that they should be left

On Wednesday, April 17th, the attack would begin. Messengers had already been sent out to the towns loyal to him to prepare for battle. Opechancano's Pamunkey warriors would converge with the Mattaponis and possibly Opachisco's Chiskiacs to form about a one hundred and seventy-five man force, ready to attack those who dared to plant on the York River.[121] The Chickahominies, of whom Herquapink may have been war captain, Ascomowet's Weyanokes, the Appamattocks, and Powhites amounted to approximately one hundred and ninety warriors, and were to attack the settlements near the falls of James River and its tributaries in Charles City and Henrico counties. The Nansemonds, with about a hundred warriors of their own, were poised at those in their vicinity in an effort to reclaim their river, though the possible recent division in the tribe may have halved this number.[122]

---

alone, presumably because they did not participate in the assault. The Rappahannocks and Accomacs also later sided with the English as scouts. See Robinson, "Notes From the Council and General Court Records," 64-73; and Act 9, February 17, 1644/5, Acts of the Assembly, in Hening, *The Statutes at Large...*293-294; Rountree and Davidson, *Eastern Shore Indians of Virginia and Maryland*, 58-59.

[121] The Chiskiacs are never mentioned for the entire length of the war in any record, so their role is unknown. However, it is known that they engaged in hostilities against settlers on the Piankatank River shortly before the war and were assigned a reservation immediately following the war, so logically they were most likely involved in some capacity.

[122]Beverly's account on where the attacks fell most severely, together with references in the June 1644 Assembly meeting, gives information on which I inferred the tribes that were attacked and by whom. Ascomowet and Opachisco were noted in 1649 documents, and I inferred that they were likely the chiefs during the war. The Chickahominies had no centralized chief and operated under a council system, but Herquapink was a lead man noted in documents in the early decades following the war. The warrior counts are my own decidedly rough estimate. There are no population records between 1612 and 1669, but by plotting the general rate of decline between the two points, and understanding that this decline did not happen evenly but did so after various bouts of disease and war (making any population study problematic), a general and tentative

The first difficulty was keeping it a secret. English traders and other visitors were frequently living in the Powhatan towns. These traders were not altogether friendly toward the Powhatans, though they were "as familiar in their houses as those of the family." References to traders such as these in later times describes them as those who would cheat Indians in trade, run them into debt and take advantage of Indian women. If resident traders caught wind of the plan, the Powhatans would lose the element of surprise. They had to be silenced. As many as possible were likely hustled out of town discreetly in advance, but apparently some traders remained. Business went on as usual, until a time when the traders least expected it. Perhaps when they were sleeping that night, or perhaps they saw it coming, but "they killed all, by sudden surprisal, living amongst them," as the first act of reclaiming their land and their sovereignty. There was no going back after that.[123]

---

estimate can be given. See Beverly, *The History and Present State of Virginia,* 61; and "Acts, Orders and Resolutions of the General Assembly of Virginia," in *The Virginia Magazine of History and Biography* Vol. 23, No. 3 (July, 1915), 225-255.

[123]Winthrop, *History of New England, 2:*168.

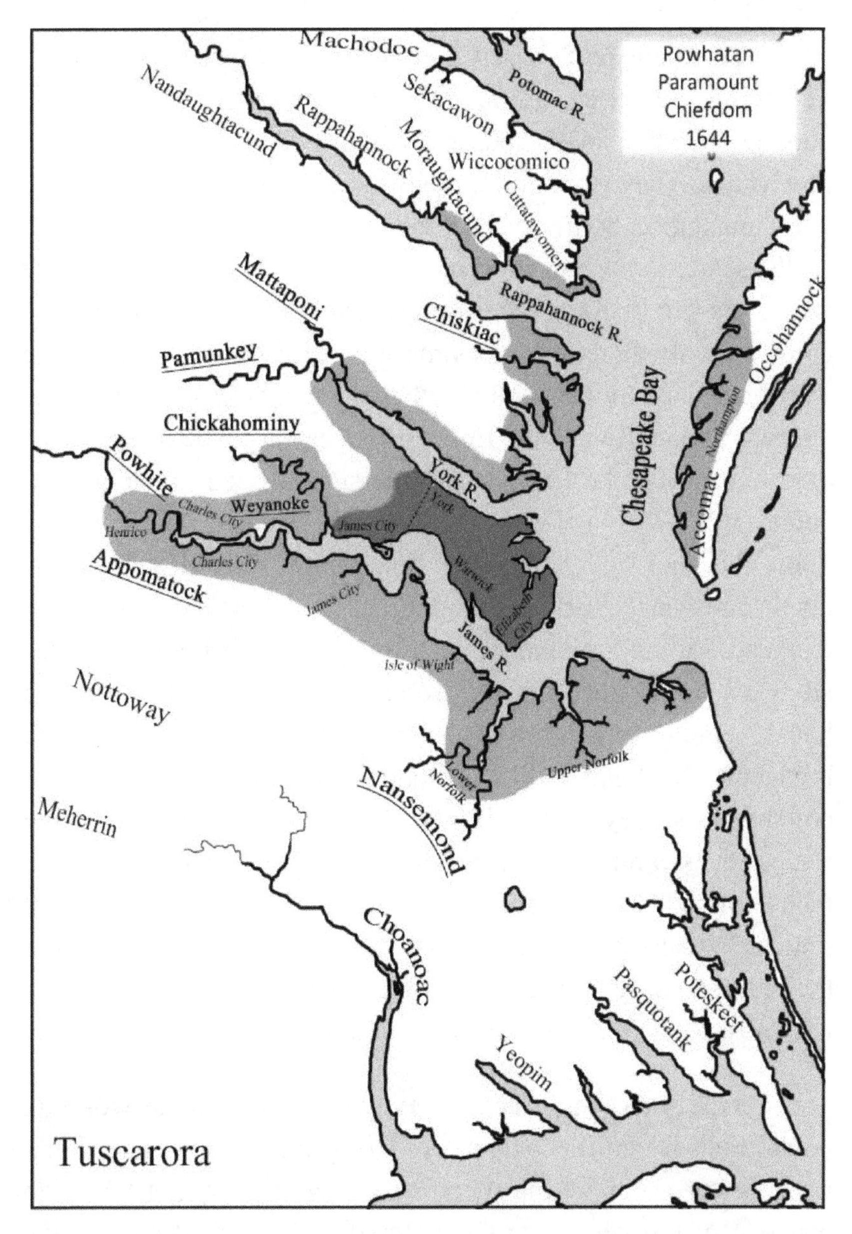

Figure 14. By 1644, many earlier chiefdoms had been reduced and absorbed by neighboring towns. Virginia's settlements had expanded to surround or butt against virtually every remaining native group. Dark gray indicates an insular non-Indian area, and light gray is the outer frontier. Map by the author.

At about 6:00, when the sun was not yet risen and the lightening sky cast a dim, grey light through the trees, the outlines of the small houses became visible to the waiting Powhatans. They were unimpressive structures, not at all the fine white plantation homes of later centuries, with "most of it being seated scatteringly in wooden clove board houses." These simple wood frame houses were single-level little cabins with a chimney, only three or four rooms at most and a storage loft. The warriors stayed hidden, and may have one or two posted near the doorway, which "beset the English houses a little before break of day, waiting for the first person that should open the doore and come forth." They got ready as they heard stirrings in the house. Soon, the door opened and the first person walked out into the open. The warrior behind the door made a quick club strike to the head, killing him instantly, "beating out their brains," or else an arrow sailed out from the woods. Then they rushed into the house, going from room to room, using edged weapons and bludgeons "and slew all they found within," except women and children that they took prisoner. They worked quickly, taking scalps, arms, ammunition and other supplies. Usually they would then destroy the plantations by "firing the houses… in fearffull flames." Others, if they didn't have time to remove all the goods, they left standing until they could revisit it later. As one traveler later observed, "many by fire were undone."[124]

One such family undone by the assault was the Worleigh household on the York River, bordering on Pamunkey territory. Little is known about the specifics, but Mrs. Margaret Worleigh was one of the women to be captured and marched back to the Pamunkey capital town of Menmend. The Worleigh surname was

---

[124]Ibid; Plantagenet, "A Description of the Province of New Albion," in Force, *Tracts and Other Papers,* 2:6.

very uncommon in Virginia at this time, so she was probably the wife of George Worleigh, a former burgess who lived in Charles River County [now York and New Kent Counties]. He died during the course of the war, probably in April 18 attack that saw his wife taken captive. Margaret would have been bound and grouped together with other women and children captives under a guard of warriors to be taken back to Pamunkey territory.[125]

Firearms probably weren't used at the outset as they would serve as warning to other plantations. From farm to farm, the war parties worked as quickly as they could in a massive assault that stretched from the "South-side of James River," to the "Heads of the other Rivers; but chiefly the York River, where Emperor Opechancanough kept his Seat of his Government."[126] The first attacks probably didn't take as many prisoners because it would be cumbersome to carry them along while the element of surprise was still necessary. The farms were usually widely spaced from each other, so this element of surprise was probably maintained throughout the morning, and maybe into the afternoon. Eventually, however, the plantations became acutely aware of what was taking place as piercing screams reverberated through the trees, an occasional shot was futilely squeezed off by a defending Englishman and the smoke of burning houses rose in the air. Settlers then made a panicked retreat to escape the

[125]Margaret Worleigh is only known because of nineteenth century historian Sebastian Streeter, who had access to records that were later destroyed during the civil war. George Worleigh appeared as burgess in 1642, and in a suit against his estate it was stated that he died after 1644 and before 1646. He lived in the same area that Margaret was captured and was, in fact, the only man recorded in Virginia with that surname at the time. That said, the connection between Margaret and George Worleigh is probably but speculative and cannot be specifically proven for genealogical purposes. See Streeter, *Papers Relation to the Early History of Maryland,* 78-79; Fleet, *Virginia Colonial Abstracts,* 52, 58; Stanard, *Virginia Colonial Register*, 62.
[126]Beverley, *History and Present State of Virginia,* 61.

onslaught. Frightened survivors would shoot three shots in quick succession as a warning signal to neighboring settlements and attempt to flee with their servants and families through the woods to larger plantations that had more people and were better defended.[127]

One bedraggled group was scrambling through the woods and reached a plantation they thought might be safe, only to discover that it was already ablaze and the Powhatans had moved on. Discouraged, they began to leave, but stopped in their tracks when they "heard a pitiffull out-cry of a poor Child, crying, I burn, I burn!" The girl had probably hidden from the warriors while her family was under attack. The survivors knew they were behind enemy lines and taking even a few extra moments could be their death. None could leave the girl, however, and "although they could have willingly made haste away, yet the miserable out-cry of this poor babe, caused them to hast to the house, and rescure [sic] it forth the flames, that was even almost ready to scorch it." They carried her to the rest of the group, where they continued on their way, eventually finding safety.[128]

All day this went on, the Powhatans pushing their advantage. The Pamunkeys, along with their allies, apparently dealt out the worst assault on York River, "cutting them off by whole Families" and burning houses as they went. The Chickahominies, Weyanokes and Appamattocks worked together

[127]Three shots fired as a warning was the standard alarm on the frontier of Virginia at this time, as noted in Berkeley's instructions from King Charles and subsequent acts of the assembly. That the survivors fled and sought each other out, settling into "great families," is seen in Johnson's narrative and acts of the assembly. See Johnson, Wonder-Working Providence, 266; See Anonymous, "Acts, Orders and Resolutions," 234, and Hening, *The Statutes at Large...*, 1:285-86.

[128]Johnson, *Wonder-Working Providence,* 266.

to inflict massive casualties, especially at the falls of the James near present day Richmond, where they "surprise[d] and kill[ed] under the feigned masque of Friendship and feasting,"[129] all the English that could be found. Henrico and Charles City counties were severely depopulated so as to be of little use in later counter-attacks. These attacks, though most severe at the falls of the rivers, stretched for nearly the entire length of the riverbanks, stopped only at the eastern half of the Lower Peninsula, where government buildings and prominent plantations were well-protected by palisades.[130]

According to tradition, one family managed to save themselves from the impending attack of the Appamattocks. Sarah Woodson and her two children were at home with a local shoemaker named Ligon as a houseguest. Her husband, John Woodson, was a doctor, and was making his medical rounds when the Appamattocks attacked. Mrs. Woodson quickly barred the door and handed Ligon an old musket that hung over the door. Ligon moved to a firing position while she stoked the fireplace to prevent entry from there. As she did this, her husband rode in from the woods, which the Indians quickly dispatched as she watched in horror. Quickly, she grabbed her children and hid them, one in a wash tub and the other in a potato hole in the floor. Ligon by this point had managed to squeeze off several shots with deadly effect, but two warriors managed to

---

[129]Anonymous, *A Perfect Description...,* 11.

[130]The Puritans of New England heard that the attacks had spread out for nearly 200 miles along the rivers. This is clearly an exaggeration as such a figure, if taken from the falls moving toward the coast, would encompass all of Tidewater Virginia and into the bay, but clearly the attacks were wide-ranging, beginning at the falls and moving eastward, gradually losing momentum as better defended positions were encountered. See Johnson, *Wonder-Working Providence...,* 266; and Beverley, *The History and Present State of Virginia,* 61.

come down the chimney. Mrs. Woodson dumped scalding water on one and used a roasting spit to inflict a deadly blow to the other. Having encountered resistance, the Appamattocks moved on, but Ligon killed two more as they retreated.[131]

The success of the different war parties varied. Though settlements at the falls "crumpled inward [eastward]," the attacks on them were less severe and more sporadic as they went downriver. In one case, the assault appears to have been discovered beforehand and prevented almost altogether. On the south side of the James, the Nansemond Indians were a divided people. The pro-English faction and the traditionalists may have had a disagreement over the assault. The Pochicks, as the traditionalists would call themselves, remained loyal to Opechancano while the pro-English group was more acculturated to English society.[132] The Pochicks went ahead with the assault, but the Puritans living on Nansemond River caught wind of it before it fell out. As Edward Johnson described, "in this massacre, when it came toward the place where Christ had placed his little flock [Nansemond River and eastward toward the coast], it was discovered & prevented from further proceeding."[133]One wonders if it was the pro-English Nansemonds who were the informants. The Pochicks were repulsed, as described by the man who earlier had seen a sign

---

[131]This story is obviously embellished, especially in several romanticized versions I have read, but they do bear several marks of underlying truth. The people mentioned, namely John and Sarah Woodson with their two sons, can be positively identified as real people during this time period. The family kept the gun as a cherished artifact and it still exists today. Additionally, the details of the story do not disagree with the written record and in fact are consistent with what is known of the 1644 assault. For one of many examples of this story, see Grose, S.E., *Appomattox County History and Events,* (Marceline, MO: Walsworth Publishing Company, 2001) 193.

[132]Rountree, *Before and After Jamestown,* 170.

[133]Johnson, *Wonder-Working Providence,* 266.

from God when his wife's wash water turned into blood. He described that, "having some kinde of intimation of some designe of the Indians… I provided for defence, and though we were but five men and mistrusted not any villany towards us before: yet we secured our selves against 20 savages which were three houres that day about my house. Blessed be the name of God."[134]

The day finally ended withsurvivors banding together for defense and building makeshift defensive works around larger plantations while more settlers likely filtered in through the woods during the night. Others were not as lucky and had to spent the night alone and shivering in the woods. Those few older planters who had lived through the assault of 1622 probably told the others of their experiences, namely, that the last attack was bad, but lasted only one day, and then the Powhatans had retreated. Hopefully, this time, too, they would find the morning free of attacks so they could begin to pick up the pieces of their shattered lives.[135]

Dawn finally came. It was Good Friday, the day that Christ was crucified as a sacrifice for their sins. They wistfully remembered that Berkeley had appointed a colony-wide fast that day, and to pray for the good success of the King. Well, the fast they would likely be keeping, though the King's problems now seemed a very distant concern. Gazing out into the dark forests,

---

[134]Ibid.

[135]Exactly how long after the assault the garrisons were established is unclear, but I feel they beginnings of them were immediate. Banding together for defense would come naturally without much thought in the face of such an attack, and if they hadn't, I believe the casualties would have been much higher. In any case, these "great families" were mentioned in the October acts of the assembly. See Hening, *The Statutes at Large…*, 285-86.

they hoped that the attack had run its course. It had not. The crackling of muskets soon erupted as Opechancano revealed the hidden weapon that had long been feared: a stockpile of arms and ammunition that he had been building up for some time. The sounds of gunfire, both near and distant, signaled a renewed assault as warriors chased down those unfortunate enough to still be trapped in the forests. Though firearms were used by Powhatans previously, by the 1640s the black market trade made their use fairly widespread among the chiefdoms and individual Powhatans were better trained in their use than ever before. Now, the Powhatans had a full-fledged arsenal. A general assembly meeting later that year recognized that "the Natives have beene furnished both wth Gunnes Powder and shott with other offensive Instruments [knives and swords] thereby tending to our utter ruine."[136] It was apparent that Opechancano's orders were being carried out to the letter as the Powhatans continued to press in, this time on a level playing field with the English. Though specifics are lacking, it is clear that the second day was just as deadly as the first, and instead of a general massacre, it became a massive, disorganized battle as firefights erupted between bands of survivors and armed warriors. Eventually, most of the English who were left behind in the forests had either made it to the garrisons or were killed. Some sorties were apparently made by the English against Powhatans as well that day, for several prisoners were able to be taken, and reference was made to the English expending more ammunition than was expected.[137] No doubt there were those who wanted to kill the captives right then and there, but control was maintained and the prisoners were kept alive for later questioning. It is doubtful that

[136]Anonymous, "Acts, Orders and Resolutions of the General Assembly of Virginia," 3:236

[137]Anonymous, "*Acts, Orders and Resolutions,*" 236.

frontal assaults of the garrisons took place other than sniping, and it eventually became apparent to Opechancano that his assault truly had run its course and they would get no further.[138]

Governor Berkeley was likely in a state of shock as the reports continued to come in to Jamestown. It was difficult to separate fact from rumor as passions flared and panic reigned. One thing was clear. The frontier of the colony "had upon this second Massacre beene utterly deserted and ruinated."[139] He needed more information, but communication between Jamestown and the survivors was nearly impossible. He didn't even know yet where they were all located. As he tried to untangle the mess from Jamestown, the exhausted Powhatan warriors returned to the unburned farm houses to finish plundering the goods before returning to their families, who were then living in dispersed camps as they always did during the early spring. They had done it. They had won. There can be little doubt that they reveled in their victory in celebrations and feasting on English stores, as well as mourning those warriors who had lost their lives in the assault. Having hardly slept in days, the men needed a long rest to recuperate. They couldn't

---

[138]A 1642 law prohibited the trade of firearms to the Powhatans, indicating that a steady black market trade was already going on. Also, the surviving records do not indicate the length of time the attack went on for. Later on, only one day, April 18, was deemed a new holiday, but with it known that the Powhatans pressed on until garrisons were brought together and were stopped by their firepower, and the government taking over a week to respond, may indicate that more violence on a lesser scale happened for the next few days following the main assault. Also see Ben C. McCary, *Indians in Seventeenth Century Virginia,* (Williamsburg, Garret and Massie, Inc., Virginia 350th Anniversery Celebration Corporation, 1957) 80; Act 23, March 1642/3, Acts of the Assembly, in Hening, *Statutes at Large...,* 255-256; Billings, *The Papers of Sir William Berkeley*, 60-61.

[139]Anonymous, "A Perfect Description...," 11.

rest long, however, because though the English were boxed in, they were still a lethal enemy who would surely seek vengeance. Care needed to be taken if Opechancano's plan was to work.

Many in the garrisons, and even in the areas that didn't receive an attack, began to have a different perspective of things in the wake of the assault. In one instant most feelings of distrust toward one another, whether Puritan or Anglican, Londoner or Royalist, dissipated. As one Puritan said, "We are at peace among our selves and have beene so ever since the massacre," whereas they were at the point of open armed rebellion a week earlier. It was his opinion that "the massacre (though a judgement) did divert a great mischief that was growing among us by Sir William Barclay's courses... so that it is the opinion of judicious men that if the Indians had but forborne for a month longer, they had found us in such a combustion among ourselves that they might with ease have cut of[f] every man if once we had spent that little powder and shot that we had among our selves."[140] That is not to say that the preexisting issues disappeared, but having a common enemy put these on hold for the moment.

A great many cattle and hogs were left out in the open as their owners either died or retreated. As Opechancano ordered, many Indians took advantage and killed or led off a lot of cattle in the wake of the attack; the hogs could be hunted later, like wild animals. All through June the Powhatans would be "fed and encouraged" by this new food supply. The cutting of English families' growing corn may also have been successful. By June the colony anticipated a future want of corn and "by woeful experience" knew that if they didn't do something the colony

[140]Frank, "News from Virginny," 86.

would starve. At that point they also enacted a resolution to keep night watches and sentinels, indicating there may indeed have been successful nighttime corn slashing attacks by the Powhatans. Indian ambushes in the woods were generally feared for months, so that few dared "to goe over the forrest alone."[141]

The wide ranging estimates of the casualties inflicted that day may give some sense to the kind of unsure intelligence Berkeley was receiving from the field. In New England, John Winthrop had heard that "300 at least," had been killed, while his peer Edward Johnson thought it was "five or six hundred." Robert Beverley would later guess "near Five Hundred Christians," an anonymous contemporary Puritan letter thought that "400 of our people," had fallen, and the June 1644 assembly meeting estimates "neare fower hundred," with an unknown number of wounded and captured. The anonymous Puritan letter-writer and the Assembly meeting estimates are the most reliable, since they are the earliest and closest to the events.[142]Interestingly, this is more people killed than in the first assault of 1622, when about 350 colonists lost their lives.[143] That was at a time when the Powhatans outnumbered the English. It is remarkable in 1644 that even though weaker, outnumbered, and only able to enter the plantations at certain points, they were still able to inflict casualties worse than nearly any other time in American Indian history. Firepower certainly had something to

---

[141]Anonymous, "Acts, Orders and Resolutions of the General Assembly of Virginia," 3:235; Robinson, "Notes From the Council and General Court Records…," 70; Fleet, *York County Records,* 40.

[142]Beverley, *The History and Present State of Virginia,* 60; Frank, "News From Virginny," 85; Anonymous, "Acts, Orders and Resolutions," 229; Winthrop, *History of New England,* 167; Johnson, *Wonder-Working Providence,* 266; Morton, *Colonial Virginia,* 153.

[143] Fausz, J. Fredrick *Powhatan Uprising,* 362-400.

do with it, rage being another. They knew that they had to give it everything they had, for if the attack was ineffectual, the English would retaliate quickly and their offense would amount to nothing.

In October, the new communities at the plantations of the "great families" who gathered together for defense were addressed by the Assembly and allowed to exist as such, but only "in places of danger," with at least ten men sufficiently armed at each small community.[144] Likely, these groups of families of varying size built some kind of defensive works, and also planted corn and tobacco communally. Few dared to go out into the forest alone and increasingly relied on each other for support. It was an interesting social dynamic for a rather anti-social society that valued individual estate-building over community interests.

Banding together, however, came both instinctively and by royal order. Berkeley's instructions from King Charles specifically stated that in case of Indian attack people were to give out a signal of three successive shots to alert the community and seek each other out for defense. How this exactly played out on the day of April 18 is difficult to say, but mention of the three successive shots to be fired is mentioned in laws passed soon thereafter and specific mention is made of people settling by groups for better defense, so it would seem that King Charles's orders were in fact implemented and may have saved lives.[145]

As the days went by, colonists who had formerly despised each other began to think more about what happened in a religious context. The Puritans had been saved. They had been

---

[144]Act 5, October 5, 1644, Acts of the Assembly, in Hening, *The Statutes at Large...*, 285-286; Morton, *Colonial Virginia,* 154.

[145] Billings, *The Papers of Sir William Berkeley*, 31-32.

given divine signs from the Almighty before the attack occurred. The Anglicans had been slaughtered. Perhaps the Puritans had been right all along. Soon, Puritan leaders and pastors began preaching this message to attentive ears, and their churches began to swell in numbers. Over a hundred people were turning out on Sunday services at the Nansemond church under the Rev. Mr. Harrison, whom Berkeley despised. In Berkeley's trips around the colony to organize his people, he made sure to visit the church at Nansemond to make sure they knew he still wanted Harrison gone, but the people, in defiance, upheld him as their minister in Berkeley's presence.[146]

Many people began to view the assault as a divine judgment for the rejection of the Puritan teachings. They began to heed that message and turn their hearts toward God. Others who were able managed to find a way to escape Virginia. Groups of refugees boarded ships to leave that place forever. Many Puritans escaped north to New England, who gave the leaders there the news of the assault and of Berkeley's persecution of the Puritan churches in Virginia.[147] Based on these refugees, John Winthrop remarked:

> "It was very observable that this massacre came upon them soon after they had driven out the godly ministers we had sent to them, and made an order that all such as would not conform to the discipline of the church of England should depart the country by a certain day, which the massacre now prevented: and the governor… a courtier, and very malignant towards the way of our churches here… had appointed a fast to be kept through the

---

[146] Johnson, *Wonder-Working Providence...*, 266.

[147] Winthrop, *History of New England,* 168.

> country upon good Friday (as they call it) for the good success of the king, etc., and, the day before, this massacre began."[148]

The Rev. Edward Johnson echoed Winthrop when he energetically wrote:

> "It were much to be desired, that all people would take notice of the hand of God against this people, after the rejection of these Ministers of Christ: and indeed it was none other but the thrusting [of] Christ from them; and now… all you Cavaliers and malignant party the world throughout, take notice of the wonderworking providence of Christ toward his Churches, and punishing hand of his toward the contemners [sic] of his Gospel. Behold ye dispisers [sic], and wonder. Oh poor Virginia, dost thou send away the Ministers of Christ! with threatening speeches? No sooner is this done, but the barbarous, inhumane, insolent, and bloody Indians are let loose upon them."[149]

By April 30, twelve days after the attack, Governor Berkeley finally had enough information, and had reestablished channels of communication with colonists of the frontier. The prisoners that were taken had been brought in for questioning. These warriors may have expected torture, which was consistent with their culture surrounding warfare practices. They may have received it. In the end they spelled out exactly what caused them to be so angry as to bring on the assault. It was the land. The English took the land away from the Powhatans, and they would

---

[148]Ibid.

[149]Johnson, *Wonder-Working Providence…,* 265.

stop at nothing to get it back. What's more, these captives boasted, all the Indians within six hundred miles were confederated together against the English. The English have no hope. It was a bluff, but Berkeley bought it, and this impression would make them think that they were at war with the entire Indian world.[150] He gave basic orders and instructions for marches against the Powhatans and began getting the colony on a war footing.[151] This show of military activity may have disconcerted the Indians, who had hard experience of English style warfare, and began to abate on their attacks and altogether look after their individual tribal interests rather than Powhatan affairs on a larger scale. The English interpreted this as cowardice. It was written that "they had not the heart to follow the Counsells their King commanded: but to the admiration of the English, prosecuted not their opportunitie, nor were constant to their owne Principles, but fled away and retyred themselves many miles distant off the Colony: which little space of time gave the English opportunity to gather themselves together, call an Assembly, secure their Cattell, and to thinke upon some way to defend themselves."[152] Opechancano must have been horrified that the most critical part of his plan to lay siege was no longer being followed. Perhaps like the later Japanese who bombed Pearl Harbor, he may have known that he had awakened a sleeping giant. It is a mistake however, to say that no further strikes were made by Opechancano's forces. To the contrary, as will be seen, he still had fight left in him, and while he was abandoned by some of his followers, most remained loyal and

[150]Winthrop, *History of New England,* 167-68; Anonymous, *A Perfect Description...,* 11.
[151]Robinson, "Notes From the Council and General Court Records...," 70.
[152]Anonymous, "A Perfect Description...," 11.

would continue to wreak havoc on the Virginian frontier in coming months.

“Irreconcileable enemyes:” Virginia’s battle plan

Sir William Berkeley had known war before. He had supported the King as a field officer during the Bishop’s Wars against Scotland prior to the English Civil War, though at one point passing along faulty intelligence, disgracing himself.[153] While European–style combat had little meaning against the Powhatans, Berkeley’s military experience proved valuable as he began calling out orders and instructions to the militia commanders. Though over a week passed before any record of military action surfaces, there was no doubt of much activity. Before any counter measures could be taken against Opechancano, the colony needed to take stock of its losses and secure whatever provisions it could find. Corn supply was suddenly a concern, and some of the braver sort had to make the dangerous trek to their abandoned plantations to try and secure supplies. One such man was Captain Ralph Wormely, who “emediatly after the Masacre” travelled north of the York River, probably with a squad of armed men, to retrieve six barrels of corn from Thomas Shaw’s house.[154] Another dying man requested papers in a trunk in Jamestown be delivered to Captain John West, “now finding the tymes Dangerous giving my [gun?] to goe over the forrest alone.” [155] Likely there were many others as well, some of whom may have fallen prey to Powhatan ambushes.

Militia commanders would have had a difficult task as they took stock of their county’s casualties and organized the

[153]Billings, *Sir William Berkeley,* 26-28.

[154]Fleet, *York County records*, 36.

[155]Ibid., 40.

men into an organized state of readiness. Slowly, the numbers began to filter into Jamestown and a horrified Berkeley took stock of the losses. Nearly four hundred dead and counting, with many more missing. They could almost forget about a corn and tobacco crop that year, except for what they could manage to plant late and communally in their gathering places. His main concern, however, was powder and shot munitions. There wasn't nearly enough. Supplies were already low before the attack, and the settlers had expended a great deal in defending themselves, so that now ammunition was "extremely wanted." Tobacco prices had already plummeted and that cash crop wasn't nearly as valuable as it once had been. Without being able to plant safely that year, the colonists would hardly be able to grow enough tobacco to sustain the purchase of more ammunition, not to mention soldiers' salaries, care for the wounded plus orphans and widows, the erection of fortifications, none of which would be cheap. Letters of credit would have to do.[156]

Finally, twelve days after the assault, Berkeley got the governor's council together to take the first decisive steps. On April 30, he issued an order "for 4 score [eighty] men at middle plantation," to be permanently stationed there for the defense of the lower peninsula at modern-day Williamsburg. The Lower Peninsula wasn't the main theatre of conflict as few, if any, attacks had taken place there. Still, some viable plantations and cattle ranges were within the palisades that more or less blocked off the eastern half of the peninsula. This area would have to feed the rest of the colony for the foreseeable future since the best of the agricultural land was open to enemy attack. It had to be protected. It is easy to imagine a certain amount of impatience on the part of the frontier plantations south of James River and on

---

[156]Anonymous, "Acts, Orders and Resolutions," 237-238.

the York as they remained in makeshift garrisons, keeping watch at night, wondering when the next attack would come or if their friends and family were still alive.[157]

Berkeley further appointed Lieutenants and Deputy Lieutenants in each county and gave them "Particular directions for marching against the Indians," though specifics about those directions are not recorded. Before any marching was to happen, however, the militia needed to be fully squared away as the colony moved to full battle readiness. These new militia leaders were therefore given instructions in May to compile a list and present it to the "governor and counsel on the 1st Monday in June, of all persons from 16 to 60" to be deemed tithables, or in other words, taxpayers who were eligible for the draft and for the levies that were sure to come as war costs rose. This data would also serve to estimate the casualties sustained in the assault. The May council meeting also made an order against using "improper language in time of War" addressed the needs of those newly widowed and orphaned, and dealt with the property and cattle and other property "of persons lately slain."[158]

---

[157]Robinson, "Notes From the Council and General Court Records," 70-71.

[158]Ibid.

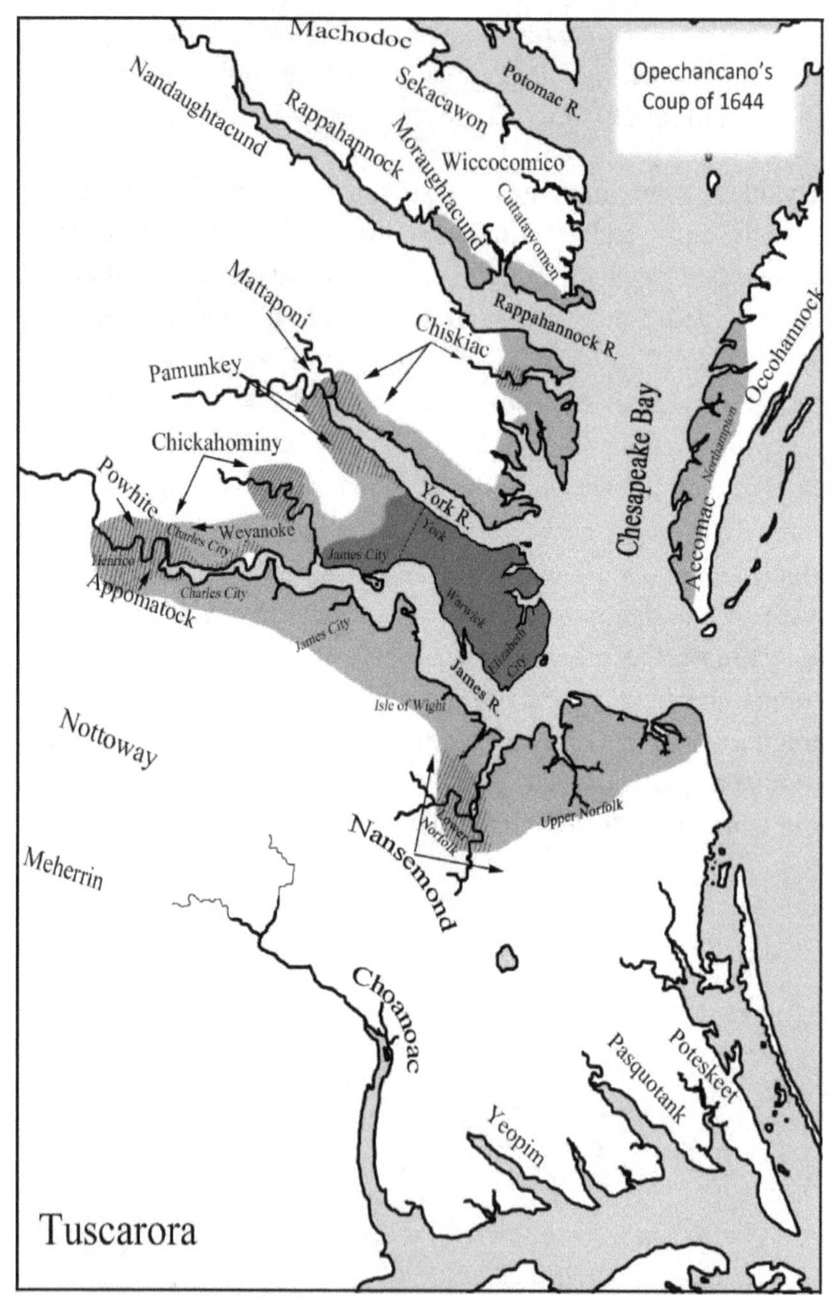

Figure 15. The assault of 1644. Organized groups of Powhatans struck simultaneously, beginning at the heads of the major rivers and progressing inward as far as possible. Map by the author.

The actions of the Powhatans are little known in these opening months following their initial strike on the colony. According to an anonymous author in 1649, possibly authored by Governor Berkeley, they showed cowardice and withdrew immediately following the attack, which gave the English time to regroup and effectively counter-attack.[159] A letter written by Richard Kemp in 1645, however, gives the distinct impression that the Powhatans had in no way backed down and still made sorties against frontier settlements, though this may only apply to later in the autumn and imply that any mid-summer attacks were not at the intense level that Opechancano desired.[160] Even so, the June Assembly meeting shows indications that the Powhatans continued to be a danger in the forests and freely killed English cattle.[161] As far as the settlers' actions were concerned, the month of May was spent in a flurry of activity as the Lieutenants Berkeley had appointed prepared reports for him and the council, giving a full accounting of their manpower, and more importantly, their powder and shot levels. Military leaders, the Lieutenants and Captains, were in a large part comprised of veterans of the 1622-32 Powhatan war and probably began training their newly conscripted men in the Indian-style fighting that they had learned. Though not called rangers in this war, later records suggest ranging techniques were practiced as smaller squads of men ranged the woods as scouts to keep the frontier as safe as possible. Many of these young soldiers, perhaps most, were new immigrants from England who had come over as indentured servants and poor farmers. They were largely in their early twenties, though soldiers were drafted as young as sixteen

---

[159]Anonymous, "A Perfect Description of Virginia," 11.

[160]"Richard Kemp to Sir William Berkeley, 27 February 1644/45," in Billings, *The Papers of Sir William Berkeley,* 62-66.

[161]Anonymous, "Acts, Orders and Resolutions," 235-236.

and as old as sixty. Many had scarcely ever shot a gun before, let alone fought a frontier Indian war.[162]

Berkeley called another council meeting for the first of June, immediately prior to convening the General Assembly. The news the council heard was not good. One by one the new Lieutenants made their reports and Berkeley became more and more convinced that they could not handle this war alone. Opechancano had planned well, and Virginia was in deep trouble. What Berkeley and others had expected was true, that there was in no way enough powder and shot for any kind of effective resistance, let alone an active counter assault. And even if there was a large scale assault, that would use up the last of their powder and provisions. Then there would be nothing left. On the other hand, by not assaulting the enemy, the Powhatans would probably become emboldened and step up their attacks as they realized the dire straits the colony was in.[163]

After much contemplation and advice from his council, Berkeley decided that a full assault was necessary nonetheless. The English would not be bullied by what they considered to be an "inferior" nation of "savages." He and the others of the council exited the back room and entered the main hall of the assembly building in Jamestown. The room was stuffy in the

---

[162]Later in the war, small forts were erected to house garrisons of soldiers who kept constant patrol of the woods in search of hidden Indian targets. They could not move about in this way if they were in the rank-and-file European style warfare. Similar scouting expeditions were also noted in other places such as Lower Norfolk County. See Walter, *Lower Norfolk County, Virginia Court Records,* 197. For information on ages and occupations of incoming indentured servants, see Horn, "Servant Emigration to the Chesapeake in the Seventeenth Century," in Tate and Ammerman, *The Chesapeake in the Seventeenth Century,* 51-95.

[163]Anonymous, "Acts, Orders and Resolutions," 225-255; Shea, *The Virginia Militia in the Seventeenth Century,* 61-62.

Virginian heat as the bedraggled burgesses from the various counties mingled with each other, recounting the harrowing tales of the attack on their homes. Some had little to tell as those like William Whitby of Warwick and John Holden of Elizabeth City experienced no violence, whereas men like John Chewe, Edward Hill and Mathew Gough from York, Charles City and Henrico had to travel through a war zone, leaving their families behind in the garrisons in order to attend the meeting. Berkeley and the council took their seats and called the meeting to order.[164]

No doubt starting with a speech (Berkeley was known for his eloquent oratory), the colonial leaders began working out a plan to protect themselves and defeat their enemies. Opening with a statement of intent, the Assembly recorded a mission statement that would guide their actions over the next several years:

> "Whereas the Indians have justly made themselves our Irreconcileable enemyes by the late Bloody Massacre having most treacherously and cruelly slayne neare fower hundred of the Inhabitants of the Collony. Bee it therefore by this present Grand Assembly recorded to Posterity. That wee will for ever abandon all forms of peace and familiarity wth the whole Nation. And will to the uttmost of our power pursue and root out those wch have any way had their hands in the shedding of our blood and Massacring our People."[165]

---

[164]Ibid., 228-229.

[165]Ibid., 229.

In pursuing their goal to utterly destroy the Powhatans, (which today would be called a genocide) it was resolved to be the main mission of the summer to cut off the Indians' food supplies by "use[ing] our uttmost endeavrs to cut downe the Indians Corne generally this Summer in all places subject to Opochanckanough," but particularly to do it to the Pamunkeys themselves. Recognizing their own supply problems, however, these attacks could only be taken "as farre as our abilityes and Ammunition shall enable us thereunto."[166]

In a vote by the whole Assembly, probably after Berkeley's nomination, Capt. William Claiborne was made "General and Chief Comannder in this expedition." Claiborne was a good choice, having military experience from the last Powhatan war, and having acquired some cultural knowledge from being engaged in the fur trade. Berkeley was "pleased" to give him a commission, in which Claiborne was "enabled to order all things belonging to this Warre According as he shall receive Instructions and directions from tyme to tyme from the Governor & Councell during his Imploymt therein." He also had power to "press and take such men and such neccessaryes at the publique Charge as shall be expedient for the service," and all captains, junior officers and constables were to view him as their superior.[167]

This main assault was to take place in mid-July, concurrently with attacks on smaller chiefdoms made by county expeditions. Upper Norfolk County, which encompassed the Nansemond River, was ordered to "sett out a sufficient company of men," to attack not only the Nansemonds, but also the

[166]Ibid., 230.

[167]Ibid.

(formerly) nearby Warrasquoyacks and the more distant "Seacocks, . . . Chawanoke or any other neare unto them." The Chowanokes are known to have been active at this time, but they occupied land to the well to the south in what is now North Carolina. The Wariscoyacs are thought by scholars to have been eliminated in the last war, and while Martha McCartney has speculated that the Seacocks represented the Secotan people from Carolina, I think it more likely that it was a reference to Seacock Creek, in present day Southampton County, within marching distance of Upper Norfolk. Perhaps these Seacocks were traditionalist Nansemonds, moving southwestward to avoid the English In all; I find it unlikely that any but the Nansemonds were actually attacked at this time, although these orders did set the stage for more southerly expeditions later in the war.[168]

Henrico and Charles City counties were among the hardest hit during the assault, and their subsequently reduced population size prevented them from carrying out massive assaults. They were deemed strong enough, however, to launch a raid against the Weyanoke town south of the James, and continue harassing others in their vicinity such as the Chickahominy as a distraction to try to draw warriors away from the Pamunkey heartland. A diversion of Indian manpower would give William Claiborne a better chance of success as his three hundred-man army, the largest ever assembled in Virginia to that point, slammed into Opechancano's center. Following the Pamunkey assault, the assembly planned a final expedition to destroy the Chickahominy town in an effort to protect the weak Henrico and Charles City counties.[169]

---

[168]Ibid.; McCartney, "Seventeenth Century Apartheid," 53.

[169]Anonymous, "Acts, Orders and Resolution," 231.

The Englishmen on the Pamunkey expedition were to furnish themselves with one pound of powder and four pounds of shot per man, not to mention the ammunition to be spent against the Nansemonds, Weyanokes and Chickahominies. Recognizing that "the Late Bloody Massacre by the Indians hath occasioned more shott to be spent then was expected... and that shott [is] being extremely wanted to suppresse the enemy," orders were sent out by the Assembly to melt down any and all lead supplies in possession of private colonists, even to the extent of tearing off building materials from their houses and melting down lead weights.[170] In light of this emergency, the Assembly implored Berkeley to travel back to England with letters of credit and use his good standing with King Charles to procure provision, powder, shot and royal support. Hopefully by the time the assaults were carried out, the Powhatans would be in a state of withdrawal and Berkeley would promptly return with enough ammunition for defense and further offensive campaigns. It was a gamble, but there were few other options. The colony may have had strength in numbers, but if their supplies ran out, they would wither on the vine. Berkeley must have had the English Civil War in his mind as he made preparations to set out, wondering if he could reasonably convince King Charles to part with any amount of supplies while he was fighting a war of his own.[171] An Act of the Assembly enacted that June, that:

> Whereas New Matters of Importance hath nowe most unexpectedly interposed itself, as allsoe the deplorable estate of this afflicted Country being unable to Mannadg the affaires that doth continually aryse by reason of this present Warre

[170]Ibid., 236-37.

[171]Ibid., 238.

> being now [no] ways furnished with a fit proportion of Armes and Ammunition, for the preservation and safety thereof, But that in all likelyhood may decline to a sodain Ruine and Desolation. It is therefore ordered by this present Grand Assembly that the Governor bee entreated to repaire for England, and emplore his Mejesties gracious assistance for our Releife which Motion and desires of ours he having willingly embraced.[172]

Also at this point, another agent of Virginia named Cornelius Loyd was commissioned to take a shipment of tobacco (and even some corn, despite the potential shortage) to the northern colonies of New England, the Dutch and the Swedes, and exchange it for arms and ammunition. Loyd was a merchant who had previously assisted in providing light leather armor to Norfolk County troops in 1639, and now he provided this tobacco and corn out of his personal supply. He was to be repaid by the colony out of the public levies later on.[173]Almost as an afterthought, Berkeley introduced legislation to reconvene the county commissioners and have them resume administering the oath of allegiance, which had been halted in the face of the assault, before adjourning the Assembly on June the third.[174]

Following the Assembly, Berkeley made final arrangements before departing on the next available ship. Richard Kemp was appointed interim governor in Berkeley's absence in civil affairs while General Claiborne handled all things military. Splitting the civil and military affairs of his duties between two people shows that Berkeley did not trust any

---

[172]Ibid.

[173]Ibid., 238-239; Shea, *The Virginia Militia in the Seventeenth Century,* 52.

[174]Anonymous, "Acts, Orders and Resolutions," 238.

one man to have too much power.[175] In regards to future plans of raids, Berkeley and apparently most of the council took a stance of lashing out, once supply enough was procured, against even the Rappahannocks and Patawomeks, who do not appear to have taken part in the attack. Claiborne's opinion was "different from the others in relation to the propriety of war upon the Indians between the Rappahannock and Potomac." No doubt the others pointed out that he had a personal financial interest in maintaining trade relations with these people that he didn't want damaged, but the issue was dropped and the Rappahannock River nations would be left alone, for the time being.[176] Berkeley made final preparations and departed without further delay, though as Shea stated, "it is unclear what help he expected from an England locked in civil war."[177]

Richard Kemp is an interesting character. One would think that because he supported former governor John Harvey when no one else on the council did, that he would be shunned by the others thereafter and that he would lose his place of influence. To the contrary, he became Berkeley's right hand man in the same way that he was Harvey's, and there is no evidence that he was in enmity with any other councilmen. Being handed the care of the entire colony in a time of war was no small thing, so he must have been a trustworthy and capable person. From his lengthy discourse written in the following year, he managed to keep control of the colony even as opinions shifted, passions flared and loyalties swayed. Nor did he write this discourse in a self-congratulatory way, but rather self-critically and

---

[175]Ibid., 230; Shea, *The Virginia Militia in the Seventeenth Century,* 62; Billings, *The Papers of Sir William Berkeley,* 60; Billings, *Sir William Berkeley,* 96-99.

[176]Robinson, "Notes From the Council and General Court Records," 70-71.

[177]Shea, *Virginia Militia in the Seventeenth Century,* 62.

apologetically, constantly conscious of incurring royal wrath by ignoring certain royal orders for the good of the colony. [178]

Kemp would come to face a very trying time. In fact, a delicate balance between supporting either the King or Parliament now rested on him and his abilities to mediate between the political factions that had risen up back home. If he was worried, he had good reason to be, for at the same time that the Virginian general assembly was finalizing their war strategy, Parliament's House of Commons in London had received word of Berkeley's previous refusal to acquiesce to the commissioners they had sent in March. Now seeing where Virginia stood, they began discussions "to consider what Course is fittest to be taken for reducing the Plantations of Virginia and Barmoudies [Bermudas] to the Obedience of Parliament." Kemp not only had Opechancano to contend with, but he had to tread very carefully, otherwise there was a real possibility of facing an invasion from Parliamentary England as well.[179]

As Berkeley neared England he would have heard more about the civil war from the crewmen, but as he stepped off the dock into Bristol and asked around, he would have received very discouraging news. While the King was far from defeated at this point, the conflict was dragging out longer and on a much broader scale than anyone could have anticipated. What was thought to have been a simple matter of one glorious and decisive battle had become a constantly shifting series of campaigns that constantly changed the maps of Parliament and

---

[178]Martha McCartney, *Virginia Immigrants and Adventurers,* 439-440; "Richard Kemp to Sir William Berkeley, 27 February 1644/45," in Billings, *The Papers of Sir William Berkeley,* 62-66.

[179]House of Commons, *Journal of the House of Commons: volume 3: 1643-1644* (1802), pp. 523-525.

Royal-held territory as both sides pushed back and forth against each other. Earlier that year, King Charles had made a truce with rebellious Irish Catholics in order to free up troops for his campaigns on the mainland. This caused many of his supporters to fall away from him as rumors of Catholic conspiracies ran rampant. At the same time, Parliament made an alliance of its own with the northern Scots, who combined with Parliamentary forces and after an epic series of battles, captured the city of York, forcing the King to retreat to western England.[180]

At least Bristol, where Berkeley landed, was in the same general region in which the King was conducting his campaigns. It is unknown how long Berkeley spent seeking out King Charles, but at this time King Charles was chasing down the Earl of Essex's army, attempting to corner him on the coast. Finally getting audience with him in the midst of the battles, Berkeley pleaded Virginia's case, but what he feared was true. King Charles supported Virginia morally, but in terms of actual supplies he had none to spare. He gave Berkeley letters stating his support, as well as instructions and concessions for prosecuting the war, but on the whole little of use could be had from the crown. Berkeley was no doubt discouraged, but for some reason decided to stay in England for an extended period, to help the King in his campaigns, according to Billings. It is equally possible he had been trying to procure supplies from other sources during this time, or that he could not find transport back to America, but little is known about his time away from the Virginian war for the entire next year. Surely he knew that if

[180]Gaunt, *The English Civil Wars,* 21-43.

he didn't return with adequate supplies, Virginia would be in serious trouble.[181]

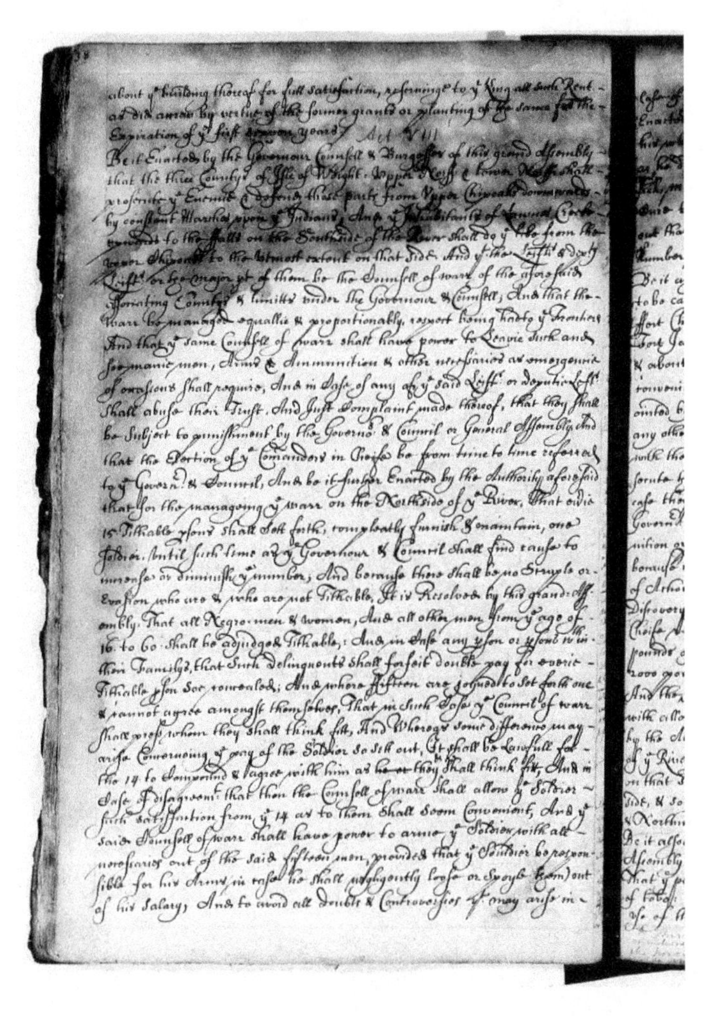

Figure 16. 17th century copy of original orders for Upper and Lower Norfolk Counties to launch attacks against the nearest Indian nations to them, most notably the Nansemond. Thomas Jefferson Papers. Courtesy of the National Archives.

[181]Ibid.; Billings, *Sir William Berkeley,* 96-99; Billings, *The Papers of Sir William Berkeley,* xlvi; Bliss, *Revolution and Empire,* 51,76.

Traitorous and Seditious Murmurings

While the English prepared for counter-attack, the Powhatans were busy in their season of Cohattayough, the *earing-of-corn* season, in which the corn was halfway grown. The men had just finished harvesting fish from the yearly sturgeon runs while the women were gathering wild fruits and tubers until the green corn was ready. While the English were preparing frontal assaults on known town sites, the Powhatans were actually in dispersed and mobile camps, making it difficult for the English to locate them.[182]

Each county's militia officers and sheriff began appointing and training the men they deemed most fit for the marches and gathering supplies throughout June and early July. Upper Norfolk, Charles City and Henrico Counties were not as strictly regulated as other counties in their supplies for their marches against local indigenous communities, but the three hundred man expedition under General Claiborne was a well-supplied and protected force. Each man was required to have a full pound of powder and four pounds of shot, in addition to three weeks' worth of food. Besides a gun in good repair (usually a matchlock musket as opposed to state-of-the-art flintlocks), each man also carried a sword or cutlass for close-quarter combat or corn-slashing, and defensive armor with a headpiece.

In accordance with the times, "armor" did not necessarily mean metal armor, although perhaps the wealthy officers donned such, but more likely referred to heavy leather buff coats, which typical English soldiers of this time would wear under chain

[182] Rountree, *Pocahontas, Powhatan, Opechancanough,* 239-240.

mail. The headpiece was also usually a tight-fitting leather cap with straps secured under the chin. This assemblage of armor may have done well enough against blunt weapons and stone implements, but Powhatan arrows had already been demonstrated to be able to completely penetrate wooden shields with arrows better than a pistol could, not to mention the fact that they had acquired firearms. These soldiers' counterparts in England had different tactics and equipment than those in Virginia. On the mainland, English armies used large companies of pikemen (men who carried long spears for anti-cavalry purposes) who guarded their musketeer company, who often had the newer flintlock rifles. In Virginia, pikes were useless and disregarded, making every man a musketeer. High-quality equipment such as flintlocks and metal armor would have also been hard to come by in Virginia, their forces still using the older matchlocks, with officers carrying pistols, and every man carrying a cutlass. It was an assemblage unique in one of the first real attempts to adapt English tactics and technology to frontier Indian fighting.[183]

By early July, most of the counties had their forces together. Each county had its own pinnace or shallop for the transport of their men to the rendezvous, somewhere near the entrance of the York River. The most populous counties like James City, York and Isle of Wight contributed fifty men each, while Elizabeth City and Lower Norfolk each contributed forty,

---

[183] There are numerous texts on English weaponry and tactics during the English Civil War. For an example, see Gaunt, *The English Civil Wars, 28-31;* Powhatan arrows were demonstrated as having superior penetrating power to English pistols when, near the time of first contact, a wooden shield was set out to test the Powhatans. An English bullet stuck into the wood, but the Powhatan arrow went completely through it, to the shock of the English. A metal shield was used next, shattering the Powhatan arrow, causing a conflict. See Rountree, *Pocahontas's People,* 31.

and Warwick and Northampton sent thirty-five for the total of three hundred men. Once at the rendezvous, the officers began organizing and training under General Claiborne.[184]

Meanwhile, Upper Norfolk had finished organizing their troops and launched raids against the neighboring Nansemonds on July 8.[185] The Nansemonds were among the most dangerous of Powhatan chiefdoms, with about one hundred warriors between the two towns and scattered hamlets, though with ongoing factionalism within the nation their full strength is difficult to estimate. They are one of the first Indian nations in the region, indeed in America, to have roundly defeated an armed European force in a sustained series of skirmishes and battles in 1609, when the first attempt at the settlement of the Nansemond River was turned back with their tails tucked between their legs. They have consistently been characterized by early sources as a warlike and aggressive nation, intolerant of infractions against their sovereignty.[186] Times were different now, and though the details are not known, Upper Norfolk set out against them and any other Indians in their vicinity to slash their corn and burn their homes.[187]

Shortly after the Nansemond raids, Charles City and Henrico Counties joined their meager forces together to attack the "Great Weyanoke Town," on July 15, which had already been surrounded by English settlements, so that its whereabouts were precisely known.[188] Although details are unclear, the raid was entirely successful. The town was destroyed, and the

[184] "Acts, Orders and Resolutions," 231-32, 234.

[185] Ibid., 230.

[186] John Smith, *Generall Historie...*, 269-270.

[187] Ibid.

[188] Ibid., 231.

Weyanokes never again inhabited it. They may have been successful in holding back English forces long enough to carry off their supplies, however, for later accounts show they purchased new land from the Tuscaroras with roanoke shell beads and planted new corn, showing that they were able to save enough trade goods and grain to start over. Likely many Weyanokes had been in seasonal dispersal during the attack and met up with each other from various points. Travelling all together, they evacuated their homeland to an unknown future to the south as their town burned behind them.[189]

Knowing that the Weyanokes were to be attacked on the 15th in a move meant to distract Opechancano, General Claiborne launched his army in seven shallops up the York River with Henry Luellin as Surgeon General (with several assistant surgeons) and one Mr. Cleverio as chaplain.[190] Charles City and Henrico Counties were to continue to harass any Indian targets in their vicinity following the Weyanoke assault, to draw warriors away from the Pamunkey heartland, though to what success this was achieved is not known.[191] The action by Norfolk against the

---

[189] The Weyanoke evacuation south and their subsequent actions in purchasing land from the Tuscaroras and planting corn can be found in "The Indians of Southern Virginia, 1650-1711. Depositions in the Virginia and North Carolina Boundary Case," No. 4 (April 1900) 7:337-338; and "The Indians of Southern Virginia (Concluded)," VMHB No. 1, (July 1900) 8:1-11. They have also been commented on by Rountree in "Ethnicity Among the 'Citizen' Indians of Tidewater Virginia," in Porter, ed., *Strategies for Survival,* 173-209;Rountree, *Pocahontas's People,* 86; and Rountree, "Trouble Coming Southward: Emanations through and from Virginia, 1607-1675," in Robbie Ethridge and Charles Hudson, eds., *The Transformation of the Southeastern Indians, 1540-1760,* 65-78.

[190] Anonymous, "Acts, Orders and Resolutions," 233.

[191] Charles City and Henrico were instruction to attack other Indians in their vicinity following the Weyanoke assault, "the better to divert them from Pomunckey as farre as

Nansemond, Henrico and Charles City against the Weyanokes, and Claiborne's army against the Pamunkeys, has been described by William Shea as a three pronged assault, who stated, "The most interesting aspect of the campaign was the unusual degree of specialization and coordination among the three task forces: a single-county holding action south of the James, a modest diversion above the palisade, and a powerful attack against the main enemy stronghold."[192]

Although three hundred men may seem small by modern standards, it was more than sufficient at the time, since most Indian towns in the region had only about one to two hundred total inhabitants at most, including women and children. Salt pork and beef with cornmeal were the standard English rations, along with a supply of dried peas. Sometimes bits of cheese found their way into the supply, but the standard soldier's diet was fairly bland. Kemp described an extreme want of clothing in the following year, so bad that many colonists were practically "naked" with rags hanging off their bodies. These soldiers must have seemed a ragged bunch compared to the regular British armies, but the hopes and prayers of the colony went with them as they departed for the Pamunkey capital of Menmend.[193]

Claiborne followed strategies similar to what he learned in the last war of amphibious assault against the Pamunkeys. While most soldiers were transported in boats, it seems from a description in a land deed that the army actually divided and took

---

theire Amunition and Abilityes will enable them." See "Acts, Orders and Resolutions," 231.

[192] Shea, *The Virginia Militia in the Seventeenth Century,* 63-64.

[193] For supplies of the army and its size, see "Acts, Orders and Resolutions," 231-232; The Pamunkey Capital was called Menmend in a 1662 map referencing the old town. See Rountree, *Pocahontas's People,* 110-11.

two routes, one by water and one by foot soldiers on land, probably because the ships didn't have enough room for the entire force, and also so that thirty horses that were pressed into the service could be used to help transport baggage.[194] The fleet met up with the supply train and infantry "about six or seven miles up the narrows in Charles river alias York or Pomunkey river... where the foot Company met with the Boats when they went pomunkey March under the Command of . . . William Claiborne."[195]

The Pamunkey and other Powhatans were a keenly observant people and probably knew that the army was coming, likely having posted scouts all along the major routes along the river, and especially since a large part of the force went on foot. In many cases in the past, approaching English boat squadrons were often met with retreat before they ever arrived so that the English had to content themselves with burning crops and buildings instead of actual combat. However, later references cite that "diverse men were hurt and Maymed & disabled" and that there were several "Boats lost & damnified," showing that the Pamunkeys, under Opechancano's leadership, held their ground and contested control of their town in the Battle of Menmend. [196] The battle on the part of the Pamunkey warriors may also have been a protecting action meant to stall the English to allow their women and children to escape into the woods. Although no battle reports detail exactly what took place, Richard Kemp bragged that the town was destroyed; the houses burned, "even theire kings owne house and theire treasure house," and their

---

[194] Shea, *The Virginia Militia in the Seventeenth Century,* 62.

[195] Nugent, *Cavaliers and Pioneers,* 162.

[196] Act 5, October 5th, 1644, Acts of Assembly, in Hening, *The Statutes at Large...,* 285-286.

growing corn was slashed.[197] As the Pamunkeys retreated to their fallback position, however, something may have loomed in the distance that could threaten to stop the army in its tracks. According to a later map drafted in 1662, a short distance above Menmend was a large "Indian Fort."

Martha McCartney, a leading researcher associated with the discovery of the map, is of the opinion that the designation is meant to identify Fort Royal, a fort constructed in 1645 that was used as a trading post after the war. She stated that there were no examples of an Indian fortification with squared walls elsewhere in the east, and land deeds show this area to be in the vicinity of where Fort Royal would be, so this must be an English fort.[198] More recently, however, Helen Rountree suggested that this may indeed have been of native construction, and that Opechancano used it as a major factor in the Battle of Menmend, though she cites little evidence to support the argument.[199] While this mystery can't be fully solved without a thorough archaeological excavation or further documentation, I tend to agree with Rountree that a native origin to the fort is probable, or at least possible. McCartney's argument that no ethnological evidence of square-shaped American Indian fortifications exists is untenable. For example, archeological and documentary evidence of a Tuscarora fort in North Carolina that withstood an English siege in 1712 shows clear squared corners, protruding bastions, a

---

[197] Kemp to Berkeley, February 1645, in Billings, *The Papers of Sir William Berkeley,* 65

[198] Martha W. McCartney, "The Draft of York River in Virginia: An Artifact of the SeventeenthCentury," in *Southeastern Archeaology* 3(2), (winter, 1984).

[199] Rountree, *Before and After Jamestown,* 154. Dr. Rountree has informed me that having walked the grounds of the former fort with an archeologist colleague; she has become doubtful that there was an Indigenous-made fort in the area. Dr. Helen Rountree, personal communication, 24 January, 2016.

blockhouse and even subterranean siege bunkers, all built by native hands.[200] Further up the coast in New England, defending Narragansets during King Philip's War of 1675 constructed a five-acre fortress containing five hundred wigwams with forward positions of blockhouses using English architectural inspirations.[201] Even in the Virginia-North Carolina border region, the Nottoway Indians became one of the strongest surviving nations by the 1700s, and constructed for themselves an innovative palisade. One English visitor stated that "This Fort was a Square Piece of Ground, inclos'd with Substantial Puncheons, or Strong Palisades, about ten feet high, and leaning a little outwards, to make a Scalade more difficult. Each side of the Square might be about 100 yards long, with Loop holes at proper Distances, through which they may fire upon the Enemy."[202] Obviously, squared fortifications were not such a strange thing by 1700s, and Opechancano may have constructed the first such example.

If Opechancano directed the construction of this fort in anticipation of an English advance, then it was most likely here that the most of the English casualties were sustained. In fact, according to Rountree, this may have been ultimately a Pamunkey victory, though Kemp would later claim success in his letter to Berkeley. Claiborne continued to operate in the area for three weeks, seeking and destroying houses and corn fields, and

---

[200] Heath, Charles L. and. Phelps, David S., "Architecture of a Tuscarora Fortress: The Neoheroka Fort and the Tuscarora War (1711—1715)," (Paper Presented at the 63rd Annual Meeting of the Society for American Archaeology, January 1998, Seattle, Washington).

[201] Shultz, Eric B. and Tougias, Michael J., *King Philip's War: The History and Legacy of America's Forgotten Conflict,* (Woodstock, VM: The Countryman Press, 2000) 252.

[202] William K. Boyd, ed., *William Byrd's Histories of the Dividing Line Betwixt Virginia and North Carolina,* (New York, Dover Publications, 1967) 114.

returned to Jamestown by August 5, but Opechancano had escaped again.[203]

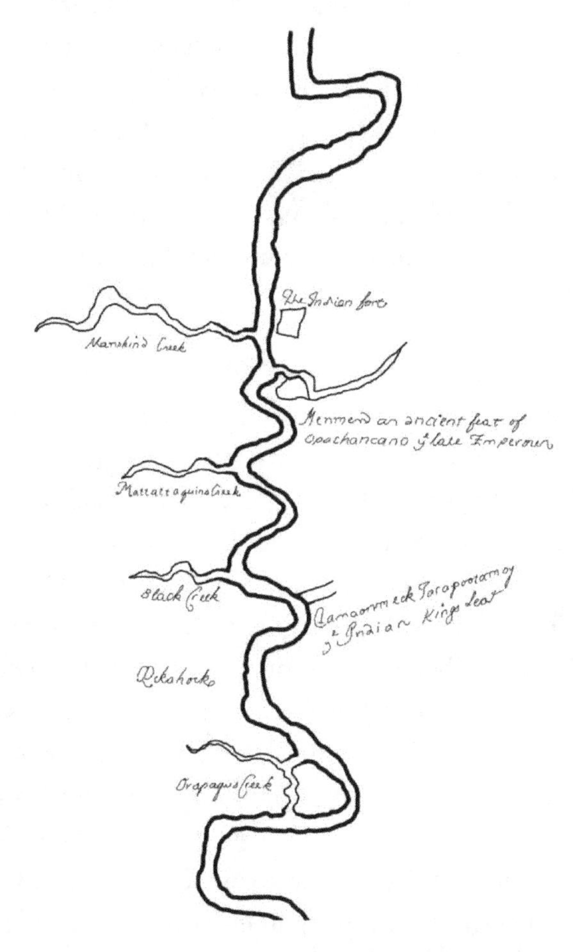

Figure 17. Draft of York River, ca. 1662. This map has been shown by Martha McCartney to locate several important archaeological sites, among them, Opechancano's probable fortress. Redrawn from the 1662 Langston map (McCartney) by the author.

[203] A three week campaign based on the soldiers carrying three weeks of provisions, and their return by August fifth was mentioned in the Governor's Council Minutes. See Anonymous, "Acts, Orders and Resolutions," 231; Shea, *The Virginia Militia,* 62-64; Rountree, *Pocahontas's People,* 85; McIlwaine, *Minutes of the Council,* 501.

General Claiborne sent messages and probably wounded soldiers back to Jamestown to keep his superiors apprised of the campaign, who must have been encouraged by news of Menmend's destruction. As those attacks proceeded, the lower counties kept up their raids as well, possibly hitting the Appamattocks and Powhites. All of the attacks were continuous and relentless. As Kemp said, "Wee suffered none of them about us to rest." It probably seemed to both the Powhatans and English that Opechancano's plan had backfired and all was ruined for the Indians.[204]

The final major assault of the summer of 1644 was against the Chickahominy town of Oranioc (erroneously called Warrany by the English) in August by a small force of about fifty men.[205] This was a multi-county force again, and may have been a foot march as opposed to an amphibious assault because of its closer proximity to Jamestown. Capt. Ralph Wormeley, who seems to have led the expedition, rode a horse into battle and apparently went ahead of his men with sword drawn. Little is known about the rest of the force except for Thomas Ward, the company surgeon, whose wages for his service would later be garnished to pay his debts, which was becoming increasingly common in the colony. Richard Kemp described Wormeley's actions as "the best and maine of the service," of the whole summer, where he "did very gallant service, and with his owne hands killed two and brought in one prisoner by the locke [of his hair] to the great joy of the Armye, and was of greate

---

[204] Anonymous, "Acts, Orders and Resolutions," 230-231; Kemp to Berkeley, February 1645, in Billings, *The Papers of Sir William Berkeley,* 65; Shea, *The Virginia Militia,* 63-64; Rountree, *Pocahontas's People,* 86.

[205] Shea, *Virginia Militia in the Seventeenth Century,* 64.

Consequence to them in guiding them to their townes and Corne feildes."[206]

Figure 18. The shores of a section of the Chickahominy River, not far from the town site or Oranioc. The town was the site of a major battle of the Third Anglo-Powhatan War. Photo by the author.

Interestingly, as the march progressed toward Oranioc, Governor Leonard Calvert from Maryland arrived with a small quantity of ammunition and sailed his small ship up the Chickahominy River to assist the army in their assault, in what was probably a repayment for all the times Virginia had sent supplies and men to help with Maryland's Indian marches.[207] It seems Oranioc fell, therefore, by both cannon fire from the Maryland gunship and an infantry advance that devastated the town. It would never again be reoccupied, because the Chickahominy fled north as refugees to Pamunkey territory. What was a string of successes for the English quickly turned

---

[206] Kemp to Berkeley, in Billings, *The Papers of Sir William Berkeley,* 65.

[207] Ibid, *Berkeley,* 62.

sour, however, as reality set in. "Our powder failed us" after the Chickahominy march and "wee had but one Barrell" left when Calvert came and gave "us one hundred weight of shott," which still was not nearly enough, when distributed amongst the counties, to make any new marches at all. In fact if Calvert hadn't brought the ammunition, "wee must have againe disbanded." Altogether, "Our warrs with the Natives this Sumer had good success," despite the powder shortage. [208]

But the year wasn't over yet. Opechancano would not fail to respond to this renewed assault, already surmising that their ammunition was low. The main problem for him during this firestorm was keeping his people together. In the retreat and confusion of abandoning their towns and corn fields, some of his people lost contact altogether with him. The traditionalist Nansemonds were too far to the south for effective communication and so were the Weyanokes, who had gone even farther from the James River valley. Scouts would have had to be sent out to discover their whereabouts. The Weyanoke experience is a very interesting story that will be detailed later.[209]

Meanwhile, Opechancano took stock of his losses and reorganized his remaining people. Most others hadn't abandoned him and seemed to be willing to fight for him. As long as they did not count on firearms to fight the English, the Powhatans' arsenal was made entirely from renewable resources. While they were under the withering fire of the English counter-attack, it must have seemed as if the whole world was imploding as many Powhatans, such as the Weyanokes and Chickahominies, were

---

[208] Ibid, 65.

[209] "The Indians of Southern Virginia, 1650-1711. Depositions in the Virginia and North Carolina Boundary Case," No. 4 (April 1900) 7:337-338; and "The Indians of Southern Virginia (Concluded)," VMHB No. 1, (July 1900) 8:1-11.

forced away from their ancient homes altogether and became refugees trying to keep their families alive. An interesting thing happened, however, after the Chickahominy assault. While the Powhatans may have braced themselves for more attacks, there was a sudden stillness as the Virginian guns went silent. For the moment, they were able to come together and assess the situation. It soon became clear. The colony had used up all its ammunition. Opechancano wasted no time in gathering his remaining warriors, because exploiting this window of opportunity might be their only hope for victory.[210]

When the Chickahominy March commenced in August 1644, an unexpected visitor brought mixed feelings from all people, burgess and small farmer alike. Leonard Calvert, the current Lord Baltimore of Maryland, sailed into James River and met with interim governor Richard Kemp. On the one hand, he brought a hundred pounds of shot, which was well received, Kemp saying that the army would have had to have been disbanded without it, and even gave his personal assistance in the Chickahominy March itself. On the other hand, the heavier hand, he brought instructions from King Charles himself concerning dealing with parliament supporters, and Calvert himself was responsible for administering the King's pleasure.[211]

Leonard Calvert, despite his assistance with the Chickahominy march and ammunition, was probably the most hated man in Virginia at the moment of his arrival. He was a

[210] Most, at least those from the Pamunkey heartland, were willing to continue the war, as is seen from Kemp's statements that as soon as the English powder ran out, the Powhatans counter-attacked and fell on the frontiers again. See Kemp to Berkeley, in Billings, *The Papers of Sir William Berkeley,* 65.

[211] Frank, "News from Virginny," 86; Kemp to Berkeley, in Billings, *The Papers of Sir William Berkeley,* 62-24.

stench in Virginians' noses, his name a vulgarity. Looking at it from Virginia's perspective, he and his family had single handedly stolen Virginia's birthright by taking over northern Virginia and renaming it Maryland. He had violently fought against Virginians, killing some, in his spat with the Kent Island settlement, who by the way, were legally settled there before his "colony" was ever thought of. His colony was an economic cancer that cut hard into their tobacco profits, reaping all the rewards of Virginia's hard work, plucking the fruit of what Virginia had sown. And he was Catholic. How could the King allow a Catholic to do all these things?[212]

Calvert knew that Virginians disliked him, but it seems that he didn't realize the extent of their hatred, to the point of being a threat to his personal safety. From Kemp's letter, he appears to have invited several Virginians to his ship and gave them much wine and merriment, disregarding Kemp's warnings about threats to his person. But in this condition, he naively produced the King's commissions for Kemp's cooperation. As Kemp read the commissions, perhaps hoping for word that Berkeley had made inroads with the King and that supplies would be forthcoming, he quickly became horrified and aghast at what he was being asked to do.[213]

By Royal order, he was to seize all London ships, confiscating all cargoes, in the King's name. If that weren't bad enough, he was to confiscate all estates of Parliament supporters

---

[212] The Calvert family controlled Maryland, and was a family universally hated by Virginians, primarily for taking over the northern part of Virginia for themselves, battling and killing Virginians in the Kent Island dispute and heavily competing for tobacco. Kemp described him as "odious to the country," in Kemp to Berkeley, in Billings, *The Papers of Sir William Berkeley,* 62.

[213] Ibid.

in the colony, reducing them to poverty, punishing them for their disloyalty to the crown. Such an order had no hope of being accomplished, not with the current state of things in Virginia. Surely, the orders were out of date, for at the time the King wrote them, he was not aware of the Powhatan war or of the crippling supply situation in Virginia. If he had known, he never would have issued them, Kemp reasoned.[214]

> "I entered into due consideration of the meanes wee had to execute these Commands, as alsoe of the ruine which might succeed a rash attempt without further ability then onely show a will to doe. I was not a stranger to the inclination of the people bent to better theire conditions under any Masters, the cropps in most places were all together neglected and stagnent discourses of good plunder in this and that house, the invasion of Londoners rather wished for then feared, and these hopes incouraged by rumours from New England of the declyninge of the Kings partye and the prevailing of the other, Soe that upon all collections finding myself destitute both of Fortification and ammunition, and neyther fitted for offence or Defence nor with men but such as were rather to be doubted then trusted in such a cause..."[215]

Kemp said all this to Calvert, and "desired Capt. Calvert to desist from further prosecution, and that his Majesties Comands might be silenced and suspended until further pleasure knowne." But Calvert was unmoved. It was not as if he had made it up himself; he was under orders from the King and was

[214] Ibid.; Also described in Frank, "News From Virginny," 86-87.

[215] Kemp to Berkeley, in Billings, *The Papers of Sir William Berkeley,* 62.

responsible for their execution regardless of consequence. Frustrated, Kemp "added indeed this reason truly and you will say without flattery that upon my knowledge hee [Calvert] was a man soe odious to the Country that if there were no other cause in it, theeire eversion to him would foile the business. But when soe many obstacles and impossibilities which stood [in the way of success] ... these reasons weighed nothing with Capt. Calvert," who replied, "doe it I must and the service would be required at my hands." Kemp, getting angrier, later said that, "his end, his hopes, his interest, lay in the accomplishment of the designe in the purchase of the Shipps [that were seized] with theire Kargoes without concernment to him if the Colony for overtoppinge Maryland." He further reflected that "I would not affirme anything beyond knowledge, but this most Contantly [sic] I can, that if Capt. Calverts propositions had taken, Maryland had bene raised by the dispeoplinge of the Kings Colony [Virginia]."[216]

Kemp wanted to silence the commission altogether without making any public spectacle of it, for he knew that if the people found out that the King had given Calvert such a commission to flex the royal muscle around them, they would be up in arms, even despite the Indian war, and the whole colony might go over to the Parliament side. Calvert wouldn't drop it, however, so "After many reasons Controverted between us I acquainted him that though my opinion were rather to scilence [sic] the Comission then divulge it, yet since that would not satisfie I would acquainte the Councell," who was summoned for a special meeting.[217]

[216] Ibid., 62-63.

[217] Ibid., 63.

Kemp read the commissions aloud with Calvert present in the room and, most likely, the room exploded in a vile storm of vulgarities as they reacted to the commissions. The councilmen, probably especially with openly Parliament men like Richard Bennett and William Claiborne, "unanimously gave theire opinions that it was impossible to execute and unsafe to divulge his Majesties Commands at present," to the public. Calvert then said that he already had told several people of his orders, having "let slip some words of power and trust he had received from his Majestie concerning this Colony," probably to those who drank wine with him on his ship. The meeting adjourned for the present, but quickly the council found that the few people Calvert had told his plans to had let rumors spread like wildfire, "whereupon Whisperings and Rumours were spread among the people that the King had sent a Papist to be Governor (reflecting upon the person of the Governor of Maryland) which Monstrous inferences from thence of the Kings disaffection to Religion, and now they gave Creditt to the Pamphletts which declared his Majesties addiction that way [that he was a Catholic supporter]." 218

These pamphlets were apparently hand written tracts by anti-crown Parliament supporters that had been circulating for some time, interestingly, in York County. One might expect such a thing south of James River in the Puritan colonists' heartland, but it was apparent that anti-crown sentiment was spreading through the Anglicans as well. Hearing these rumors of Calvert gave some credit to these pamphlets, which apparently hadn't been taken seriously before. Hearing "of theise traitorous and seditious Murmurings," Kemp "sent out Proclamations to vindicate his Majetie of theise aspersions and threatening the lay

[218] Ibid.

against the County Commissioners if they suffered the Authors or Divulgers of such reports to pass with impunity." He personally went to York County to meet with the County Commissioners so that they would investigate who was behind the pamphlets and traitorous speeches. [219]

Calvert finally began to see that the country truly hated him for more than just political reasons. "The distempers began to move which might have advised Capt. Calvert to relinquish all hopes of prevailing with the Country," but he did not give up, though he switched tactics by giving further instruction concerning the erection of fortifications, which surely they could agree on, and thereby find some common ground. He asked Kemp to call an Assembly to "cause them to understand the necessitie of fortification," and to clear the air concerning the King's commissions.[220]

Kemp agreed, and was planning to call an early Assembly in any case. Originally planning on a November assembly, which was turning out to be too late to levee the tobacco from the new crop to support the letters of credit they had earlier given Berkeley, an October assembly was necessary to secure the cash crop in reserve for the ammunition supply that could come at any time from Berkeley's return. He also anticipated "danger… from the Londoners to the prejudice of the Kings title" and thus called for a General Assembly.[221]

Burgesses from all over the colony met together in Jamestown on October 1st, 1644, and looked uncomfortably at Calvert sitting with Kemp in the front of the room. Kemp called

---

[219] Ibid.

[220] Ibid., 63-64.

[221] Ibid.

the meeting to order and began by agreeing with Calvert about the necessity of fortifications to be erected, giving him credit for the idea. He was surprised, however, to find that across the board, burgesses gave "many dilatorye excuses to the first point, and at length a flat answer of disability and impossibilitie for them to preforme it." As the debate continued, Kemp met privately with some of his closer friends among the burgesses to see the real reasons for their problems with the plan. He "was soone resolved by some of my nearer freinds among them that the Assembly were in jeaslousie of some designe that the Governor of Maryland had upon the Contrey and that there could bee no other meaning in urging of building of Forts in this povertye then to strengthen some practice of his who they tearmed theire enemye, especially he proffering to trust them for six carryages which he brought over with him. And therefore that they had noe harte to fall upon anything until they understood the depth of his business."[222] An anonymous Puritan observer, it seems one of the burgesses, recalled:

> "The governour of Mary-land very tenderly discovered [disclosed] a commission that he had from His Majesty to take the London ships; to seize upon all debts due to London Merchants, to build custome-houses, and to receive the custome of Tobacco heere, and also to erect Castles and build Forts for the defence of the Country, and out of this revenue hee was to pay the governour of this Colony £2000. The Assembly seemed to comply with him and pretended the accomplishment of all his desires, and when they had gotten as much out of him as they could they seemed to commend the ingenious contrivance of

[222] Ibid., 64.

the businesse, hee replied that [he] was the only agent in the businesse himself, which they tooke good notice of."[223]

He went on to say that while they complied to Calvert's face, they worked against him behind his back, in agreement with Kemp's statement. It wasn't the plan, in other words, it was the man behind the idea, Calvert. No idea coming from him could possibly have the good of the colony in mind. In their minds, he was their enemy and sought their destruction at his profit. Kemp returned to where Calvert was sitting and "communicated this Intelligence to Mr. Calverte with advice to him to absent himself [from the colony] who having [been] deveived [sic] by the false seemings of those who dailye drunke of his wine, gave now credit to my advertisement." He still thought there were many who supported him, however. Even so, he dropped the issue of the forts and implored Kemp instead to read aloud the commissions of the King. Hoping that reading them would silence the rumors concerning it, he did so and asked the advice of the assembly. They in turn formed a committee consisting of several burgesses and some of the council to meet privately with Calvert to interview him further.[224]

This was probably a move made by the Londoners, since the commissions most directly affected them. In a closed door setting, "with such pretences of acceptation and with such firmness wrought upon Mr. Calvert," they pretended to be crown supporters, and "drew from him more Comisions and more secrets then he ever imparted to mee [Richard Kemp]." Calvert told them everything, and only afterward did he realize they were

[223] Frank, "News From Virginny," 86.

[224] Kemp to Berkeley, in Billings, *The Papers of Sir William Berkeley,* 64.

Londoners and "too late he found his errour, and if his Credulitye had rendered to him a scorne and mockerye to those who rather wished his hanging then the fruition of his hopes."[225]

They returned from the closed room and resumed the course of the assembly, easily passing several tobacco levies. Kemp knew something was wrong, however, soon finding out disturbing information from his informants and "gathered doubts of some violence that would be offered to his person [Calvert's], In soe much that I thought fit to interpose my authoritye by admonition to the Assembly that however his Message was not pleasinge yet they should look upon him with respect due to the Kings Messenger, and therefore charged them that no violation should be offered to his person." Moving right along, the assembly dealt with many other issues concerning the prosecution of the war, but "indeed I injoyed noe peace in my minde until he was cleare of the Countrye for I might justly feare that amonge soe many, one desperate hand might murder whome they all alike hated, and looked upon now [no] otherwise then upon betrayer of their liberties and lives."[226]

The remainder of the Assembly was mainly a meeting to address the costs of the summer campaign. The up-front costs were paid by wealthy men like Richard Bennett and William Minifie, and now general levees had to be implemented to repay them for their funding of the Chickahominy and Pamunkey campaigns. All other expeditions, scouts, or any other military action that took place over the summer was the responsibility of the individual counties, for which they would make local levies for their charge. An additional very large levee was the cost of

[225] Ibid.

[226] Ibid.

Berkeley's voyage, for the hopeful appearance of an ammunition supply. Further charges were implemented to support wounded and disabled soldiers (which were many), and also the widows and orphans of the war. In all, the population was virtually stripped of their tobacco crop that year, which was already inconsiderable, to pay for the war costs, and it plunged the colony into a further state of poverty.[227]

As the meeting neared its end, a large London ship entered the river and sailed up to Jamestown, as if to test whether they would obey the commissions of the King. The sixteen gun ship dropped anchor but "stood upon their guard," knowing in advance of the Kings commissions and of Virginia's reputation of being a Royalist colony. Word of the ship's arrival spread quickly and all wondered what the outcome would be. Prepared for a standoff, they informed Kemp of the contents of their cargo, which were mostly textiles. Calvert, who hadn't left yet, watched to see what Kemp would do. Kemp saw "the desperate wants of the people," for clothing, which were hanging in rags off their bodies, and knew he would face open rebellion if he didn't trade. Little thought was needed. "Without much Consideration inclined the Assembly to move earnestly that a Free Trade might be proclaimed with the Londoners or any other Porte within the Kingdom of England… which I apprehended as absolutely necessary for the peace and subsistence of the Colony, And therefore did accordingly." Clothing came into Virginia to the great joy of the people. Calvert, seeing that he had failed, "was now upon departure with much discontent, the people breathing infinite execrations and curses against him." Though he feared the consequences of the King's wrath, Kemp did what

[227] October, 1644, Assembly Meeting, in *The Thomas Jefferson Papers,* National Archives.

was best for the material health and political unity of Virginia, and to have done otherwise would have been to his and the colony's destruction.[228]

[228] Kemp to Berkeley, in Billings, *The Papers of Sir William Berkeley,* 64-65.

"Our hopes almost spent," The Autumn and Winter of 1644

The summer after the assault was a season of incessant violence against the Powhatans. As stated, every chiefdom under Opechancano's control was subject to counter-attack, particularly the Chickahominies and Pamunkeys, who were all forced away from their towns. However, after the surviving corn was harvested around August and a winter's store of nuts was collected throughout September, another Powhatan season of dispersal would begin as the *fall-of-the-leaf,* Taquitoc, began.[229] This was the traditional season of warfare and communal hunting, and it would be used to great advantage in pressing a new campaign of attacks and ambushes against the English. This was a key part of the war that has not yet been discussed; as it has been mostly assumed that the Powhatans offered no attacks whatsoever following the main assault. Richard Kemp's letter, a document fairly new to historical study, provides historical insights into a period of incredible difficulties for both sides of this conflict. For the Powhatans, an interesting period emerged wherein they were able to regain the momentum and shift the war in their favor. Once again, as Virginia's ammunition ran out, Opechancano convinced his warriors that victory was not yet out of their grasp, and new attacks and ambushes were launched into Virginia's frontier.

Powhatans During Wartime

The stereotype of the stoic Indian warrior has been overly romanticized in film, books, and cultural lore, but even so, it is

[229] Rountree, *Pocahontas, Powhatan, Opechancanough,* 239-240.

difficult to produce from the historic record anything but a colorful picture of men of great physical ability and mental endurance. In the days before the English came, warriors usually engaged in small-scale warfare with other tribes in the autumn and early winter, when the year's work was done and all they had left to worry about was the winter hunts. War parties would trek for surprising distances to raid enemy towns, and if possible, capture women and children both for personal honor and to bolster their own nation's population. In these expeditions few were killed compared to the colonial period, though it certainly happened as they waited in ambush for enemy war parties and vice versa. Warfare was not just for the sake of war, but was part being a man. Even one born to a "commoner" family with no hope of becoming a *weroance* could advance oneself to the level of a great councilor or war captain by distinguishing himself in this way.[230]

War parties travelled light and moved with astonishing speed. After European contact, warriors would carry with them their weapon, (a rifle if possible, otherwise bow and arrow), a knife, tomahawk and blanket. Because moccasins would wear out so quickly (in hard usage one pair may only last a day) extra leather was brought along for repair and new shoe production. Food was a simple pouch of corn meal, which was simply mixed into a cold paste and swallowed, with wild food being gathered along the way. They moved with great speed to and from their targets, staying at a trot the entire day until they reached their destination. Later white observers who travelled with them were completely winded, to the laughter of the well-conditioned Indian men, who placed great importance in physical endurance. While a European militiaman would travel at a slow and steady

[230] Rountree, *The Powhatan Indians of Virginia,* 120-125.

march (complaining loudly if there were no provisions) Indian warriors could last for days with little to no food, sleeping in the open and running all day long, which was a point of pride for them. Once at their targets, they rarely initiated an open attack, but planned a careful ambush and would lay in wait for hours. At the agreed on signal, a volley of lead or arrows was let loose with a war cry, and they would leap from their positions with tomahawks to finish off their surprised enemy.[231]

In the colonial period during the Third Anglo-Powhatan War, some things changed, while others stayed the same. On the one hand, there was certainly still the aspect of honor and personal advancement for those warriors who successfully carried out sorties against the English, but there was more personal stake in this fight than in any that went before it. Knowing that this fight was their last chance to defeat the English, warriors fought more ferociously and desperately than at any time before it, as is seen from the increased English casualties during the assault. A warrior had much more to worry about than in the past, for while he was out with the other men in a raid on a frontier settlement, the women and children were unprotected in the town or in dispersed camps, depending on the season. True, this would have been a danger even in times before the English came, but the Virginians were now larger than their neighboring hostile nations, and had shown a willingness to kill women and children in the past. Powhatans would never kill non-males, it was against their customs. Always in the back of their mind was the fear that when they returned to town, they would find smoke rising from the charred remnants of their

[231] Rountree, Helen, "The Powhatans and Other Woodland Indians as Travellers," in Rountree, Helen, ed., *Powhatan Foreign Relations, 1500-1722,* (Charlottesville, University Press of Virginia, 1993) 21-52.

houses, their corn slashed and families taken into slavery. Providing meat to their village was also more of a concern than previously as disruptions from English raids cut into their grain production, increasing the dependence on wild foods. Warriors probably were in the field away from their families much more than in the past as providers and defenders of their people, while women worked equally hard gathering Tuckahoe tubers and other wild plants. They lost sleep and were hungry, but were still able to wreak havoc on the Virginian frontier.[232]

The Weyanoke Rebellion

Though attacks against the English had gone well, Opechancano still had problems of his own. He had given specific orders that every attacking nation follow up the assault immediately with follow up attacks to prevent the English being able to group together. This stood apart from his previous 1622 assault. Rountree has stated that because some of the nations under him withdrew completely following the attack, it was a symbolic "protest" to white encroachments or one final spectacular blow before giving up their homelands and taking their chances elsewhere. If that is the case, then many had chosen to follow Opechancano for their own reasons, instead of a feeling of cultural obligation to him.

One such nation, and the best example, were the Weyanokes. Their story during this time is remarkable in that it

[232] This depended on which chiefdom was where, for the situation with the Pamunkeys was different than that of the Weyanokes, who were in retreat. In such a case, the warriors would stick close to the town to protect it, as opposed to the Pamunkey, who still were on the offensive and may have ranged for further distances to lay ambushes.

was almost entirely recorded by native testimony (albeit several decades later) as opposed to English observations. Having a native perspective on a conflict such as this, especially so early in Colonial history, is a valuable gem. In the early 1700s, a border dispute between Virginia and North Carolina had reached the boiling point, and everyone was wondering where in the world was Weyanoke Creek, a place which by royal charter was the border between the two colonies. The question arose because neither of the two possibilities, Wiccacon Creek or Nottoway River, any longer bore the name of Weyanoke, but both places had been the living place of the Weyanoke Indians following their retreat south of the James River. Therefore, in this investigation, much testimony from Indian elders of various nations was recorded showing exactly where the Weyanoke went and what Opechancano's response was.[233]

According to Nottoway elders in the year 1710, "The Wyanoke Indians Left Wyanoke on James River after the Massacre for fear of ye English." Hopelessly surrounded by English settlements, there was little way for them to even subsist, let alone defend themselves from English strikes. Anticipating this, probably under the leadership of chief Ascomowet, they retreated from their ancient town, crossing the broad James River and settling at a new camp on the Warreek Creek, it seems a branch of the Nottoway River. After they "went to Warrick & planted Corne,"[234] Virginia learned of their whereabouts, probably via a scouting expedition. Soon a raiding force was sent out and, according to Nick Major, the chief of the Meherrins, "the English Driving them from thence" in a strike that left them

233 Gleach, *Powhatan's World and Colonial Virginia,* 177.

234 Anonymous, "The Indians of Southern Virginia (Concluded)," in Virginia Magazine of History and Biography No. 1, (July 1900) 8:8.

without a crop for the year, "they went to Roanoke River to place called by ye Wyanoaks Towaywink."[235]

Being around Nottoway River was an understandable defensive measure since their old town was well within the English settlements. The most remarkable step, however, took place when they decided to quit their loyalty to Opechancano altogether. They could have remained loyal by continuing to communicate with other Powhatan loyalists and launch raids from their new southern land base, but Ascomowet chose not to do so. Instead they retreated far away from the main fronts to their old trading partners, the Tuscarora. Opechancano would not let them go so easily, however. Sometime before their descent to the Roanoke River, he organized and launched a strong eighty-man war party to seek them out. These "fourscore men [went] to look [for] them & bring [them] back," but the Weyanokes seem to have been prepared for such a response, and "all which Indians the Eynokes killed and fled Lower down Roanoke." [236] While it is difficult to imagine the wholesale slaughter of all eighty warriors, clearly the Weyanoke had defeated the Pamunkey detachment in open an act of war. This was a severe setback for Opechancano, for if the Weyanoke, formerly one of his core followers, could shake loose his grip, then any of the others could do the same. Being attacked by both the English and their former allies was enough for Weyanokes and for the first time in generations would act under their own authority. It would not be easy.[237]

---

[235] Ibid., 7.

[236] Anonymous, "The Indians of Southern Virginia, 1650-1711. Depositions in the Virginia and North Carolina Boundary Case," in Virginia Magazine of History and Biography No. 4 (April 1900) 7:349-350.

[237] Rountree, "*Trouble Coming Southward,*" 66.

They soon settled at the place they called Towaywink near a large Iroquoian nation, the Tuscaroras, and planted more corn. Naturally, the Tuscaroras were curious as to why they were settling on their lands and several of their chiefs came peacefully to confer with the Weyanokes. Chief Nick Major of the Meherrins knew these Tuscarora chiefs personally, as did the Nottoway elders, and agree that these chiefs were "Nicotaw Warr [or Nicotanwatts], and the other named Corrowhaughcoheh [or Corronwhankcokek], and one Tuscaroora "Queen" called Ervetsahekeh." These chiefs told Chief Major and the Nottoway Elders personally of the interaction. As the Nansemond *weroance* Great Peter would also later recount, "the Tuscaroras who possessed the lands demanded upon what they came there for, the Wyanoke answering that they wanted a place to settle upon, the Tuscarora sold them all ye land from thence to ye mouth of Moratuch [Roanoke River] and up Chowan to Meherrin River, together with all the beasts upon the land and the fish in ye water." [238]

It was said that the Weyanokes settled at Towaywink for two to three years before moving north, but this does not agree with later English records which accurately find them at Wiccacon Creek (still called by that name; further north along Chowan River) prior to that.[239] More native testimony states that

[238] Anonymous, "The Indians of Southern Virginia (Concluded)," in Virginia Magazine of History and Biography No. 1, (July 1900) 8:5-8

[239] Chief Nick Major of the Meherrin said the Weyanokes lived at Towaywink for two years before going to Wiccacon, and the Nottoway elders said it was three. See Anonymous, "The Indians of Southern Virginia (Concluded)," in Virginia Magazine of History and Biography No. 1, (July 1900) 8:7-8. The English court records of Lower Norfolk County, combined with testimony of early soldiers, make it clear that a Weyanoke settlement was at Wiccacon by 1645. See Lars Adams, "The Battle of

later at Wiccacon there weren't enough natural resources and so they settled in two towns instead of one settlement, with several families also living dispersed around the territory. I believe this also applies to the time at Towaywink, and the Weyanokes took full advantage of the new territory "purchased" of the Tuscaroras, spreading into several towns, the principal one at a place known to the Tuscarora as Quararakek while maintaining agricultural production at Towaywink. Several elderly Weyanoke women, some of the last of their people, who were living among the Nottoway, "heard from theyr fathers & ye old people [that]" Quararakek was "[re]named by Wyanoak Indians, Wicocons, which in ye Wyanoke language signifies a little River or Creek, during theyre abode there their chiefe Towne & fort was in that forke, but they had corn fields in severall places downe ye creeke & along Chowan River." The Weyanoke were there to stay.[240]

The Main Fronts

Meanwhile, Opechancano faced a huge problem as the English further assaulted the heart of his territory at Pamunkey and Chickahominy, and made smaller attacks against the other nations as well. He may have been thinking to himself, *if they had followed my instructions and kept up the attacks this would not have happened!* Remarkably, however, he regained control of many of his followers, especially in the York region where he lived. The Chickahominy had likewise given up their territory at

Weyanoke Creek: A Story of the Third Anglo-Powhatan War in Early Carolina," in *Native South,* (September 2013).

[240] Anonymous, "The Indians of Southern Virginia (Concluded)," in Virginia Magazine of History and Biography No. 1, (July 1900) 8:4-5.

Oraniok but had joined him with the Mattaponi in the upper waters of the York where the majority of loyal Powhatans then resided. It is more difficult to say whether the south-side of James held their same level of commitment from the Appomattocks and Nansemonds, but English attacks were kept up against them and they held their ground, though they probably had to change location frequently to avoid attack.[241]

Kemp reported that they employed corn slashing techniques as part of their offensive, and this is confirmed by orders of attack made by the general assembly, but if Kemp is to be believed, they could not find the Indian fields until they captured a man who they forced to be a guide. This suggests that the Indians knew that their fields would be attacked that year and put them in secret locations beyond the view of the river highways. The fact that warriors continued to attack English plantations in the autumn of that year further testifies that they were fed well enough that year despite English attacks. Altogether, even though there was a severe setback immediately following the assault, the war was not over and Opechancano shifted the momentum in his favor as he reformed the new refugees into war parties and sent them out with new resolve in September.[242]

Back in Jamestown, Richard Kemp was fretting over how to wage a war with no ammunition and keep the people from rebelling against the crown at the same time. As stated previously, it may well be that the war itself was the only thing

---

[241] The movements of the Chickahominy, Mattaponi, Pamunkey and Chisciac were not specifically recorded in the early narration, but by studying land deeds and other tribal records, Dr. Helen Rountree has successfully reconstructed their movements following the assaults on them during the war. See Rountree, *Pocahontas's people,* 105-127.

[242] Kemp to Berkeley, in Billings, *The Papers of Sir William Berkeley,* 64-65.

that held the people together well enough to prevent open rebellion. Some African servants had already disaffected in what is possibly the first African American "uprising" in the English colonies as the black indentured servants of one Mrs. Wormeley (Ralph Wormeley's wife?) revolted against her exhibiting "riotous and rebellious conduct," and was discussed in a council meeting on September third. A week later, these servants were all arrested, and their fate is unknown. Other strange proceedings occurred during this time as well, such as when Nathaniel Moore was given the death sentence, "being convicted of unnatural crimes" with a cow. The "Calf in [the] case [was] ordered to be burnt." Himself a servant, Nathaniel's master and wife had snuck up and discovered him in the act of these "unnatural crimes." There were few women on frontier Virginia.[243]

What Kemp didn't know was that in England, even with the distractions of Civil War, the topic of what to do with Virginia was still being discussed. Parliament had previously debated the best way to reduce them to subjugation, but did not then have the resources or inclination to carry on a full assault.[244] Berkeley, for his part, had failed to furnish supplies from Royal sources, and word had gotten out to London about Virginia's Indian war and the desperate straits the colonists were in. This made London decide on tactics to win Virginia over to Parliament by enticement rather than force. As it was, several London merchants sought means to not only relieve Virginia and assist Parliament, but also make a handsome profit in the undertaking. William Harris and Thomas Deacon, leading traders, organized a group of merchants in eight vessels. Among

---

[243]Robinson, "Notes From the Council and General Court Records 1641-1659,"in Virginia Magazine of History and Biography No. 1(Jul 1900) 8:70-73.

[244]House of Commons, 10 June 1644, Journal of the House of Commons, 3: 523-525.

them was Richard Ingle, captain of the Reformation who earlier had a scuffle with Argall and Francis Yeardley off the coast of Accomack. Bringing a petition before the House of Commons, they wished to "have Liberty to transport Ammunition, Cloaths, and Victual, Custom-free," in addition to obtaining letters of marque to attack any ships from foreign countries, especially Holland, that might be caught trading there, as well as being able to confiscate the property of certain planters whose estates had been sequestered.[245]

Parliament debated, but was quick to give permission for the trading venture. Since it was primarily "for the Supply, Defence, and Relief of the Planters," they could do this free of customs. The issues of being able to interrupt the trade of Holland ships or confiscate sequestered property were issues not so easily decided since they were trying to win over the Virginians rather than subjugate them, so they were referred to other committees. Because no one could be trusted in these times of war, however, each captain had to enter a bond into the court that would be returned only when they returned directly to London. At least, however, the merchant fleet could begin to fit out their ships and organize themselves for the voyage. It seemed that the relief Virginia so sorely needed would be on its way soon.[246]

At the time, however, Virginia couldn't have known this. The autumn and winter of 1644 was the hardest time of the entire war for Virginians, excepting the assault itself. Ammunition, food and clothing were all at dangerously low levels and apparently, Opechancano knew it. The hundred pounds of shot

[245]House of Commons, 26 August 1644, Journal of the House of Commons, 3:606-608; Riordan, *The Plundering Time,* 164.

[246] Ibid.

brought in by Calvert would not go far among so many soldiers, and all major troop movements came to an end. Kemp records that "our powder failed us, which without doubt they imagined by our lying still. And then they pressed hard upon the frontiers killing divers of our men who travelled negligently, as also many Cattell and hogs in so much that the people cryed oute loud for marches, which they should have needed to doe had I not wanted ammunition which was not by them considered." The upper hand may have been had by the English during the summer, but the Powhatans were not out of the fight yet. In fact, having penned the English in without a source of supplies, they seem even to have reversed the momentum of the war in their favor, and winter belonged to the Powhatans.

Despite the lack of ammunition and clothing, low-level defensive measures were taken to counter Opechancano's recent offensive. In September discussion was brought up concerning going against the Rappahannocks, but again, nothing came of it, probably thanks to William Claiborne's arguments. It may be at this time, in fact, that communications were opened up with them regarding the possibility of joining forces, since the colony was in dire straits and needed help from wherever they could find it. [247]

Operating under the constraints of limited ammunition, more soldiers were levied against the Powhatans in late October, though their target or operating capacity was not mentioned. More parties were ordered to go against the Indians in late November as well. At this same time, orders were given against Englishmen going hunting for food, indicating both a continued perception of danger against individuals going alone in the

[247] Ibid.

forest, and also the low supply of food beginning to be felt as settlers began to try to find other means to feed themselves.[248] Finally, in December, an expedition or expeditions was led by Lieutenant Nicholas Stillwell, again with his targets being unknown, though he was described by one historian as "an intrepid and active forest ranger."[249] Also sometime in the winter, official negotiations, probably led by William Claiborne, opened up with the Rappahannock and Accomack Indians, who had not participated in the assault, and they agreed to supply the English with scouts and to give them intelligence whenever they could regarding Opechancano's movements. This would be a very valuable service in later times.[250]

No English expeditions whatsoever are noted from late December through mid-February, probably because of difficulty of travel during the worst of the winter months, but also according to Kemp, because of the critically low ammunition supply, which was worse than ever following these few autumn expeditions, which used virtually the last of it. With the civil war in Britain raging, fewer and fewer ships came to Virginia to trade and therefore any chance of resupply came from the possibility of Berkeley's arrival and an occasional Dutch ship. While few and far between, these Dutch merchants became vital to keeping Virginia afloat, as Berkeley would later write, "We can onely

---

[248] Ibid.

[249] Morton, *Colonial Virginia, 154;* Robinson, "Notes From the Council and General Court Records 1641-1659,"in Virginia Magazine of History and Biography No. 1(Jul 1900) 8:73.

[250] This may have been the point at which contact was made with the Accomacs and Rappahannocks because sometime prior to the next February, contact was definitely made, as it was stated in the assembly, "it is an undisputable truth, that ye Service of Some Indians either of Accomack or Rappahannock be treated with & entertained for the further Discovery of ye Enemie." See Act 9, February 1644/5, Acts of the Assembly, in *The Thomas Jefferson Papers,* National Archives.

feare the Londoners, who would faine bring us to the same poverty, wherein the Dutch found and relieved us; would take away the liberty of our consciences, and tongues, and our right of giving and selling our goods to whom we please." Still, only three Dutch ships are recorded trading in Virginia during this period, and the hope of Berkeley's arrival became dimmer and dimmer in people's minds.[251] In fact, they were beginning to think, said Kemp, that something horrible happened to him and that he perished, or worse yet, he thought, the King was incensed that Kemp had not followed his order to seize all London shipping and refused to let a relief supply come. The end of winter was truly desperate. Spring was a time of renewed campaigning and spring planting, but they could hardly do either in the face of no resupply and continued Powhatan attacks. As morale decreased, the soldiers began to grumble. One man known only as John had charges brought against him for "slandering the army," and even Argall Yeardley, an esteemed member of the council, had proceedings against him for contempt.[252]

Finally "about the latter end of January when our hopes were allmost spent that... Sir William Berkeley would arrive with a supply of Ammunition," the fleet of parliamentary merchant ships sailed up James River and moored not far from Kemp's own house.[253] Captains William Harris and Thomas

---

[251]The only Dutch vessels coming to Virginia in 1644 were the Looking Glass, Water Duck and the t'Moorhoofd, and further trading from 1645-46 is poorly recorded. See Riordan, *The Plundering Time,* 168.

[252]Kemp to Berkeley, February 1645, in Billings, *The Papers of Sir William Berkeley,* 62; McIlwaine, *Minutes of the Council,* 502.

[253]The names of the ships were the Trade's Increase, Virginia Merchant, Globe, Honour, Reformation, Mary, and the Elizabeth and Ellen. See House of Commons, 26 August 1644, Journal of the House of Commons, 3:606-608.

Deacon "arrived in one fleet, and Anchored in the Bay, and sent a Boate directly to my house with a Letter from the Speaker of the House of Comons [William Lenthall] directed to the Governor and Councell with letter was noe other in effect then a desire from the house to affoard the Londoners a Free and peaceable trade with us and Justice in our Courts."[254] Lenthall had written this letter with Parliamentary approval in October, about the time the ships were ready for the voyage.[255] These ships carried a large supply of ammunition, and this letter from William Lenthall, Speaker of the House of Commons was clearly an attempt to counter the King's orders as conveyed by Calvert. Kemp faced another difficult decision whether or not to obey the King's orders, refuse their sales and continue to wait for Berkeley's arrival, or to give in and accept their business for the good of the colony. For all he knew, Berkeley was lost and they wouldn't have another chance for resupply for a very long time. It could be the end of them. Additionally, since these merchants carried letters of marque, they would probably justify themselves of violent action to plunder the good they desired. Kemp called a council meeting, and together they agreed to open up trade and get the ammunition they sorely needed.[256]

At least one of the ships was clearly recognizable to many Virginians. The *Reformation* was a strong 200-ton ship with a thirty-man crew and twelve guns, captained by Richard Ingle, a privateer merchant who had gotten into fights with royalist supporters in Virginia before. From ashore, William Claiborne saw the ship, and at some point he and Ingle had a

---

[254]Kemp to Berkeley, February 1645, in Billings, *The Papers of Sir William Berkeley,* 62.

[255]House of Commons, 16 October 1644', Journal of the House of Commons, 3:666-667.

[256]Kemp to Berkeley, February 1645, in Billings, *The Papers of Sir William Berkeley,* 64.

secret meeting. Claiborne gave Ingle a copy of the commissions that Leonard Calvert had recently brought over. Recognizing that Calvert had authorization to capture any London ships in Virginia, Ingle now had information enough to exercise the power given to him in his letter of marque against Maryland. As for Claiborne, he wanted Kent Island back, which had been forcefully taken from him by Calvert years before. Ingle would get his revenge on Maryland and the profit of whatever he could plunder.[257]Almost immediately after their meeting, Claiborne abandoned his post as general of Virginia's armies and began organizing an expedition to Kent Island. He and Richard Ingle would attack Maryland from two directions in the name of Parliament, and hostilities commenced immediately. Ingle sailed into Maryland's harbor and attacked several docked ships before attacking the town of St. Mary's (and inciting many Maryland colonist to rebel against Calvert), while Claiborne attempted a failed attack on Kent Island.[258] The news soon spread to Virginia, and one anonymous Virginian Parliament supporter wrote to a friend in London that "Certaine newes is brought hither by a credible person, That [Richard] Ingle hath taken and plundered all the Papists except the governour of Mary-land, and some few that are gone away among the Potuxant Indians for refuge, and that he hath sent 40 men by land, and 6o by water to fetch them by violence." The naval attack soon turned into general rebellion that would virtually destroy the colony. The English Civil War had officially spread across the Atlantic Ocean and was beginning to tear the colonies apart.[259]

---

[257]Riordan, *The Plundering Time,* 172.

[258]Ibid., 181-91.

[259]Frank, "News From Virginny," 86, Riordan, *The Plundering Time,* 191-249.

A Reversal of Fortunes

As Ingle broke from the main fleet of trading vessels to attack Maryland, the remainder of the merchant vessels stayed to truck for tobacco. Kemp "returned Answere to the Shipps without reflecting upon Mr. Speaker his letter, that Course was taken by the late Asembly to Incourage all freedome of trade and therefore they should not doubt the infringinge of the Act for that purpose. Upon this assurance they all came in, without which supplye wee had bene irrecoverably a lost people." He lamented that they had totally run out of tobacco in the treasury with which to pay for these new supplies. Would they be willing to take letters of credit for future payment? Harris and Deacon's reply was no, they required payment in full, up front. This presented a new problem. They had tobacco, yes, but only the amount previously levied to defray the letters of credit already written to underwrite Berkeley's voyage. They now had no choice but to use it, but it required an act of the assembly to change the use of those funds. Accordingly, Kemp and the council called for an emergency session, and very quickly got permission from the burgesses to divert the tobacco for Berkeley's supply to current trade with these London ships. He was fearful of the future consequences of disobeying the King's orders, but the conditions of the colony "Cleearly prove[d] the necessitie of suspendinge the execution of his majesties Comands." [260]

So finally, mercifully, a large quantity of powder and shot made its way into the public store, enough for a complete resupply of the whole army. In an instant, the hopes of the colony were restored. While they now had a supply of food as well as

[260]Kemp to Berkeley, in Billings, *The Papers of Sir William Berkeley,* 65.

ammunition, ongoing food production was a serious issue. They had gotten by the previous year with a bad crop, but they couldn't hope to do so for a second, and so spring planting needed to be done in earnest and in safety. No one, however, felt safe enough to work in the fields without sentinels at the ready. Kemp's memory harkened back to Leonard Calvert's suggestion of the construction of fortifications the previous year, and he was struck with an idea.[261]

He called for a regular session of the General Assembly to meet February 17, and proposed a rather grand scheme to construct a series of three forts, not located near English plantations, but in the heart of Powhatan territory. If several small forts or blockhouses could be constructed for the safety of a garrison of soldiers, then they could constantly attack the enemy and keep them away from English settlements, so that Indian families would have to rely on harder-to-find foods, thereby taking the pressure off of the English plantations. With this resupply of ammunition, they might not get the chance for another offensive for a very long time. If it failed, the cost of the forts and garrisons would be unbearable and the colony would sink further into despair, economic depression and famine. If Powhatan attacks subverted the forts and continued attacks on crops that year, then starvation would be a real possibility. If successful, however, it could turn the tide to English favor and victory might be within sight.[262]

Also proposed was a continuation of the old way of mustering soldiers for these forts, in that a selected number of

---

[261]Ibid., 64-65.

[262]Ibid., 65; Act 9, February, 1644/5, Acts of Assembly, in Hening, *The Statutes at Large...,* 293-294; McCartney, "Seventeenth Century Apartheid," 53; Shea, *Virginia Militia in the Seventeenth Century,* 64-65.

tithable persons would be chosen as a support group to supply and pay one soldier for service. One difference was that before the war, in the 1630s, this number was one soldier for every twenty tithables, whereas now it was one soldier for every fifteen tithables, showing a heavier burden on fewer people. They also expanded the definition of exactly who tithables were, to include not only every man from ages sixteen to sixty, but also all "negroes and women," making all people, servant or free, black or white, equally responsible for the war's prosecution. This also meant that all African-American men, though a minority at that time, were also eligible to be selected for service in the army. It must be assumed therefore that there were indeed black soldiers serving in the Third Anglo-Powhatan War, in what is probably the first time in colonial history that such a thing occurred.[263]

Finally, in order to provide for flexibility and more proportional distribution of the charge of the war, the colony was divided into sectors of local commands where campaigns would be prosecuted by localized "Councils of War." By far the largest sector was the north side of James River, where the forts would be located, and where the greatest enemy population centers were (i.e. the Chickahominy, Pamunkey, and Mattaponi. Southside of the James was prosecuted differently. Upper Norfolk, Lower Norfolk, and Isle of Wight counties banded together and pooled resources under the ultimate command of the Puritan leader Richard Bennett to prosecute war against the traditionalist Nansemonds and any other Indian groups found near them by "by constant Marches upon ye Indians." All other

[263]For the system of tythable supporters of soldiers, see Shea, *The Virginia Militia,* 65-66. For reference to African American tythables, and therefore their potential to volunteer or be selected as soldiers, see Act 8, February, 1644/5, Acts of Assembly, in Hening, *The Statutes at Large…,* 292-293.

residents south of James from the Falls to Lawne's Creek (about midway between the James River's falls and its mouth), were likewise to band together to fight the Appamatocks, Powhites, or any others such as the Weyanokes who may be found about them.[264]

Figure 19. A portion of the Great Dismal Swamp, a likely area were some Powhatans, especially the Nansemonds, probably hid out and launched raids from following English counter-attacks. Great Dismal Swamp State Park, North Carolina. Photo by the author.

[264] Ibid.; Kemp to Berkeley, February 1645, in Billings, *The Papers of Sir William Berkeley,* 65; Frank, "News From Virginny," 85; Shea, *The Virginia Militia,* 64-65; Boddie, *Seventeenth Century Isle of Wight County Virginia,* 98.

It was a good strategy, and risky, but necessary. The amount of deliberation within the Assembly is unknown, but in the end they passed acts to support Kemp and the Council's plans. They knew the risks, and knew that this year would make or break them. As a group, they planned for three forts. Captain Francis Epps would command a fort at the falls of James River called Fort Charles and Captain Ralph Higginson at Fort James "on ye Ridge of Chiquohomine." Captain Ralph Wormely, who had gained a reputation as a war hero for hacking to death several Chickahominies, was assigned Fort Royal in Pamunkey River, which was the most strategically advantageous and dangerous of the three posts.[265]

The burgesses also had considered the Powhatan assault and all their miseries since then to be a divine judgment on them; a punishment for their sins. With a Puritan flavor, they passed a series of laws making every April 18 a holiday for "thanksgiving and deliverance," and likewise that the last Wednesday of every month, "to beg and that God might avert this heavie Judgements that are now among us," was to be "sett apart for a Day of ffast & humiliation, And leat it be wholly dedicated to prayers." Getting right in God's sight was just as important as military victory, for victory would be a sign of God's favor on them.[266]

Other acts passed included measures against corrupt local Sheriffs, who had been found to be embezzling funds from the levies being imposed on the people, but also gave them more power to imprison debtors if they were delinquent. Free trade with any that would give them supply was continued to be

---

[265]Kemp to Berkeley, in Billings, *The Papers of Sir William Berkeley,* 65; Act 9, February, 1644/5, Acts of Assembly, in Hening, *The Statutes at Large...,* 293-294.
[266]Acts 1-3, February, 1644/5, Acts of Assembly, in Hening, *The Statutes at Large...,* 289-290.

encouraged, and so that powder and shot would continue to flow into Virginia. Merchants Richard Bennett and George Minifie were entrusted "with themselves jointly or severally or by any whom they shall think fit in behalf or ye Collony" to find and purchase "powder and shott at the Cheapest Rates they can." The governor and council would "have power to dispose thereof for the furnishing of the Forts & setting out of Marches as they shall think fit." They would work with the local sheriffs to get the tobacco they needed for the ammunition purchases.[267]

Later that month, as preparations for the spring campaigns were under way, Richard Kemp found some rare quiet time to sit down and pen a letter to Sir William Berkeley, wherever he was. Because he didn't know if Berkeley was even alive, he also addressed it to Sir William's brother, Sir John Berkeley, then in England. He began, "That you Sir William are not att this date arrived or any supply from you hath much increased our fears and almost made desperate our hopes of your safetie yet amonge soe greate distractions which now fill the world many impediments may retard your dispatch which cannot fall into our conjecture here." He recounted everything that had happened from the time Berkeley left until that point, from arrival of Leonard Calvert and the difficulty of those times, the prosecution of the Powhatan War and Opechancano's counter-attacks, the scarcity of supplies and his personal struggles as leader of the colony. In a heartfelt statement, Kemp admitted, "My burden is intolerable. Sometimes the wants and nakedness of the people loudly voiced among them imploy my thoughts, then the Consideration of the war with noe other supply internayneth mee. At other tymes doubts of treachery from the

[267] Act 18, February, 1644/5, Acts of Assembly, in Hening, *The Statutes at Large...*, 297.

Londoners with some back from the [rent?] startle me, and not without some smoake. But all these are nothing Compared to the affliction which I have in mind least some powerfull information incense his Majesty against me, to whome all I am or have is due, and shall in faithfull service out of a true sense of Confidence be paide. And in this pointe I am something Comforted in your undoubted freindshipp to a good cause." He concluded the letter with a personal note to Berkeley, saying that "Your people are in good health and safetie att the Greene Springe [Berkeley's plantation]" and sent the letter off in the next ship to leave for England.[268]

His wasn't the only letter to leave for England with these ships. The editor of the parliament-supporting newspaper, Mercurius Civicus, published two such letters written by Puritans a few months later in May, 1645, which blamed the reasons for all the difficulties solely on Berkeley's shoulders, saying that Berkeley had imposed oaths on them in support of the King against their wishes and that most Virginians were in favor of parliament.[269] The authors agreed that the Indian attack was a judgment but that at least it forced them to work together despite their differences and that peace had been established, finally, with one other. Further, the anonymous author of the pamphlet "A Perfect Description of Virginia" written following the war references three letters as source material written during and after the war, showing that many more letters and narratives were written at the time than have survived for modern scrutiny.[270]

---

[268]Kemp to Berkeley, February 1645, in Billings, *The Papers of Sir William Berkeley,* 66.

[269]Frank, "News From Virginny," 84-87.

[270]Anonymous, "A Perfect Description of Virginia," 11-12.

Besides preparations for the construction of forts and the mustering of a new army, the newly associated counties south of the James River also met separately in their own councils of war to discuss their strategies. Those in the upper half of the south-side seem to have planned a fairly straightforward approach to attack the Appamattocks, but the associated counties of Isle of Wight, Upper and Lower Norfolk counties seem to have planned something a bit more audacious. It could be that they thought traditionalist Nansemonds had already largely retreated into the Great Dismal Swamp or further southwest (excepting the friendly Christianized segment) and they therefore had fewer Indians to attack locally, but for whatever reason, their attention was diverted to seek out and attack the Weyanokes, who had retreated into the Carolina wilderness. Chief in their minds, from the many reports they had received in decades past, was the wide open land of the Roanoke region, long-contemplated for future settlement. This war gave them a perfect excuse to stake a claim in these southlands. [271]

[271] Walter, *Lower Norfolk County, Virginia Court Records*, 180.

"The Southward March"

The associated counties south of the James River (Upper and Lower Norfolk with Isle of Wight counties) met together in a "Court of Warre holden [held] at the howse of Richard Bennett Esq: the 12 Mar"of 1645. Bennett was not only the chief supply man for Virginia and member of the Governor's Council, but was establishing himself as a capable military leader. While minutes of this meeting were either not kept or lost, examination of later references from court orders can reconstruct some of the proceedings. Those attending the meeting decided that scouts were to be frequently deployed for the defense of the settlements, indicating they felt there was still a perceived threat from the Nansemonds. Accordingly, "all persons whatsoever being inhabitants of this County for theire safeguard and defence upon the salvages [savages] according the number of people in theire severall famylyes were proporconably [proportionably] allotted to sett our [out] and mayntaine men in manner of a scout..."[272] These scouts were to be equipped and financially supported by planters selected by Bennett's war captains. The soldiers seem to have been conscripts, but were nonetheless paid for their services by those fourteen planters selected to support them. These scouts were chiefly poor farmers and laborers.[273] They were supplied

[272]Court order, Nov 3, 1645, in Walter, ed., *Lower Norfolk County, Virginia Court Records,* 198.

[273]Few members connected with the expeditions are named, but the few that are were noteworthy as being chronically in debt. Thomas Ward, for example, was a surgeon and attorney, however five separate lawsuits were carried against him for a collection of massive quantities of debt. He was jailed at one point for an unknown misdemeanor and all his wages from the Carolina expedition and a former Chickahominy march were garnished to pay some of his lenders. Walter, *Lower Norfolk County, Virginia, Court Records,* 83, 138, 145, 201, 202, and 208. George Rutland, a foot soldier, was considered so financially unstable that he was forced to put up a security to the court so that his

with "provisions of powder and shott and other necessarryes," such as "cheese" and "tob [tobacco] or corne."[274]

A critical issue facing the meeting seems to be the Weyanokes who had migrated somewhere south of the Great Dismal Swamp, an effective barrier between Virginia and land not settled since the Roanoke colony over fifty years earlier. The English had already disrupted the Weyanokes when they camped at Wareeks Creek south of the James, but since then they had retreated further into the Carolinian wilderness. Precisely why they took such an interest in the Weyanokes is not explained in the text. The Weyanokes had already been retaliated against and had retreated to a land virtually unknown by English people. Nevertheless, plans were drawn up to find and assault them, wherever they may be. Revenge does not appear to be the motivation; as stated retaliation had already been carried out and the expedition would be financially quite costly. Bennett may have gotten wind that the Weyanokes had made an agreement

---

children would not fall under the care of the parish. Four other lawsuits were brought against him to collect on his debt. See Walter, *Lower Norfolk County, Virginia, Court Records,* 136, 146, 194, and 195. Information on other soldiers is not available, though lack of information on them may simply have meant that many of them were indentured servants. Truly, the fact that soldiers were only paid ten pounds of tobacco total for the several weeks long expedition certainly shows that they were not the upper crust of society. These were the same type of settlers who would first colonize North Carolina. See Noeleen McIlvenna, *A Very Mutinous People: The Struggle for North Carolina, 1660-1713* (Chapel Hill: University of North Carolina Press, 2009), 15-27; Kirsten Fischer, *Suspect Relations, Sex, Race and Resistance in Colonial North Carolina* (Ithaca NY: Cornell University Press, 2002), 19-29; Milton Ready, *The Tar Heel State* (Columbia, University of South Carolina Press, 2005) 39; Jonathan E. Barth, "'The Sinke of America': Society in the Albemarle Borderlands of North Carolina, 1663-1729,"in *The North Carolina Historical Review* 87 (January 2010): 2.

[274]Court order, November3, 1645, in Walter, *Lower Norfolk County, Virginia, Court Records,* 198.

with the Tuscaroras and feared an alliance of nations. Furthermore, if the Weyanokes used the southern land as a base to launch raids against the English, or worse yet if they forged an alliance with the Carolina Algonquians or Tuscaroras, the English could face a major roadblock to a successful outcome to the war or future settlement of Carolina, which the Virginia government had been contemplating for decades.

As reported by an exploratory party twenty years prior, the land was deemed prime for settlement and the local natives were friendly.[275] More intelligence seems to have been needed before making a decision regarding future military action to the southern lands. Thus, "it was ordered… that everyone that setts out a man for the Southward March [a scouting expedition] should paye & sattisfye unto him that went worke for his paynes equally and proporconably during the tyme of his absence from home upon the said service."[276] Captain Edward Wyndam went throughout the three colonies, selecting the men that would serve, and also selecting those who would financially and materially support these soldiers. The Weyanokes were not specifically mentioned as a target, and veterans of the two expeditions later said simply that they marched "against the

---

[275]William Powell ,*John Pory: 1572-1636, The Life and Letters of a Man of Many Parts*(Chapel Hill, University of North Carolina Press, 1977), 101. John Pory made it known that the land was full of ample lumber and good land. He met with the Chowanoke people and expressed that the Chowanoke *weroance* desired to enter into a league with the English.

[276]George Rutland v. John Cole and Geoffrey Wight, August 14, 1645, in Walter, *Lower Norfolk County, Virginia, Court Records*, 180. Both Cole and Wight were selected by Captain Edward Windham to equip and pay George Rutland for the scout.

southern Indians,"[277] however it was certainly the Weyanokes, as the events of the expeditions would later reveal.

Almost no detail is given for this detachment, but because it was financially backed in the same way as scouts were (the second expedition, a full assault, was handled as a general levy), it can be established that this was a scout and not a large troop movement. I believe this expedition was for reconnaissance purposes to ascertain the location of the Weyanokes and their relationship to the surrounding Indians. Also considering earlier orders to attack any Indians in their vicinity, including the Choanoacs, they may have considered raids on Carolina Algonquian towns, depending on their reaction to the English. Other scouting parties ranged in size from fifteen to forty men, so it is reasonable to assume that about twenty or thirty men made up this detachment.[278]

Once organized, the scout departed the Nansemond River for the southern wilderness "by land under the Command of

[277]Deposition of Henry Plumpton; Deposition of Thomas Ward, November 3, 1645, in Walter, *Norfolk County, Virginia, Court Records,* 201.

[278] In Rutland v. Cole and Wight, George Rutland brought forth suit against two defendants who had neglected to pay him for service on the land expedition. In a similar case for a separate and unrelated scout, thirty-nine men were selected to "sett our [out] a man" for service, and finally, a court order was issued relating to the fact that many of the men selected to support these scouts were negligent in paying and equipping the soldiers. Because the march into Carolina was handled in this same way and because of the short duration of the march, it can be concluded to have been a small detachment in the manner of a scout. See George Rutland v. John Cole and Geoffrey Wight, August 14, 1645, and the November 3, 1645 court order to "those 39 men… allotted with Mr: Burroughs" in Walter, *Norfolk County, Virginia, Court Records,* 180, 197-98. For a reference to a fifteen-man march, see the court order of July 17, 1639, in Walter, *Norfolk County, Virginia, Court Records*, 19.

Major Genll Bennett."[279] The fact that Bennett himself headed the scout clearly shows the interest he took in the southern land. Later court cases involving two members of the expedition detail that they departed overland on a "Southward March" to the eastern side of the Chowan River, continuing southeast until they reached the Yeopim River and presumably some of the Algonquian peoples in the area (Weapemeiocs, whom the English called Yawpims). For just over a month, ample time to meet the Choanoac and Yeopim people and gather intelligence on the Weyanokes, they explored a land that hadn't been seen by Englishmen in decades.[280]

Thomas Ward, a financially desperate surgeon who had previously served in the Chickahominy assault, also was selected to provide medical attention during this scout. He later stated specifically that they "serve[d] in an expedition against the Indians to Yawopyin [Yeopim] als Rawanoake as Chirurgeon [surgeon] to the whole company and did divers Cures upon severall men in the said service."[281] This is the first known reference to the Yeopim River, where the Yeopim Indians lived. Other records of that river are not recorded until the 1657

---

[279]Deposition of Henry Plumpton, March 25, 1708, in William Saunders, ed., *Colonial Records of North Carolina* (Raleigh NC:P.M. Hale, 1886), 1:676.Richard Bennett was not a major general at the time; he was promoted in later years.

[280]Rutland v. Cole and Wight, 180. Rutland was owed wages for two and one half days each from both Cole and Wight for the time he was absent on the march. At this time, however, a total of fourteen tythable persons would pool resources to support one soldier, so Cole and Wight would be the only two out of the fourteen who failed to pay. When two and a half days wages per supporting tythable is tallied, an expedition of thirty-five days can be calculated. This was ample time to explore the eastern shore of the Chowan River south to the Yeopim, establish contact with the Chowanoke and Yeopim people and gather intelligence on the whereabouts of the Weyanokes.

[281]Deposition of Thomas Ward, November 3, 1645, in Walter, *Norfolk County Court Records,* 201.

Comberford Map.[282] It is reasonable, therefore, that the detachment learned the name of the river from the indigenous people, interacting with them in some capacity. Quite probably they gained information regarding the Weyanokes and their location.

There is no record indicating that there was any violence on this first expedition. For example, a financial statement of the second expedition shows expenses accrued for a wounded man, but no such record exists for the first march.[283] Also, Henry Plumpton, a member of both expeditions, later gave a short narrative of his experiences. He only briefly mentioned the scout, giving no detail, but he explained the second in some detail since a battle was fought and a man was killed. Additionally, a Bass family record written decades later shows that "Edward Basse sonne of Nathll and Mary Basse. . . took in marriage one virtuous Indian maydn by the Christian name Mary Tucker and went to live amongst the Showanocs [Choanoacs] in Carolina in 1644 AD."[284] Edward, a resident of Upper Norfolk, might have been a

---

[282]William P. Cumming, *North Carolina in Maps* (State Department of Archives and History, 1966).

[283]Thomas Ward did perform "diverse cures" upon men in the first march, but there is no indication that these were wounds caused by violence. If they were, then most likely they would have been noted in county financial statements to compensate them for missed work, as is seen with a later levy toward costs for the assault later that year.

[284]Bass Family Prayer Book Record, photocopy from original, 8 leaves, call number 26371, Library of Virginia, Richmond. As this record was written three decades later, seemingly by Edward's brother, John Basse, the date of 1644 may have been mistaken in recollection for the true date of 1645. Note that Henry Plumpton, from whom much of this information has come recalled "to the best of his remembrance" that the expedition was in 1646, which is easily proven to have been actually 1645. Edward Basse eventually returned to Virginia with his Chowanoke wife, renamed Mary, and moved back to Carolina with Mary and their children sometime before 1696, shortly before his death. In native culture, a marriage such as this one was used in much the same way as a treaty of peace, unifying two peoples. This was the first interracial marriage recorded in

member of this expedition, and this marriage clearly shows a friendly relationship to the natives of Carolina during this time period.

The Weyanokes turned out to be at Wiccacon Creek on the west side of the Chowan River, which is extremely broad, and there was no way for the scout to get to them in any case. Thus, with Ward's statement, the explanation that best fits the known facts is that the party met with the local Algonquians (the Chowanokes and Yeopims), learned that they were not allied to the Weyanokes and learned their location. They left the Carolina Algonquians, seemingly as friends, and returned to Virginia discuss the next steps.[285]

The intelligence that the detachment brought back must have been well received in Jamestown. There existed no alliance between the Weyanokes and the other southern Indians. In fact, the Chowanokes and Yeopims may have been eager to join forces to eliminate the Weyanokes who had encroached on their territory. It is unlikely at that point that the Virginians perceived the Weyanokes as a threat since first-hand intelligence had finally been gathered, yet plans for a further assault continued.

Carolina and only the third instance since Virginia's founding, although certainly other unrecorded marriages occurred.

[285]There is no record of the Weyanokes ever being east of the Chowan River. They appear to have travelled west and north of the Chowan, at odds with most of their English and native neighbors. See Rountree, *Pocahontas's People,* 84-88, 100.

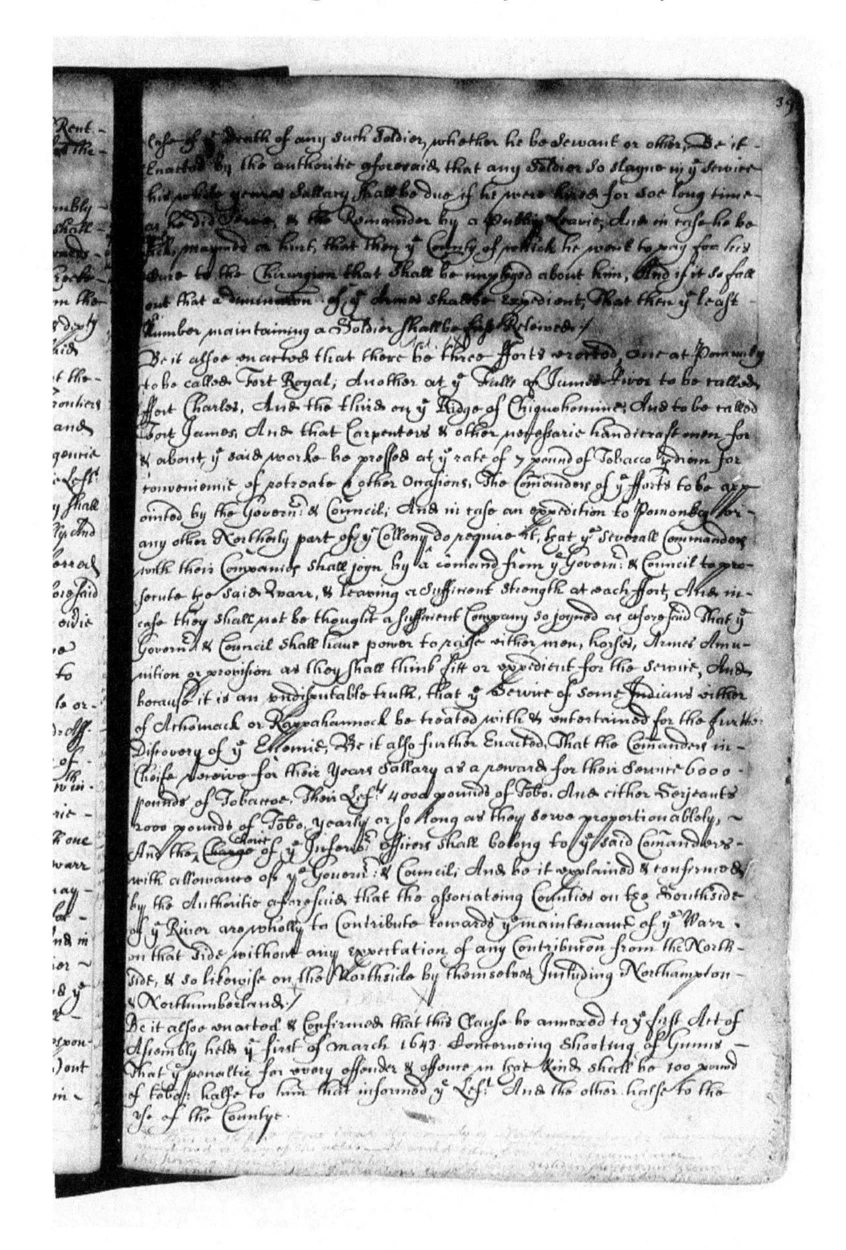

case of ye death of any such Soldier, whether he be servant or other, Be it
Enacted by the authoritie aforesaid that any Soldier so slayne in ye service
his whole yeares Sallary shall be due if he were hired for soe long time
as he did serve, & the Remainder by a publique Leavie; And in case he be
[illegible], maymed or hurt, that then ye County of [illegible] he went to pay for his
cure to the Chirurgion that shall be imployed about him, And if it so fall
out that a diminution of ye Armes shall be expedient, That then ye least
number maintaining a Soldier shall be first Releived./
Be it also enacted that there be three fforts erected, One at Pomunky
to be called Fort Royal; Another at ye Falls of James River to be called
ffort Charles, And the third on ye Ridge of Chiquohomine; And to be called
Fort James, And that Carpenters & other necessarie handicraftmen for
& about ye said works be pressed at ye rate of [illegible] pound of Tobacco [illegible] for
[illegible] of [illegible] & other occasions. The Comanders of ye fforts to be appointed by the Govern: & Councel; And in case an expedition to Pamonkey or
any other Northerly part of ye Collony do require it, that ye severall Commanders
with their Companies shall joyn by a command from ye Govern: & Councel to prosecute ye said warr, & leaving a sufficient strength at each ffort; And in
case they shall not be thought a sufficient Company so joyned as aforesaid That ye
Govern: & Councel shall have power to raise either men, horses, Armes Amunition or provision as they shall think fitt or expedient for the Service, And
because it is an undisputable truth, that ye Service of some Indians either
of Accomack or Rappahannock be treated with & entertained for the further
Discovery of ye Enemie, Be it also further Enacted, That the Comanders in
Cheife receive for their Years Sallary as a reward for their Service 6000
pounds of Tobacco. Their Lieut 4000 pounds of Tobo. And either Serjeants
2000 pounds of Tobo. yearly or so long as they serve proportionablely, ~
And the Chardge of ye Inferior officers shall belong to ye said Comanders -
with allowance of ye Govern: & Councel; And be it explained & confirmed
by the Authoritie aforesaid, that the associateing Counties on the Southside
of ye River are wholly to Contribute towards ye maintenance of ye Warr .
on that side without any expectation of any Contribution from the Northside, & so likewise on the Northside by themselves Including Northampton -
& Northumberland./
Be it also enacted & Confirmed that this Clause be annexed to ye first Act of
Assembly held ye first of march 1643 Concerning Shooting of Gunns -
That ye penaltie for every offender & offence in that kind shall be 100 pounds
of Tobo: halfe to him that informed ye Lieut And the other halfe to the
use of the Countye

Figure 20. 17th century copy of original orders for the erection of forts for use as bases of operations against the Powhatans. Thomas Jefferson Papers. Courtesy of the National Archives.

Available evidence indicates that Virginian excursions into Carolina during the Third Powhatan War were a means to extend its southern boundary. The treaty between Virginia and the Powhatans at the end of the war, in which Virginia specified a claim to Yeopim Creek, makes clear that the English had a keen interest in the southern lands and took the opportunity to extend their borders. As Helen Rountree has stated, "it is plain that the English had investigated and were now staking a claim to some of the land south of the James River drainage."[286] I believe that Virginia wanted to establish a foothold militarily in Carolina as a precursor to settlement. Earlier reports and now firsthand experience attested to the quality of the land in the south, and a growing colonial population would soon need a new frontier to settle. This could not be done easily, however, if a hostile Indian group blocked the way of progress, and so, in the effort of removing this obstacle and staking a claim on the land, the Virginians planned a massive assault on the Weyanokes.

Meanwhile in the Lower Peninsula, major military operations were taking place as construction crews penetrated the wilderness under the protection of companies of soldiers to construct a string of three forts in a curved line from the falls of the James River through "the ridge of Chiquihomine" and on toward the burned towns of the Pamunkey. Not forts in the sense of the word we would think of, they were rather palisaded blockhouses that were quickly erected out of timber as fall back positions for garrisons of soldiers who were to remain on constant marches against the enemy.[287]

[286]Rountree, "Trouble Coming Southward,"71.

[287]MCartney, "Seventeenth Century Apartheid," 53.

Battles and skirmishes were probably associated with the blockhouses' construction as the Powhatans would have resisted this serious incursion, but nothing is mentioned of them. Archeologically, two of these forts appear to have been discovered, Fort Royal and Fort James. They were tiny, only about sixteen by twenty-four feet. Constructed out of set posts, there was hardly enough room for a garrison to sit comfortably.[288] Shea has claimed that each fort supported about a hundred soldiers, but I feel it was less, about fifty or sixty each at most, due to space constraints and compared with another fort that would be constructed the following year which was documented to hold forty five soldiers.[289] Orders were issued to maintain constant marches on the enemy, leaving sufficient men behind to defend the blockhouse. Thus they likely traded off in shifts, going on marches and defending the fort. Nothing at all is told of their specific actions against the Powhatans, nor of the Powhatans' reaction to them, but we know that it bore results, for by the following spring the constant expeditions met fewer and fewer Indians as the Powhatans were pushed further and further back. [290]

---

[288]Ibid.

[289]Shea, *The Virginia Militia,* 64-65. Reference to the forty five man garrison is mentioned in relation to Fort Henry at Appomattox River the following year. See Act 8, Acts of the Assembly, March 1, 1645/6, in *The Thomas Jefferson Papers,* National Archives.

[290]References of being constantly engaging the enemy and also the small size of the blockhouses indicates that there were probably few times the entire company was in the fort together for an extended period of time. That they encountered fewer and fewer Indians over time in demonstrated by a reference in March, 1646, that the Indians had all been dispersed from their towns and were scattered about, with further revenge nearly an impossibility. See Act 18, Acts of the Assembly, March 1, 1645/6, in *The Thomas Jefferson Papers,* National Archives.

The forts were completed by April, when the first garrisons of soldiers were ordered to occupy them. The fighting was probably hot at the outset of these operations, but it was very effective, as is seen in the fact that land grants, which had waned the previous year, now began again in earnest, though not yet in the combat zones of the frontier.[291] Also in April, in Massachusetts, a large explosion rocked Roxbury, whose residents thought it was an earthquake. It was their public storehouse, wherein seventeen barrels or powder and firearms were being stored, all going up in flames. John Winthrop lamented that "the loss of our powder was the more observable... In that, at the court before, they had refused to help our countrymen in Virginia, who had written to us for some for the defense against the Indians."[292] As this was going on, and as the associated counties south of James River planned their next offensive against the Weyanokes in Carolina, Governor Berkeley finally, after all this time, sailed up the James River and made landing at James Island, shocking the colony on June 7 with his "sudden arrival." He was probably greeted very warmly by Richard Kemp and others, but after all this time, he had brought no ammunition. None could be had from England.[293]

---

[291]There were, for example, only sixteen land patents were made in 1644 following the April 18 attack, and the majority of them were within firmly English-held territory. It was midsummer of 1645, about the time of fort construction, when land patent rates reached amounts comparable to pre-war levels. See Nugent, *Cavaliers and Pioneers,* 152-162.

[292]Winthrop, *History of New England,* 220.

[293]Conway Robinson, "Notes From the Council and General Court Records, 1641-1659," 8:64-73; Shea, *Virginia Militia in the Seventeenth Century,* 65.

The Battle of Weyanoke Creek [294]

Berkeley had managed to gain an audience with King Charles and even, apparently, assisted the King in the campaigns against the Parliamentarians.[295] Nevertheless, though the King was sympathetic and thankful to have Virginia within his loyalists, the realities of the situation prevented material support in terms of actual resupply. While Berkley was in England he witnessed the Royal forces lose more and more ground, and the king became increasingly outnumbered. In fact by the time Berkeley returned to Virginia in June, Oliver Cromwell had outflanked the Royal forces and demolished the army of the King. The remainder of the war would be a hopeless mop-up operation that kept King Charles on the run.[296] In these desperate straits the king wrote a letter for Berkeley to carry back to Virginia with instructions and moral support. The contents have been lost but within the Virginia Acts of the Assembly some reference to it has been made. It "hath pleased his most excellent Majestie to give Instructions to the present Governor for ye inlargemt of the payment of powder paid by the shipps drawing in the Collony," in other words giving permission to demand additional ammunition as duties from trading vessels. The King's letters also stated that he still expected his quitrents from the colony, though he also promised to pay the fort commanders and other officers himself by the means of subtracting from these quitrents. He also gave instruction that all people equally bear the charge of the war, meaning the privileged Council members

---

[294]The following chapter is based in a large part on my previous essay, "The Battle of Weyanoke Creek: A Story of the Third Anglo-Powhatan War in Early Carolina," in *Native South* (September, 2013): 6:170-195.

[295]Billings, *Sir William Berkeley,* 96-99; Billings, *The Papers of Sir William Berkeley,* xlvi.

[296]Gaunt, *The English Civil Wars,* 41-44.

must bear the charge the same as the rest, which they previously had been exempt from.[297]

As Berkeley was readjusting to his role as Governor and military commander, the expedition against the Weyanokes was just about ready to get under way in the region near Nansemond River. An amphibious assault was favored in the same way as previous battles, which could make for a clean entry and exit if skillfully handled. It also afforded an opportunity for further exploration. Accordingly, eight river boats were hired and fitted for the transport of troops. The voyage was provisioned with plenty of powder and shot, cheese, and other necessities. The supply requisitions mention no staples such as corn; it could be that the soldiers were expected to provide their own. Finally, a force of eighty soldiers was "hired" into service by means of conscription, which was the second largest troop movement of the war.[298] After making the necessary preparations, they launched their assault "by Water under [the command of] Coll [Thomas] Dew."[299]

---

[297]Scattered references to instructions in King Charles letters are found in the acts passed by the November assembly following Berkeley's arrival in June 1645. See Acts 5 and 17, November, 1645, Acts of the Assembly, in Hening, *The Statutes at Large...,* 301, 306-307.

[298]The first largest was the Pamunkey March with three hundred soldiers. For a basic list of some of their provisions and the number of boats and soldiers, see "Councell of Warre for the Associated Countyes," October 25, 1645, in Walter, ed., *Norfolk County, Virginia, Court Records*, 195-96.

[299]Thomas Dew was actually a captain in 1645. Plumpton related this account when he was 86 years old and the leaders he mentioned had undergone promotions since the war ended. Deposition of Henry Plumpton, in Saunders, ed., *Colonial Records,* 1:676.

So it was that the voyage departed the James River in the summer of 1645.[300] The eight river boats would have carried about ten soldiers each, along with provisions. The sheer distance travelled to carry the attack out was one of the longest range assaults ever carried out against any specific Indian target, including the Powhatans. About two hundred miles were rowed battling the Atlantic waves and often the current in this extraordinary action. Master boatmanship was required to navigate into the Chesapeake Bay and out to the sea, hugging the coast for a short distance until "they had entered Corrotuck [inlet]," the treacherous entrance to what would become North Carolina.[301] They then proceeded southward down Currituck Sound until entering the Albemarle Sound, at that time called the Roanoke Sound or just "the Sound." This was the first recorded time since the Roanoke expeditions of the 1580s that English watercraft had navigated the area. The entire voyage would have taken ten to fourteen days partly because in the latter part of the journey they would have had to stop to make camp at night along the northern bank of the sound, probably in polite contact with the Poteskeet, Pasquotank and Yeopim Indians who lived there. The water that lapped at the oars was notably fresher than that of the Chesapeake Bay. Rounded knees of Cypress roots penetrated the surface of the shallow water around the large trees, draped in Spanish moss, which grew well off shore into the shallow sound. The beauty of the land could be captivating, but danger-filled, as at one point a man was bitten by a venomous snake, though

---

[300]Estimate of early to midsummer derived from the last expedition ending around April or early May, and a later financial statement of accrued costs of the voyage recorded in October. Taking into account time to fit out the expedition and to prepare the financial statement, this was probably a summer voyage.

[301] Currituck Inlet no longer exists as it has since been blocked up with sand. See Orrin H. Pilkey, ed., *The North Carolina Shore and Its Barrier Islands: Restless Ribbons of Sand*, (Durham, N.C.: Duke University Press, 1998) 139-140.

surgeon Christopher Ackely was able to treat him successfully.[302] Finally, the boats "proceeded up the Sound to [the] Chowan [River]" where the last twenty miles of the journey were made.[303]

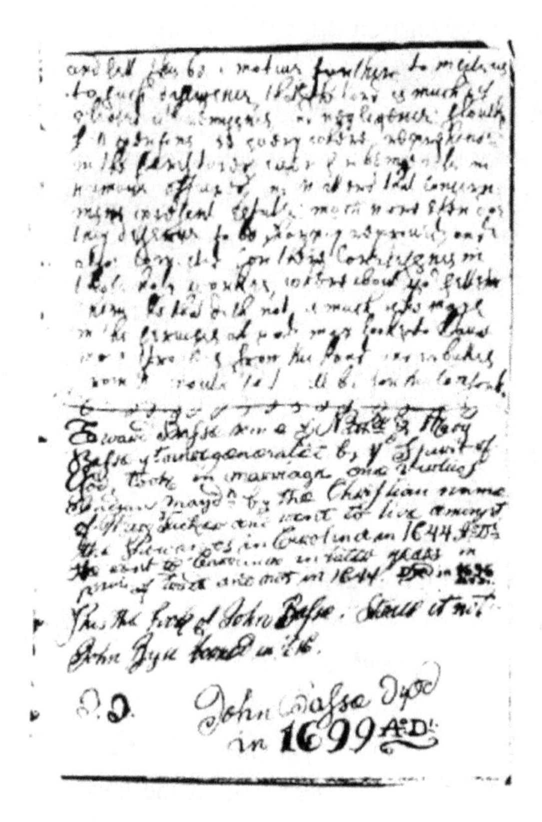
John Basse Dyed
in 1699 A.D.

Figure 21. This 17th century marriage record shows Edward Bass (whose brother had married a Nansemond woman) taking in marriage Elizabeth Tucker, a Chowanoke, and going to live with the tribe. This indicates a friendly relationship with the Carolina Algonquians during the time of the 1644 war. Bass Family Prayer Book Record. Courtesy of the Library of Virginia.

[302]For the castaway boat and snakebite victim, see "Councell of Warre for the Associated Countyes the 25 Oct 1645," in Walter, *Lower Norfolk County, Virginia, Court Records,* 195-96.

[303]Deposition of Henry Plumpton, in Saunders, *Colonial Records,* 1:676.

Historian Samuel Ashe argued that these expeditions were against the Carolina Algonquians, which allowed for future settlement. This dated view, sometimes still cited, is taken without the context of the Third Powhatan War (though I do believe he was correct regarding future settlement). When put in the proper context, the true target of the Weyanokes is more obvious, as Helen Rountree noted.[304] Looking at Henry Plumpton's narrative, he specifically names their target and the place of their battle as Weyanoke Creek, (known today as the Wiccacon), stating that they went "as far as the mouth of Weyanook Creek where they had a fight with the Indians and had a man killed by them."[305] Rivers of this time are well known to be named after whichever Indian group lived there, or vice versa. This is also confirmed by the testimony of some Meherrin Indians interviewed during the later border dispute, which drew a detailed diagram of the Weyanoke town and corn fields at Wiccacon in the dirt.[306]

The Virginians entered the mouth of the creek, which is still navigable by watercraft for a distance. Along the banks they saw the cornfields and knew they were getting close, but they never reached the town. In what seems to have been at least a sharp skirmish, if not a full-fledged battle, Ascomowet had been expecting the English and had brought up his remaining warriors as a forward defense to keep the English away from the women and children in the town. Dewe may have been off guard as he was attacked almost as soon as he entered the river mouth. As the Weyanokes unleashed a volley with a combination of arrows and shot, soldier Abraham Pitts went down with a serious wound.

---

[304]Rountree, *Pocahontas's People,* 86.

[305]Deposition of Henry Plumpton, in Saunders, *Colonial Records,* 1:676.

[306]Ibid.

Another unnamed man was killed instantly and Christopher Ackeley moved in to try and save the wounded. In the melee, one of the boats was castaway and sank, all the goods lost, and soldier John Skull lost his cutlass in the confusion. Others were likely wounded as well, but none that required enough prolonged medical attention to accrue significant cost.[307] The Weyanokes were noted as having one hundred warriors at the first arrival of the English in 1607,[308] but with much war and disease in the intervening decades, they were far reduced and outnumbered by the 80 soldiers. Colonel Dewe managed to land the boats and get his soldiers ashore to fight on foot, where Ascomowet finally relented and withdrew. Colonel Dewe faced a choice. Continue upriver to attack the town, which was miles up a winding river in which they had lost the element of surprise, or turn back now. Having critically wounded men that might not survive upriver, he turned back with his men to Virginia. Before they left, they buried a man on the site of the battle and claimed victory, but for all intents and purposes, it was the Weyanokes who succeeded in holding back a stronger enemy and saved their town from destruction. No further assaults would be attempted in the Carolina region during the war.[309]

---

[307]"Councell of Warre for the Associated Countyes the 25 Oct 1645," in Walter, ed., *Lower Norfolk County, Virginia, Court Records,* 195-96.

[308]William Strachey, *The History of Travaile into Virginia Britannia (1612)*. . . (London: Hakluyt Society, 1849), 59.

[309]Deposition of Henry Plumpton, in Saunders., *Colonial Records,* 1:676

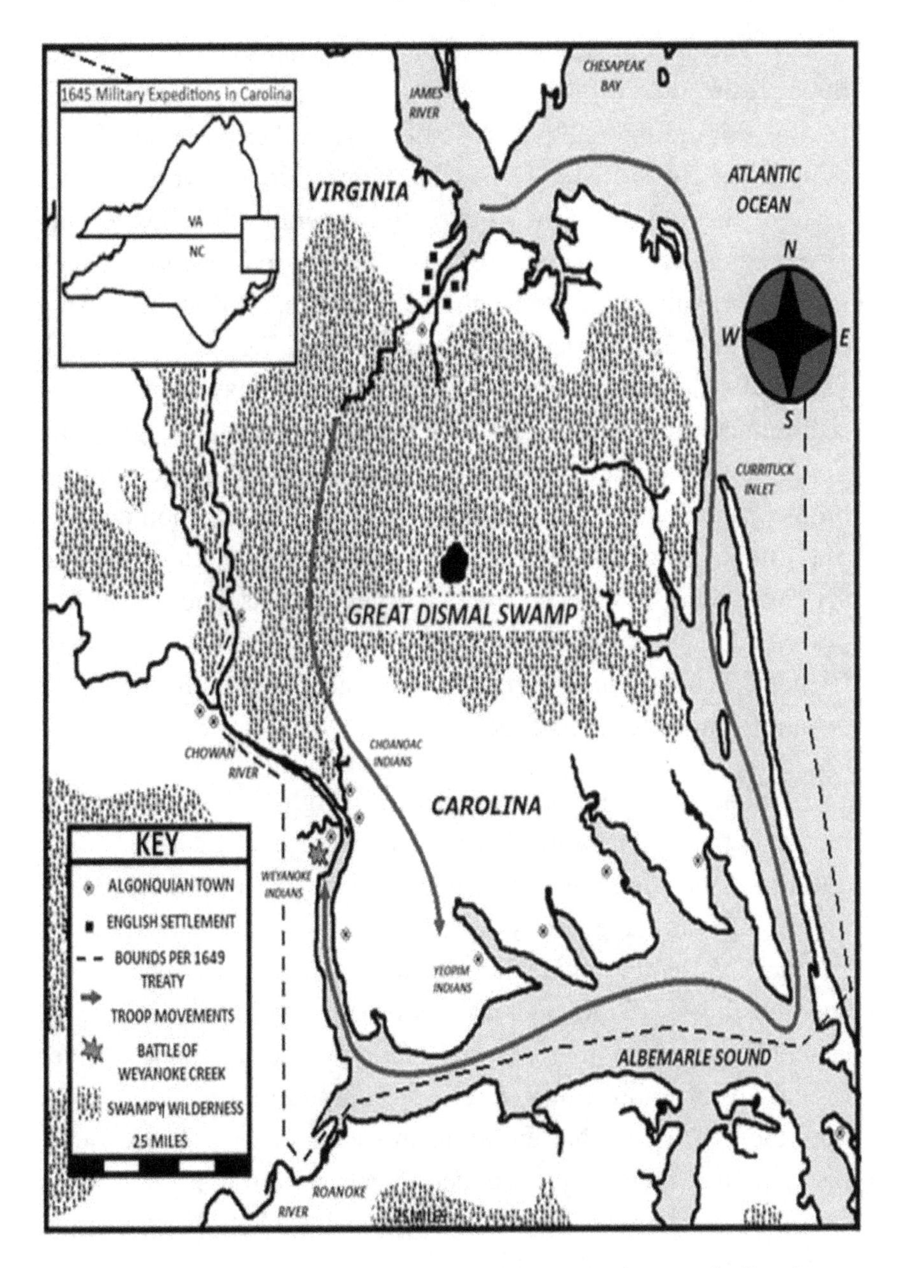

Figure 22. Military campaigns sent into present day North Carolina from Virginia. The first land scout was followed by an amphibious assault on Wiccacon Creek dwelling Weyanokes. Map by the author.

The Weyanokes remained at Wiccacon Creek for another three years, making a true determination of the victors of the Battle. Nor did the underclass settlers of southern Virginia forget their experiences there. Henry Plumpton, along "with Thomas Tuke of the Isle of Wight County and severall others" who may have been a part of the expeditions, returned to Weyanoke Creek to purchase the land from the Weyanokes.[310] The increasing burden on the underclass was getting unbearable, both financially and socially. While Virginia may have once represented a chance to better themselves and give an opportunity to reap the full rewards on one's labor, the realities on the ground were that Virginia was becoming a carbon copy of the English social system. These poor farmers, laborers and servants who saw the prime farmland of isolated Carolina perceived a fresh opportunity, and they spread the word to their friends and family in Virginia about the new land to the south, far distant from the tethers of Jamestown.

These underclass colonists of Virginia were under the increasingly unbearable costs of wartime. Sheriffs were authorized to jail anyone delinquent in paying the many heavy levies, and they apparently had been doing it frequently. In the February Assembly this increase in prisoners was recognized, and the plight of the poor farmers dealt with: "for Releife of severall poor men that are layd in the Sherrifs hands under execution for Tobb, Corne & other Commodities, which truly in kind they have not, that therefore in such cases ye Inventorie of his or their Effecte being produced upon oath in preforme of the Creditor, The Comiss shall Determine what Shall be valued for

[310]Deposition of Henry Plumpton, in *Colonial Records of North Carolina,* 1:676.

satisfaction of the Debt."[311] This had the benefit of getting these poor men home to their families, but even then, since they had no tobacco for payment, their meager belongings began to be confiscated to pay for the war. Lawsuits flooded the courts as debt cases skyrocketed and got out of control. In response, the Assembly expelled all monetary attorneys from office the next November in the hopes of reducing the caseload on the courts. The rich men on the great plantations often lost much less than the lower class due to their rank and privilege, and morale suffered as the poor farmers and indentured servants became resentful. [312]

As the summer went on, the success of the forts, although at great financial cost, became increasingly apparent as "constant marches" against the Powhatans kept them continually on the move. Shea notes that "Their duty was twofold. First, they were to try to prevent Indian raiding parties from moving down the Virginia Peninsula toward the palisade some forty to sixty miles below. Second, whenever the opportunity presented itself, the three groups were to join forces and move against Opechancano and the Pamunkeys."[313] The fort commanders kept in communication with each other, often coordinating attacks on specific targets, otherwise having their forces constantly deployed in patrols of the woods, looking for any sign of Indian activity. Clashes with the soldiers must have been fierce, especially in the construction phase of the forts, but as time went on, fewer and fewer Powhatans were encountered as Opechancano's people withdrew further up the York River,

[311]Act 11, February, 1644/5, Acts of the Assembly, in Hening, *The Statutes at Large...*, 294.

[312]Acts 6 -7, November 1645, Acts of the Assembly, in Hening, *The Statutes at Large...*, 301-302.

[313]Shea, *Virginia Militia in the Seventeenth Century,* 65.

farther from the English settlements. Finally, the Powhatan counter-offensive that had begun the previous autumn was totally turned back. [314]

Because the forts were constructed in early spring, Indian women's corn planting may have been disrupted, though it is probable that seeing the forts being built, they simply moved further inland to plant their crops out of sight of the English. At this point Opechancano's war was a totally defensive one, and his main concern would have been for the women and children who relied more heavily on wild foods while constantly on the move. While we must speculate in the absence of records, he probably made sure the forts and English patrols sent out from them were constantly under the close watch of his hidden sentinels who would give warning to main groups so that they could get out of harm's way. It would have surely had psychological impact on the young people as they learned to truly fear the English, never truly knowing when the next attack would decimate their towns and carry away their families. The next generation of Powhatan leaders like Totopotomoi and Cockaqueske of the Pamunkeys, Pattanochus and Robin Tucker of the Nansemonds, Ascomowet of the Weyanokes and countless others unnamed grew up in this constant state of fear and hunger. [315]

---

[314]By March, 1646, so few Indians were encountered any more that further attacks were considered nearly impossible. See Act 18, March 1645/6, Acts of the Assembly, in Hening, *The Statutes at Large...*, 317-318.

[315]Even if the Powhatans had secret cornfields and other stored provisions, it was not long before even these wore out, for they were noted as living in dispersed camps away from their towns, ranging the woods in search of food, robbing English frontier plantations where possible and hunting English cattle.

With no foreseeable way to reverse this new tide, Opechancano seems to have known that the war was lost. In the early summer of 1645, likely with the advice of his closest councilors and priests, he decided to treat for peace. Margaret Worleigh, who had been captive during the entire war to this point, was brought before Opechancano. Having dealt with English people for decades, Opechancano likely did not need an interpreter to convey the message that he instructed Margaret to write. She carefully inscribed it, folded the paper and handed it to a messenger, who ran through the woods to the forest's edge by Fort Royal. It took courage to be seen within the sights of the soldiers behind the fort walls, but Captain Roger Marshall maintained control of his men and received the message, passing it along to Jamestown.[316]

Sir William Berkeley was only back in office for nine days before the messenger from Fort Royal rode into Jamestown with Worleigh's letter, probably just as the Carolina expedition was getting underway. He immediately convened the Governor's Council and had the note read out loud. Though the details are lost, Margaret Worleigh "proposed by authority of that chief redemption of the captives in his hands and a negotiation for a treaty of peace." After some discussion, Berkeley decided to play along for the time being. He "ordered that Opechancanough be treated with for the redemption of the prisoners and required to redeliver them with the arms and ammunition he had taken to the

---

[316]This event is not found in any seventeenth century records. However, it was recorded by nineteenth century historian Sebastian Streeter, who had access to Virginian colonial records that would be later burned in the Civil War, and no longer available to modern historians. On examination of his entry, I could find no contradictions that would cast doubt on its historical value. Streeter died in 1864, and his papers were published posthumously in 1876. See Streeter, *Papers Relating to the Early History of Maryland,* 78-79.

English and that a cessation of hostilities be agreed upon during the continuance of the negotiations." He penned this in a letter to deliver to Worleigh, also saying that he would soon be at Fort Royal personally, wherein Opechancano should send twelve of his "principle councilors" to confer with Berkeley regarding the prisoner exchange and peace treaty. Berkeley then sent for Henry Fleet, the leading expert in Powhatan customs and language, and told him to meet him at Middle Plantation before proceeding to Fort Royal.[317]

What happened at Fort Royal the day of the proposed meeting is unclear. According to a version of events constructed by Shea, the councilors and chiefs met outside the fort at the appointed time. As they approached, the doors swung open and the garrison made a charge at the envoy, thereby striking an additional blow and ensuring that the war would continue.[318] Shea went on to say that this success "inspired a new series of raids for the 'cutting upp of the Indians Corne,' which lasted until winter closed the second season of campaigning," but this reference to cutting up the Indians' corn is not mentioned in the records until the following spring.[319] It seems that he made this connection because of a reference that at some point during the war Captain Roger Marshall, the commander of Fort Royal, made a "hot charge" in some decisive action. This reference, the mention of a passing traveler, wasn't actually connected with

[317]Ibid.

[318]Shea, *The Virginia Militia in the Seventeenth Century,* 66-67.

[319]Corn slashing was ordered in reference to attacks to be caries out the following spring, I doubt that they were inspired by this event. See Act 8, March 1644/45, Acts of the Assembly, in Hening, *The Statutes at Large...,* 314-315; Shea, *The Virginia Militia in the Seventeenth Century,* 66-67.

these peace talks.[320] Though Shea's version of events is one possible explanation, it cannot be proven that Marshall or Berkeley gave the order for a charge that day. Regardless of whether there was a fight or not, the results were largely the same. Through violence or failed negotiations, the peace talks fell through and the war would continue. For the Powhatan people, little hope could be had to defeat the English at this point. For them, military action devolved into a purely defensive one as they began to break apart into family units, moving from place to place to avoid the patrols sent from the forts. Their sole goal would have been to keep their families alive.[321]

[320]Roger Marshall, though he was a resident of Northampton County on the Eastern Shore, commanded Fort Royal and was a veteran of the Battle of Menmend. This charge was considered an important one, and Samuel Mathews told about it to passing traveler Beauchamp Plantagenet, but did not say in what campaign or battle it was connected to. See Plantagenet," A Description of the Province of New Albion," in Force, *Tracts and Other Papers,* 2:6.

[321]Shea, *The Virginia Militia in the Seventeenth Century,* 66-67.

"Imposibillity of further Revenge upon them"

The autumn and winter of 1645 seem to have passed by fairly peacefully for the English families within the protected portion of the Lower Peninsula, as life began to resemble normality. Very little concerning the Powhatans or the war in general is mentioned in the records until the following spring. No doubt, however, the fort commanders kept their soldiers on constant patrol, the war continuing in earnest on the frontier. Conceived at this point to be a defensive war, it is doubtful that these soldiers went deep into enemy territory, and unless a good target was identified, they probably stuck to continued foot patrols to keep the Lower Peninsula Indian-free. That is not to say that it did remain Indian-free. If these soldiers used the same paths at regular times, they would have made themselves vulnerable to ambush. While at this time Powhatan warriors would have probably been preoccupied with hunting to feed their families over the winter, especially since autumn was the traditional time of communal deer hunting, no doubt at least some measure of ambush and skirmish was kept up that autumn and winter as it was also traditionally the best time for Powhatans to stage attacks.[322]

Since the forts were constructed in the early spring of 1645, they not only possibly disrupted some Powhatan corn planting, but gave a measure of safety to English farmers, and thus a corn and tobacco crop was able to be produced in the summer of that year. It would have been difficult to balance corn production with tobacco planting, because while the need for food was obvious, so was the need for money, so both crops had

---

[322]Act 18, November 1645, Acts of the Assembly, in Hening, *The Statutes at Large...*, 307.

to be exploited to the fullest. It is also possible that corn was able to be traded with friendly Indians such as the Accomacs and Rappahannocks, who continued to act as scouts and spies for the struggling colony.[323]

One advantage that the Powhatans had was availability of wild food sources in times of a poor crop. Many times previously severe droughts had ravaged the land, sometimes for several years in a row. When this happened, wild foods were used more frequently than normal. During non-drought years, these wild foods were less utilized so that they could re-grow and replenish until the next drought. If the Powhatan crop was indeed disrupted this year, as it may have been, then these foods would have been taken advantage of. In the Powhatan core area where the Pamunkey, Chickahominy, and Mattaponi lived in the autumn of 1645, an large deciduous forest provided them with bountiful tree nuts that they could dry and store over the winter, as well as having available the starchy tubers of what they called *tuckahoe,* and many other available fruits and wild grains. South of James River, especially near the coast, where fewer deciduous trees and therefore less nuts. However, they had the clear advantage of a variety of fruits and tubers that grew in the swamps near the Great Dismal Swamp, as well as greater access to shellfish. They probably also used this massive swamp as a hideout for their families and a safe home base from which they could launch

[323]While there is the distinct possibility that many Powhatans were able to plant a corn crop further back from the forts, out of sight of the English, it is apparent from the Acts of the Assembly that by the following year the various Powhatan groups had largely dispersed into small hunting camps, the impression being that they were desperate for food. The forts, therefore, must have been highly effective in disrupting Powhatan subsistence.

raids and ambushes, as well as hunting grounds to take advantage of the large bear population.[324]

Morale continued to suffer among the troops on the frontier, who were pressed into the service, probably against their wishes. They were poor farmers and tradesmen who were kept away from their farms and families, and while in theory they would be compensated for time lost and injuries sustained, it didn't always play out that way as their many lawsuits during and following the war testified. They were poorly supplied in cramped conditions within the tiny forts. Lieutenant Nicholas Stillwell, who had been given command of at least one expedition in the winter of 1644, now found himself resentful of Virginia; he deserted, taking some of his men with him north to Maryland. The Assembly also said that many others also went and that more were "likely to follow," showing a general dissatisfaction.[325]

It is easy to see why many were so disaffected. In a particularly sad and increasingly common set of circumstances, "...the Hearts of divers Masters were hardened rather to suffer their servants to perish for want of fit means & applications than by seeking Relief." Indentured servants, powerless and fully dependent on their masters, were being allowed to die of sickness rather than to be treated by a physician. Considered to be "griping & avaricious men," these masters "were more Swayed by Politick respects then from Xpian [Christian] Duty or

---

[324]By far the most extensive study on the wild food sources of the different geographical and seasonal availabilities of the different locales of Powhatan nations has been in Binford, *Cultural Diversity Among Aboriginal Cultures of Coastal Virginia and North Carolina,* 10-62, though his work has also been debated in its accuracy.

[325]Act 24, March 1645, Acts of the Assembly, in Hening, *The Statutes at Large...,* 321.

Charity." In their defense, they claimed that Physicians were charging more money to give medical treatment than the whole purchase price of the servants themselves, who were beginning to look more and more like chattel property than human beings. The masters claimed that "it was the more gainfull & saving way to stand to the hazard of the servants then to entertain the certain Charge of a Physitian or Chirurgeon [surgeon]." In response, the Assembly regulated the charges of care givers so that the masters would not face the temptation of copping out of doctor's charges, and any physician hiking up their prices could be arrested.[326] It is unknown if Thomas Ward, the surgeon who accompanied the Chickahominy and Carolina marches, was one of these price-gouging physicians, but the court records reveal that he was chronically in debt and had his wages from his military service garnished to satisfy his debtors, showing the plights that the surgeons, in turn, were in. The increasing poverty of the people was leading to desertions, willful neglect, and a general downward moral spiral that the Virginian government rightly found troubling. This war needed to end. [327]

Altogether, although ambushes and skirmishes likely continued to a degree over the autumn and winter, there seems to have been a respite in violence as far as the records show. Collection of wild foods and hunting required a greater effort on the part of the Powhatan people and the defensive patrols of the English did not go deep into enemy territory. On the one hand, this was probably something of a relief to both sides, but on the

---

[326]Act 15, March 1645, Acts of the Assembly, in Hening, *The Statutes at Large...,* 316.

[327]Thomas Ward, was a surgeon and attorney, however five separate lawsuits were carried against him for a collection of massive quantities of debt. He was jailed at one point for an unknown misdemeanor and all his wages from the Carolina expedition and a former Chickahominy march were garnished to pay some of his lenders. Walter, *Lower Norfolk County, Virginia, Court Records,* 83, 138, 145, 201, 202, and 208.

other, the cost of keeping up these patrols was getting out of hand. According to Shea, the war was becoming obviously inconclusive, reminiscent of the prolonged ten year war of the 1620s. No one wanted that. By March, 1646, the Assembly put together a final plan of attack designed to finish the war once and for all. They must have Opechancano, dead or alive.[328]

Opechancano and the rest of the Powhatans had had a hard winter to deal with. Their people were hungry and living hand to mouth. Winter had brought thousands of wild fowl to the Chesapeake Bay, but the English had taken up much of the hunting grounds traditionally used to hunt the birds, so this food source may have slipped through some chiefdoms' fingers that year. As spring time came, they knew that they were likely to face a renewed season of campaigns against them, but at the same time there was reason to hope. The Cattapeuk (spring) season brought something that the English were far less likely to keep from them: fish. Herring and Shad came in innumerable amounts every spring like clockwork, migrating to the uppermost reaches of the tidewater rivers where the Powhatans hid out from the English. The long anticipated arrival of the fish was probably the best thing they had seen in months. Immediately people set out to erect fishing weirs (large reed-walled fish traps), which could capture large amounts of fish easily for feasting and future storage. Others would come out in dugout canoes for spear fishing or with line and hook. It is easy to imagine a rare moment of community thanksgiving and festivities as they also began to make an attempt at planting a crop of corn.

---

[328]Shea, *The Virginia Militia,* 67-68.

Not all nations were able to construct the weirs out of sight, however. The Appomattox River had long since been inundated by English settlements and the weirs constructed by the Appomatock Indians near Swift Creek were easily spotted and reported to government officials. The spring assembly ordered immediate expeditions set against them for "the prevention of the great Relief and Subsistance to the Salvages by ffishing in Brostill als [alias] Appomattocke River, as also for ye Cutting down their Corne or pforming any other Service upon them." For further measure a new fort was to be erected near that river's falls, called Fort Henry, in order to make constant attacks on them. This fort was to be manned by a forty-five man garrison comprised of men from all the other counties who would rendezvous at Basse's Choice plantation in Isle of Wight County to march upriver for the attack.[329] Chosen as commander of Fort Henry was newly appointed Captain Abraham Wood. Wood had arrived in Virginia as a five year old servant boy in 1620, and grew up during the ten years of constant warfare in the Second Powhatan War. He had grown up by that war's end and had probably served in some of the expeditions. Having increased his holdings in the interim, he made a successful life for himself in Virginia, and was highly regarded by his superiors. He would arise to even greater importance later.[330]

The Associated Counties of Isle of Wight, Upper and Lower Norfolk were also charged with a renewal of their campaigns against the traditionalist Nansemond "or any other neighboring Indians," recognizing that many tribes were

[329]Act 13, March 1645,Acts of the Assembly, in Hening, *The Statutes at Large...,* 317-317; Shea, *Virginia Militia in the Seventeenth Century,* 67.

[330]McCartney, *Virginia Immigrants and Adventurers,* 759; Morton, *Colonial Virginia,* 157-159.

becoming displaced and had to move from place to place for subsistence and security. Shifting from defensive to offensive patrols, these excursions may have made attempts into the Great Dismal to root out the Nansemond but likely didn't get very far. Traditionalist Nansemonds also probably travelled to the southwest to the Nottoway River, making searching them out very difficult for the English.[331]

Despite these forays, Berkeley recognized that most offensives were relatively ineffective in that while they could keep the Indians disrupted and hungry, The English simply did not have the resources to fully root them out and destroy the Powhatans completely. He wanted the war to end, with or without Opechancano. And so, having "Considered the great & vast expence of the Collony in prosecuting the warr against oE [our] Comon Enemies the Indians, & the almost impossibility of further Revenge upon them, they being disbursed & driven from their Townes and habitations, Lurking up and downe the woods in small numbers, And that a peace if honourably [obtained] would Conduce to ye better being and Comoditie of ye Country," an immediate end of the war would be sought by a sixty man company under the command of Lieutenant Travis Poythers and Captain Henry Fleet, who had recently come south from his Indian trading business in Maryland.[332]

[331]Act 13, March 1645, Acts of the Assembly, in Hening, *The Statutes at Large...,* 315; Shea, *The Virginia Militia,* 67-68.

[332]Act 18, March 1645, Acts of the Assembly, in Hening, *The Statutes at Large...,* 317-318.

Figure 23. Looking east across the Chowan River at the original town site of Choanoac. This was very near the mouth of the Wiccacon Creek and may have been the landing site of the English amphibious assault in 1645. Photo by the author.

Henry Fleet was an interesting man, who had been captured during the last Powhatan war and was a captive of the Rappahannocks for five years. He knew the language better than anybody, and personally knew many of the Rappahannock Indians who offered their services as scouts to Virginia. In fact he was a rival trader to William Claiborne and his relations with Maryland made him unpopular to many Virginians. However, the plan of this expedition seems to have been his, and he also personally offered his services, in both his large trading vessels and translating services. His advice and offer was readily accepted by Berkeley and the Assembly (despite what Claiborne may have thought) and Lieutnant Poythers was ordered to follow

Fleet's advice in leading the company, thus making it unclear who was actually in charge of the expedition.[333]

Fleet's ships were larger than the river boats that they had been using for amphibious assaults. Consisting of a Barque and a Shallop, these larger vessels could hold all sixty soldiers and were supplied for a full six weeks. Fleet, "att his owne Exp Coste & Charges," supplied 300 pounds of powder and 1200 pounds of shot, giving a needed boost to the colonial armament. Besides the vessels, expertise and ammunition, he also provided the food for all the men, though the colony was responsible for raising money for tools, men and soldiers' pay. The men were levied from all over the county, several from each county in proportion to their population. Only two from Henrico but 16 from York County and 13 from around James City. All men were to travel downriver to meet at a general rendezvous on April 20, 1646. [334] Being able to supply all this, it is obvious the level of success Fleet achieved as an Indian trader. Perhaps he wanted to patch up the old divisions between himself and the Virginia government, and perhaps he saw trading opportunities if the war ended peacefully. Nevertheless, while Virginia was happy to have him with this unexpected and sorely needed boost of momentum, they accepted it only with a provision. Fleet would be paid 15,000 pounds of tobacco for this service, but "Provided always That in Case he do not effect the aforesaid intended peace with Oppechankeno or his Indians our Enemies, that then he shall beare all such Charges & disbursements without any Consideration or Satisfaction from ye publique." The stakes were high for Fleet to do what he promised he could do.

---

[333]Ibid.

[334]Ibid.

"That great bloody Monster": The Murder of Opechancano

After fitting out the ships and gathering the troops at Kekotan, Fleet and Poythers set out, swinging around the Lower Peninsula to the northward and from there up the Rappahannock River into the Powhatan heartland. Although Fleet detailed his plan to the Assembly, the court clerks never actually explained in the surviving records what the plan was. Because this contingent was heavily armed and obviously prepared for battle, the message was obvious: choose peace or destruction; Virginia was prepared for both. Since he was the leading expert of the region in Algonquian language and customs, Fleet was ideal for the task of seeking out a peaceful meeting with Opechancano. In order to do so, it seems that he used Rappahannocks who had defected from the Powhatans or other native contacts he had as messengers to draw the aged *weroance* in. Meeting up with Rappahannock scouts upriver, they would have been able to sneak around the back end where Opechancano didn't normally expect an English advance.[335]

Once beyond the frontier, no records indicate the details or precise results of this expedition. Berkeley had given orders to Poythers and Fleet that if peace with Opechancano was unattainable, then they were to construct a fort at Rappahannock. This way, if peace failed, at least they would have a further foothold to launch more effective attacks. The voyage had a six

---

[335] Because Fleet and Poythers were ordered to construct a fort on the Rappahannock River should peace talks fail, it can be inferred that Rappahannock was their point of landing their company of infantry. There is no evidence that this river system was used as a base of attack in any previous expeditions. See Act 18, Acts of the Assembly, in Hening, *The Statutes at Large...,* 317-319.

week supply of food and plenty of ammunition, so they may have been gone a long while before meeting with Opechancano. The ships, much bulkier than the river boats, drew more water and probably wouldn't have been able to easily navigate the upper waters of the Rappahannock. Thus, again likely with the assistance of native allies, they mounted the expedition on foot from there.[336]

No one knows how long they were gone, or exactly what happened, but eventually they were able to meet with Opechancano. It is difficult to imagine the sixty-man force simply strolling into the Pamunkey camp. Messengers must have been sent ahead, probably Rappahannocks, to request the council. He had dealt with treachery from the English during peace talks several times in the past. He had been poisoned in 1624, and Berkeley may have attempted his capture earlier the year before. He had every reason not to accept the council with Fleet. Still, he wanted peace and Fleet already had a reputation among Indian people. There weren't many options left. He consented, and he went along with his closest followers.

Opechancano wasn't the same man he had been in the past. He and the rest of his people were in dire straits. Already elderly, he could no longer walk, and his closest bodyguards transported him in a litter through the woods to meet with Captain Fleet. It must have been a surprise for many of the English to see the famed chief to emerge from the forest in such a condition. With the assistance of those near him, perhaps Totopotomoi or Cockacoeske, they sat him up and opened his eyelids (he required assistance to do so). Coming forward, Fleet explained his intentions and the terms on which Berkeley would

[336] Fleet was mentioned as transporting the soldiers in his "Barque Boat & Shallop," which were large enough to accommodate all sixty soldiers. See Ibid., 318.

give peace. If the proposed treaty was anything like the one that was later agreed on at the end of the war, then Opechancano would have faced absolute subjugation under Berkeley's Virginia. He would have to admit defeat, pay tribute to Berkeley in the same way that the small nations paid tribute to him. None of his people would be allowed to ever enter the Lower Peninsula on pain of death. They would be, in a word, subservient, second class citizens in their own country. Opechancano had spent his whole adult life fighting the European threat, and giving up sovereignty in the last moments of his life was unthinkable. On the other hand, his people were hungry and dispersed. They were losing touch with each other as communications deteriorated. This war was imploding his chiefdom, and perhaps peace would allow it to be preserved, albeit in a diminished form. His response, apparently, was to not give the English an inch. He would resolve to fight to the bitter end. He would not die a vassal.[337]

---

[337] According to Robert Beverley, Sir William Berkeley was the one who, having learned Opechancano's location, swept in to capture him, which can be verified through other sources as well. Presumably, Berkeley learned this location from Fleet and Poythers, so a message must have been conveyed that the peace talks failed, detailing Opechancano's location. See Anonymous, "A Perfect Description of Virginia," 13; and Beverley, *The History and Present State of Virginia,* 62.

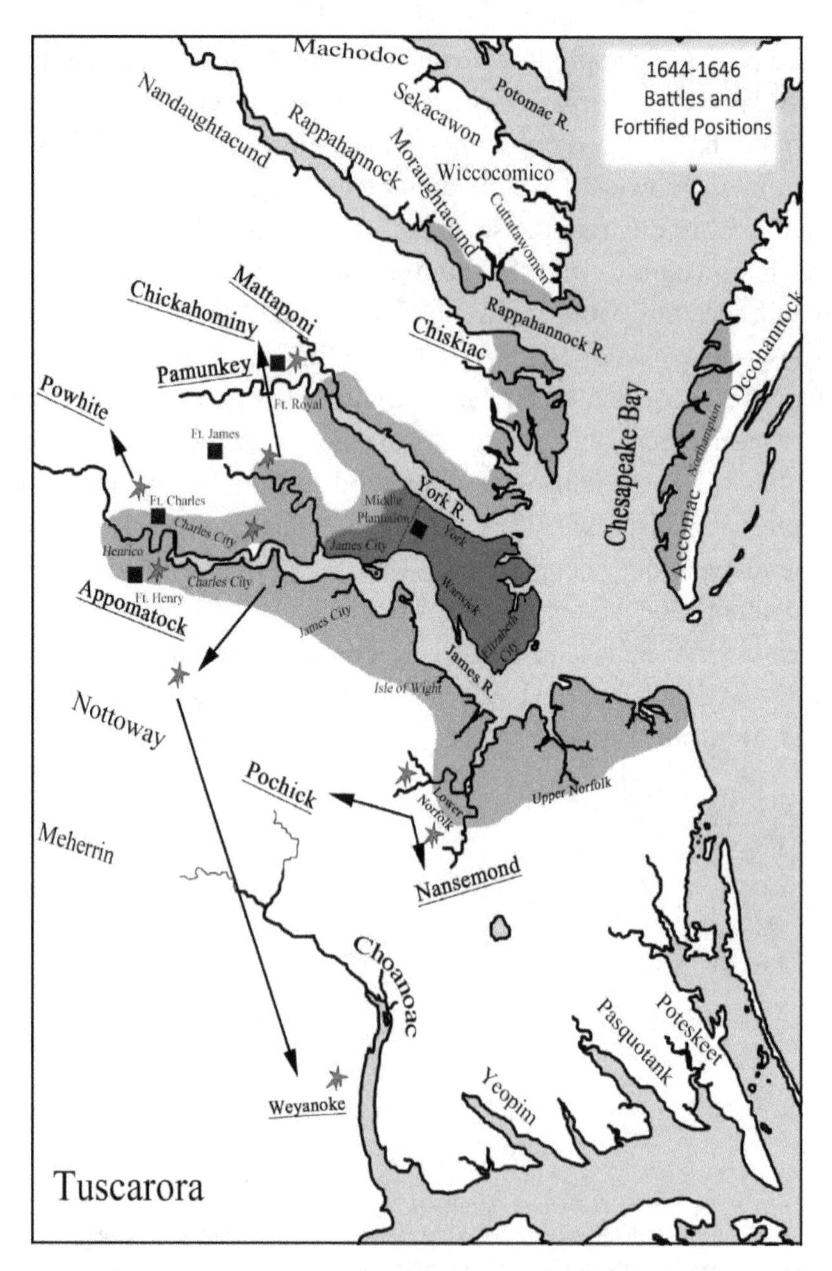

Figure 24. Partial Illustration of known battles and skirmishes of the war. While many others resulting from Powhatan ambushes and English patrols certainly occurred, spefics are not known. Map by the author.

Captain Fleet and Lieutenant Poythers were certainly exasperated at this, especially Fleet, who had 15,000 pounds of tobacco on the line that just evaporated before his eyes. The peace talks had failed and Opechancano had resolved to fight it out. Does this mean the he still thought he could win? Perhaps. No one can know for certain. But as stated, he had spent his whole life physically fighting the European threat in several different wars. There are few native leaders that rival his uncompromising resolve. Many others had fought the wars, seen the ugliness of it, and resolved to a treaty following the conflict. Opechancano never gave up, seemingly futile as it was. To Fleet's credit, there is no evidence that he attempted treachery during the deliberations, apparently allowing Opehancano's people to carry him back to his camp. But as Fleet and Poythers took stock of their losses from their failed mission, they received word, probably from their Rappahannock scouts, that Opechancano's camp was not far off, and that he was likely to remain there for a time, vulnerable to attack from being constrained to the litter that his bodyguards transported him in. The English leaders were under orders to build a fort in case peace talks should fall through, but with this intelligence, the war could be suddenly brought to an end. A messenger was quickly dispatched to Jamestown requesting orders.[338]

Sir William Berkeley and other colonial leaders nervously awaited news from the expedition. The war had grown far too costly for the colony to handle. They were sinking, unable to make a profit, for nearly every scrap of tobacco was being used to fund the war, and many poor farmers who couldn't pay their share were having their property confiscated and their persons jailed. People were deserting, and unless peace was

[338] Ibid.

attained, no end to it would be in sight. Where would this all end? Finally, a messenger emerged from the forest with a note from Fleet. Berkeley opened it, hoping for the best.[339]

At first, the news was bleak. The peace talks had failed. The war would continue. But then, the note went on, Opechancano's camp was not far away and if they hurried, they could attack and capture him. What were his orders? Berkeley thought quickly and decided that instead of Fleet initiating the attack, the glory would be all his. He hastily gathered up "a Party of Horse" and "resolved at all Adventures to seize his Person [Opechancano]." Galloping at full speed through the forest, he made a "speedy March" to meet up with Fleet in what was the first cavalry raid in Virginian history, perhaps the first in English America.[340]

Berkeley would have met first with Fleet and Poythers to ascertain Opechancano's exact whereabouts, and then, probably in company with them, galloped on toward Opechancano's camp. No doubt scouts heard the horses coming and did their best to alert the camp, but the horses were too fast and it was too late. On horseback with cutlass raised Berkeley charged among the temporary shelters of Opechancano's last camp. Scrambling, the Pamunkey bodyguards might have been able to get away had they not been hampered by the burden of carrying Opechancano on the litter as they attempted to escape into the woods. Nor could they hide in the underbrush effectively carrying their load, so, in the midsummer of 1646, Opechancano, the mighty war

[339] Berkeley learned this location from Fleet and Poythers, so a message must have been conveyed that the peace talks failed, detailing Opechancano's location. See Anonymous, "A Perfect Description of Virginia," 13; and Beverley, *The History and Present State of Virginia,* 62.

[340] Beverley, *The History and Present State of Virginia,* 62.

chief, was "surprised. . . in his Quarters," with his loyal supporters captured alongside him.[341]

It would be a treasure to know what exchange took place between Opechancano and Berkeley at the moment of the capture, but unfortunately, all that is known is that Berkeley took his prized captive back to Jamestown. In fact, if it wasn't for Robert Beverly's few lines written about it decades later, the whole dramatic event would never be known in any detail. Beverly described Opechancano at this point: "by his great Age, and the Fatigues of War, (in which Sir William Berkeley follow'd him close) was now grown so decrepit, that he was not able to walk alone; but was carried about by his Men, where-ever he had a mind to move. His Flesh was all macerated, his Sinews slacken'd, and his Eye-lids became so heavy, that he could not see, but as they were lifted up by his Servants."[342]

Berkeley had great plans for Opechancano. Not only would he force him to terms of peace, but he would be shipped off to England as a display of English prowess and proof of the good climate of the land since he was able to attain such an uncommonly great age, thought by the Virginians to be 100 or more years old. This "personal and resolute march and victory of Sir William Berkley" would be Berkeley's greatest military achievement, perhaps in his mind vindicating himself from his failure during the Bishop's Wars.[343] No doubt there were great cheers in Jamestown as Berkeley brought Opechancano in,

---

[341] Anonymous, "A Perfect Description of Virginia," 13; Beverley, *The History and Present State of Virginia,* 62.

[342] Beverley, *The History and Present State of Virginia,* 61-62; Rountree, *Pocahontas's People,* 82.

[343] Plantagenet, "A Description of the Province of New Albion," in Force, *Tracts and Other Papers,* 2:6.

known to the colonists as "that great bloody Monster." Berkeley took great pains, according to Beverly, to treat him with tenderness and respect, though at least one pair of eyes from the crowds wanted nothing to do with shipping him to England. Thinking of their family and friends killed in the assault, they wanted him dead.[344]

Opechancano thus far sat stoically, and according to Beverly, "continued brave to the last Moment of his Life, and not showing the least dejection to his captivity." Berkeley had him remanded to prison, which was probably not one with cages and bars, but rather a simple house with locked doors normally used as a debtors' prison. Obviously, he could not escape on his own, even if in more comfortable quarters. I believe that Berkeley realized there was danger to his life if he was housed in less secure conditions, and therefore put him in a prison house for his own safety until a ship could be arranged to take him to England. He placed an armed guard over him, trusting them to keep him safe and keep unwanted visitors out.[345]

Several weeks passed, and no doubt much discourse passed between Berkeley and Opechancano during this time. It is a shame that no narration survives to give testimony to it. Finally, towards the end, the guards began opening the doors to curious onlookers. Opechancano heard his door unlock and perceived many boots clunking on the wooden floor. English voices chattered to each other as they gawked about him,

---

[344] Beverley, *The History and Present State of Virginia*. 62.

[345] The primary function of prisons in Virginia at the time were debtor's prisons, which were simple modified frame structures to prevent escape. With Berkeley's plans to show Opechancano off in England it is extremely doubtful that he would lay Opechancano up in a dungeon. For refrence to debtor's prisons see Acts 11 and 13, Acts of the Assembly, in Hening, *Statutes at Large...*, 294.

probably laughing and making jokes about the captive king. Opechancano had someone near him open his eyelids to see the crowd that was gathering and saw that he was being made into a spectacle like a caged freak. Disgusted, he used all his strength to shout for Governor Berkeley, who came immediately. Opechancano "scornfully told him, That had it been his Fortune to take Sir William Berkeley prisoner, he should not meanly have exposed him as a show to the People." Berkeley probably shooed the gawkers out of the room and apologized. These would be Opechancano's last recorded words.[346]

Some research has found evidence that the prisoners that had been captured with Opechancano and in other raids met a cruel fate. Most prisoners up to this point had been turned into indentured servants and slaves, but since these captives were Opechancano's closest supporters, they could be less trusted among the Virginian settlements. Arrangements were made to ship all those over the age of eleven by boat to the "Western Island," where they were abandoned or sold. Either this island was in the Bermudas, where they were made slaves, or, according to Martha McCartney, this was the same Western Island off the shore of Accomack within Chesapeake Bay, which would have meant that they were marooned. Their eventual fate is unknown, though they probably soon made their escape.[347]

The days and weeks went on, and about a fortnight after his capture, the prison guard could no longer restrain his distaste for Opechancano. Perhaps he had only revenge for his relations who were killed on his mind, or perhaps he thought that his name would survive into the history books if he was the one to kill the

[346] Beverley, *The History and Present State of Virginia,* 62.

[347] McCartney, "Cockacoeske, Queen of Pamunkey," 261n7; Rountree, *Pocahontas's People,* 86.

infamous Pamunkey chief. Unable to look at his face, he either waited until his back was turned, or ordered him to turn around. Did the old chief have any final words to the gunman, or was he taken by surprise? It is unknown. In the dimly lighted jailhouse, "resenting the Calamities the Colony had suffer'd by this Prince's Means," the guard gunned down Opechancano, shooting him through the back. The life of the great *mamanatowick* of the Powhatans faded slowly as he bled out and died on the floor. If the gunman wanted a name for himself in history, he failed, for he remains to this day unaknoledged, whose name was never recorded, known only as a coward who shot an old man in the back.[348]

Figure 25. Reconstructed fort walls at the site of Jamestown, the probable site of Opechancano's imprisonment. Another possibility is the Middle Plantation at colonial Williamsburg. Here the author's daughter looks at a concrete cast of the original post molds. Photo by the author.

[348] Ibid.; Morton, *Colonial Virginia,* 154; Shea, *Virginia Militia in the Seventeenth Century,* 68; Feest, *The Powhatan Tribes,* 54; Gleach, *Powhatan's World and Colonial Virginia,* 178; Fausz, "Opechancanough, Indian Resistance Leader," 34; Rountree, *Pocahontas's People,* 82.

Tributary Nations: The Subjugation of the Powhatans

The news must have shot up and down Indian country like lightning. Opechancano was dead. Some, perhaps, were in a state of dismay. Others may have felt a sense of relief. Rountree has pointed out that though Opechancano's fighting spirit is admirable to those who look at his story in hindsight; this constant and unchanging policy of almost continual combat was incredibly difficult on Powhatan families. Later Powhatan claims that Opechancano was never really one of them and came from somewhere to the south may have been, in a way, disowning him for the way he led the people. No doubt the question on most people's mind was, would this war continue or would there now be peace? If there was peace, at what price would it come? This is, however, speculation. It is long-held tradition that Opechancano's body was enshrined within a burial mound next to his brother, Wahunsenaca, on the present day Pamunkey reservation. If this is true, then Berkeley transferred the remains to the Pamunkey people following his death, and his people honored his memory from that time to this.[349]

At this time a new Indian leader arose, though his background and story remains a mystery. This shadowy figure became the new leader of the Powhatan chiefdom, what was left of it, when Opechancano died. In Powhatan lines of succession only he who was in the matrilineal line of the "royal" family could be the next *weroance,* or in this case, *mamanatowick.* This means that, if the new leader was from this line, then

[349] Rountree views that Opechancano may have been unpopular in his policies by many Powhatan families, who faced the severe repercussions of English retaliations.

Opechancano was his maternal uncle or great-uncle. His name was Necatowance.[350]

Some measure of warfare may have continued beyond Opechancano's death, especially since Fleet and Poyther's company seems to have still been in the field for a time afterwards, but most likely violent encounters were kept at a minimum unless any Powhatan warriors felt compelled to strike in reprisal for Opechancano's capture. Their siege had broken. Perhaps they could move further upriver and reorganize, but having little control over the individual chiefdoms, whoever gained the title of *mamanatowick* following Opechancano's death held a great burden on his or her shoulders. Only a few would follow the Pamunkeys, not to mention they would be closer to their inland enemies, the Monacans. It was an impossible decision for one person to make alone, and much deliberation likely occurred between the councilors, *weroances* and priests.[351]

As the Powhatans reeled from the loss of Opechancano, Leonard Calvert finally came out of hiding from Fort St. Thomas to seek help from Virginia in retaking the remnants of his war-ravaged colony. While he was hiding behind palisades, the rest of the colony created a new government sympathetic to Parliament under the leadership of Captain Henry Hill. Calvert

---

[350] Necatowance is first mentioned in the treaty of 1646. See "The Necatowance Treaty," Act 1, October 1646, Acts of the Assembly, in Hening, *The Statutes at* Large..., 323-326.

[351] Ibid.; Maureen Meyers, "From Refugees to Slave Traders: The Transformation of the Westo Indians," in Ethridge and Shuck-Hall, *The Mississippian Shatter Zone,* 92; Gleach, *Powhatan's World and Colonial Virginia,* 178; The Treaty was ratified in October, so the treaty negotiations must have happened sometime in the previous summer.

appealed for a force of men to accompany him to retake Maryland for the King. Berkeley, while he disliked Calvert and hated Maryland, was loyal to the King and was sympathetic to Calvert's aims. Still, they were impoverished themselves were still under a great cost to operate their forts, and therefore could not offer any state-sponsored support. All they could do was give permission for Calvert to try and enlist for himself as many men as he could and pay them from his own purse. Calvert spent the rest of the summer and autumn in a recruiting campaign to strike a blow for the King.[352]

In the meanwhile, Necatowance met with Berkeley to discuss terms of peace. Likely similar to the terms previously offered to Opechancano, Berkeley spelled out under what terms he would accept peace. Known today as the Necatowance Treaty, this thirteen point document allowed no room for Powhatan sovereignty as they were reduced from a free-governing polity to a tributary nation. Act one allowed Necatowance to keep his "kingdom" as a vassal of the King of England. Virginia would protect them from any lawless "rebels" on their part, and the Powhatans would give twenty beaver skins to the governor every year "at the going away of the geese."[353]

The next eight articles of the treaty outline a separation of the English and Powhatan people with strictly enforced "Indian-free" zones in what Martha McCartney described as a "Seventeenth Century Apartheid."[354] The hallmark point was that no Indian whatsoever, at any time, could ever enter the Lower Peninsula, on pain of death. Any Englishman with a gun in his

---

[352] Riordan, *The Plundering Time,* 260.

[353] "The Necatowance Treaty," Act 1, October 1646, Acts of the Assembly, in Hening, *The Statutes at* Large..., 323-326; Shea, *Virginia Militia in the Seventeenth Century,* 68.

[354] McCartney, "Seventeenth Century Apartheid," 47-75.

hand could freely shoot any Indian he saw in this area between the York and James River with one exception, that messenger to the governor could wear a special striped coat to signify his official business. According to what Necatowance understood, his people would always be free to live and hunt north of York River. When the treaty was ratified, however, the burgesses did not like this aspect and had it revised wthout the knowledge of the Powhatans, which Englishmen would be freely allowed to travel there to fell trees and hunt hogs without fear of the Powhatans so long as they possessed a license. The assembly continued to change the treaty to state that as soon as they were ready to reestablish themselves north of York River, they would, but that "Necotowance be [first] acquainted therewith." This, of course, would not be the last time an Indian nation would be tricked during treaty negotiations. In further detailing new territory being staked out by the English, Berkeley laid claim to the southern country of Carolina where several expeditions were sent out by Richard Bennett the previous summer against the Weyanoke refugees. No Powhatans were allowed to visit or even hunt within the "limits of Yapin [Yeopim, at the Albermarle Sound]" north to the Blackwater River, and west to "Old Monakin Town." This meant that the "Indian-free zone" extended south of James River well into the Carolina region. Since Maryland's claims prevented much northward expansion, their interests would now turn to the southward in this newly conquered territory.[355]

Finally, it was well known that many Indian "servants," who were actually prisoners of war, or Indians who fell into debt before the war, had run away to, or were liberated by the

[355] "The Necatowance Treaty," Act 1, October 1646, Acts of the Assembly, in Hening, *The Statutes at* Large..., 323-326; Rountree, *Before and After Jamestown,* 154.

Powhatans. Many runaway or captured African servants were also in their protection. Most of these Africans were born in Africa or were raised by native Africans and were themselves a culturally relatable people. Being in a state of forced labor, they likely ran away to the Powhatans for their freedom as well. One remembers the uprising of Mrs. Wormeley's African servants and their subsequent arrest previously in the war. Necatowance was ordered to return all these servants and slaves to the English and continue to return them if any more ran away to them, as well as any guns still in their possession. Also, any Indian children under the age of twelve were encouraged to live among the English to be taught how to live "properly" in the English way.[356]

With that, Necatowance agreed, and signed away the Powhatan chiefdom as a free government. He had little choice. Any further combat would only destroy them further. Perhaps he was answering to the call of hundreds of voices that urged him to make peace. Perhaps he was looking after his own interests. He may have thought that at least the chiefdom was still together, but within a few years he made his last appearance in the historical scene as he paid tribute, saying, "the Sunne and Moon should first lose their glorious lights and shining, before He, or his People should evermore hereafter wrong the English in any kind, but they would ever hold love and friendship together."[357] In truth, however, the treaty was never designed to keep the Powhatan chiefdoms together, and in fact, the English had

[356] "The Necatowance Treaty," October 1646, Acts of the Assembly, in Hening, *The Statutes at* Large…, 323-326.

[357] Necatowance is last mentioned in 1649, when he presented tribute to Berkeley with five of his lesser weroances. This is the very last historical record of the Powhatan Paramount Chiefdom, for all the small nations composing it would act independently thereafter. See Anonymous, "A Perfect Description of Virginia," 13.

opposite plans the entire time. Thomas Ludwell, a colonial official from later in the century, recounted that "upon Governor William Berkeley's conquest of Apechancanough it was by him and the government thought the safest way by settling all the lesser nations at Liberty from that obedience they paid to the house of Pamunkey to keep them divided and indeed the effect may be more advantageous to us for they like to war with each other and destroy themselves more that we can do it."[358]

Soon after the ratification of the treaty an early and particularly sharp winter struck the region, completely freezing up James River, and "the ships were frozen up six weeks."[359] As the already weakened Powhatans struggled against the cold, the realities of the new treaty sunk in, and difficulties emerged for Necatowance. He wasn't able to hold the level of respect that Opechancano enjoyed. Perhaps it was because of his pro-English attitudes or because of the sovereignty-killing treaty he signed, but his advice and orders were ill-received by the Powhatan people. In fact, as he would later relate, "my countrymen tell me I am a liar when I tell them the Englishmen will kill you if you go into their bounds."[360] No one would ever dare call Opechancano or his older brother Wahunsenaca a liar to their face. Obviously, while one could inherit the title *mamanatowick,* it was another thing to be able to earn that office in the sight of the people.[361] Soon, three warriors decided to test both

---

[358] Martha McCartney, "Cockacoeske, Queen of Pamunkey," 257-58.

[359] Winthrop, *The History of New England,* 263.

[360] Beauchamp Plantagenet, "A Description of the Province of New Albion (1648)," in *American Colonial Historical Tracts,* (Rochester, New York: George Humphrey) 1898, 14.

[361] This calls to mind the way in which Opechancano became *mamanatowick.* The position passed from Wahunsenaca to the next brother in line, Opitchapam, by right of inheritance. As Opitchapam was considered dicrepid and lame, however, allegiance was

Necatowance and the English by entering the Lower Peninsula, perhaps thinking they could freely hunt there or reestablish trading relationships in the face of winter hardships. As soon as they were spotted, "valiant Captain [Bridges] Freeman made him no liar," by gunning all three of them down, because they were "without badge…encroaching."[362] While this incident made it clear to the Powhatans that they had truly lost the Lower Peninsula forever, their respect for Necatowance did not increase.[363]

Another aspect of this war from which Virginia learned lessons was in the area of slavery. At this time, there were few slaves other than indentured servants who were often kept in slave-like conditions. Historian C.S Everett has stated that during the Third Anglo-Powhatan War, "countless" slaves were taken in raids and either kept as personal slaves or shipped away to Barbados for a lucrative sum. Even while the Necatowance treaty would make such actions illegal in peacetime, a black market trade in Powhatan slaves continued and threatened to drag the colony back into war in later years.[364] Rountree is more cautious, saying that while Indian slaving during the war occurred, documentary evidence does not indicate that it was

given instead to the next brother in line, Opechancano, who managed to maintain the loyalty of the people even while elderly and invalid.

[362] Plantagenet, "A Description of the Province of New Albion," 14.

[363] This incident probably fell out somewhere west of Jamestown near the Chickahomny River, as this was where Captain Freeman had his plantation. This was related by, it appears, Samuel Mathews to traveler Beauchamp Pantegenet. See Plantagenet, "A Description of the Province of New Albion [1648]", in Force, ed., *Tracts and Other Papers,* 2:25.

[364] C.S Everett, "'They shalbe slaves for their lives,': Indian Slavery in Colonial Virginia," in Allan Galay, ed., *Indian Slavery in Colonial America,* (Lincoln, University of Nebraska Press, 2009) 67-108.

widespread.[365] I believe that while it is true that scanty records defy efforts to fully comprehend the extent of Indian slaving, the treaty terms making such actions illegal following the war make it clear that it did happen during the war, though to what extent is not yet known. As such, this is one of the earliest examples of English slaving in the Americas.[366]

While the Powhatans' first two wars with the English were inconclusive, with no clear victor, and while Opechancano had far greater success at the outset of this war than has previously been allowed, it cannot be denied that this was, in the end, a resounding English victory. In the words of William Shea, "The Second Tidewater War [Third Anglo-Powhatan War] was the high point in the military history of seventeenth century Virginia. Never again would the militia perform so well or achieve such an overwhelming victory. The conflict was seen as a kind of holy war against the deadliest enemy, indeed, the only enemy, most Virginians had ever known. A sense of common purpose seems to have united the settlers and spared them from becoming embroiled in social and political turmoil such as was wracking England. Internal differences were put aside for a little while."[367]

War in England still raged, and rumors were beginning to get stronger in Virginia that the King was not doing well. Indeed, as time went on, King Charles was beaten back further and further in a series of hopeless and pointless battles until he was

---

[365] Rountree, *Pocahontas's People,* 86-87; Rountree, "Powhatans and the English: A Case of Multiple Conflicting Agendas," 194-95.

[366] The "honors" of the best and earliest example of large-scale Indian slaving goes to the Puritans, who virtually destroyed, enslaved and exported all the Pequots in the 1630s.

[367] Shea, *The Virginia Militia,* 71-72.

captured and beheaded in 1649.[368] On hearing the news, Berkeley was beside himself and quickly declared that the late King's son, Charles II, who was in hiding, was now the rightful King and parliament still had no power over Virginia. In his crackdown, one group of parliament-supporting Puritans quit Virginia altogether and established a colony of their own on the Severn River in Maryland under the leadership of Richard Bennett. The unification that the Powhatan War brought between the English factions was over. [369] The other Indian wars in Maryland and New Amsterdam had also concluded, giving some peace of mind to men like Swedish governor Johan Printz, who wrote in 1647 that "the savages in Virginia, New Netherland, and North England have made peace with the Christians, and our own savages have been quiet ever since."[370]

Also in 1649, Necatowance paid his last visit to Berkeley as *mamanatowick* and is never seen again in the pages of history. The reduction of the Powhatan Chiefdom was observable as what was once a thirty-nation alliance was now a loose organization when only "five more petty Kings attended him [Necatowance]" as he paid his tribute of beaver skins to Berkeley, after which he disappears from further records.[371] In his lifetime Necatowance declared his continued loyalty to England and stressed to the Powhatans the importance of

---

[368] Gaunt, *The English Civil Wars,* 12, 81-85.

[369] Beverley mentions this crackdown in his history, but remarked that there were no Puritans in Virginia at the time. Since the Puritan presence is now well known, this shows that he did not have a complete grasp of the inner conflicts of the colony during this period. See Beverley, *The History and Present State of Virginia,* 63. For Bennett founding the Severn River settlement in Maryland, see Land, *Colonial Maryland,* 49.

[370] Printz, "Report of Governor Johan Printz, 1647," 125.

[371] Anonymous, "A Perfect Description of Virginia," 13; Feest, *The Powhatan Tribes,* 57.

observing the Indian-free zones, but he never managed to maintain a following, as one passing traveler reported:

> ". . . Virginia is used but to kill them [Indians]; insomuch that the Emperor Nicotowance's saying was, 'my countrymen tell me I am a liar when I tell them the Englishmen will kill you if you go into their bounds,' but valiant Captain Freeman made him no liar, when lately he killed three Indians so without badge, encroaching. And therefore fair and far off is best with heathen Indians, and fit it is to reduce all their trading to five ports, or pallisadoed trucking houses, and to kill all stragglers and such spies without ransom. Then shall Christians and their cattle be safe and quiet, and severely putting to death all that sell the Indians guns, arms, and ammunition, then Indians are sooner ruled, civilized, and subjected…"[372]

The Powhatan Empire had crumbled, but Powhatan people did not, and as seen above, began to endure a long period of unfair killings, lack of sovereignty, decreasing land base and increasing racism. In 1652, a squadron of parliament ships arrived off the coast carrying a group of commissioners familiar to the colonists, among them Richard Bennett and William Claiborne. Berkeley anticipated their approach and had assembled a thousand-man army to meet them, (the largest army assembled in Virginia to that point), and there they stood at a standoff. Many hands wrung together as either reconciliation or a bloody battle would take place, and no one knew which it would be. The demands of parliament to the Assembly were

[372] Plantagenet, "A Description of the Province of New Albion," 14.

surprisingly liberal. Very little of Virginian life would be interrupted or regulated. Mainly, they simply wished them to pay allegiance to them rather than the King. Virginia was the last province to bend knee to parliament, and Berkeley exhorted those around him to stand their ground, but it was in vain. Knowing their subjugation was inevitable and a battle would only get many people killed, the Assembly gave in to the commissioner's requests, swore allegiance to parliament, and Berkeley lost his job. Richard Bennett took his place as parliament's picked man for the role of Governor. The English Civil War had finally ended in the colonies.[373]

[373] Beverley, *The History and Present State of Virginia,* 63-65; Billings, *Sir William Berkeley,* 107-112; Morton, *Colonial Virginia,* 171-173; Gleach, *Powhatan's World and Colonial Virginia,* 184-85.

Conclusions

While many historians tend to consider their research areas as of far greater importance than is warranted, I will attempt a balanced analysis of the effects and impact of the Third Powhatan War. I am first drawn to what the English learned of American frontier tactics that were very different from those employed in England at the same time. Equipment lists, financial statements and events surrounding the expeditions are quite revealing. In England, as the English Civil War raged, a large group of pikemen armed with long lances would protect the group of musketeers from cavalry charges while the musketeers would pour shot into the enemies formations, organized in the same way. In Virginia, pikemen were altogether discarded and there is no evidence that they were ever attempted. The Virginian frontier was recognized as a unique battleground of vast forests bereft of open fields. Tactics learned from the 1622-1632 war were brought to bear on the Third Powhatan War, and were perfected as some of the first known ranging techniques were employed. Though not called rangers, patrols of men travelled through forests searching out Indian targets and defending the frontier in the same way as later rangers would do.

Horses received their first real debut in English-American warfare from 1644-1646 as well. Though used sporadically in the past as an occasional mount for an officer there were simply not yet enough horses in the colony for effective military use. With the largest assembled army to that point in 1644 with 300 men, horses are seen used as pack horses as the supply train for the army. Horses also saw some of their first recorded American combat, first as Captain Ralph Wormely attacked the Chickahominy town Oranioc on horseback, and then in the last raid of the war when Berkeley gathered what might be called the first company of cavalry in Virginia and rode them in a sweeping attack that ultimately won the war.

While Powhatan towns were sometimes noted as having a palisade for protection, it appears that the first true Indian fortress may have been constructed and employed during the Battle of Menmend. According to the Langston Map, this fort was immediately above Menmend, and possibly square in shape. Forts such as this one would later become more common during wars against the English or even in inter-tribal warfare if firearms were involved. The Nottoways were later noted as having a huge square fortress for defense against interior Indians. Wampanoags built an impressive structure during their Great Swamp Fight in King Philip's War of 1675 and the Tuscaroras built an English-style fort during their later war in 1711 with the help of an escaped African slave. These fortresses were modified from their earlier palisaded towns to be effective against bullets, not arrows, and were much more difficult to storm and capture. While little studied as of yet, it appears that the first of these European-influenced Indian fortresses may have been built by Opechancano in the Third Powhatan War.

Also instrumental in defeating the Powhatans were other Indians. This, perhaps, was the most wide-reaching lesson that would be learned in this conflict. At the outset, Indians outside of Powhatan control such as the Rappahannocks and Chowanokes were contemplated being attacked in an all-out war against any Indians whatsoever. By the latter half, however, it was felt that it would be more prudent to keep them as allies instead. Rappahannocks and Accomacs were soon used as guides and scouts, which made it possible to find Powhatan cornfields and town locations that the English couldn't have known otherwise.

Likewise, there is evidence that the Chowanokes and Yeopims from today's North Carolina assisted the English expeditions south in 1645. Ultimately, I believe the Rappahannocks were the ones who organized the meeting between Henry Fleet and Opechancano, and the ones who disclosed his camp position making it possible for Berkeley to capture him. In most wars following this, ways were conceived to play off of inter-tribal conflicts in order to set one nation against another.

One institution that had some if its roots in the 1644 war was the later institution of slavery. While shown at this point to be servants rather than full-fledged slaves, conditions had been getting worse and often illegally crossing the fine line into actual slave conditions. Firstly, what appears to be the first ever recorded act of revolt by African Americans occurred as the African servants (slaves?) of one Mrs. Wormeley rebelled against her, exhibiting "rebellious and riotous conduct." As the issue was brought before the governor's council, orders were issued for their arrest, and nothing more is known of the incident. Following this, there appears to be an exodus of African slaves who ran away to the Powhatans, and the Powhatans, in turn, accepted them. While white servants ran away frequently as well, only the African servants are specifically noted in the treaty of 1646 as being required to be returned to the colony. It is plain that conditions were getting worse for them. While white servants were at least usually known by name, African ones were simply called Negroes; their names were not considered worthy of mention. This is indicative that they were seen and treated with fewer rights than English servants, even in this early time before the racist attitudes of later centuries matured. Additionally, early examples of American Indian slaving are observed as "countless" captives in raids were sold to defray war costs. While a brutal and exceedingly large Indian slave trade would later be centered on South Carolina, it began earlier in Virginia and New England (in their Pequot War). I believe these earlier slaving incidents were influential to the later South Carolina slavers, and ultimately, the African slave trade.

The most immediate effect of the war, of course, was the removal of the Powhatan Chiefdom from power. While once a serious contender not only to the English, but also other Indian nations, their influence was no longer consequential, especially after 1649 when the chiefdom was fully dissolved and reservations were assigned to individual nations. This had a dual effect. On the one hand (to the delight of the English) they were now free to move their settlements further west and south than had ever been done before. Major exploratory parties were able to be sent out, and new plantations were established above the fall line and south into Carolina. On the other, with Opechancano out of the way, a power vacuum was created that allowed other powerful Indian nations to come in from the interior and probe the English. The Powhatans had practically encircled Virginia previously so that they had an insulating effect, but now, with the insulation gone, new groups of Indians that had never been seen before would clash with the Virginians.

The best immediate example of this is the Battle of Bloody Run. Nobody is certain of who the Indians were, but in 1656 a large body of Indians, five hundred strong, came from somewhere north and settled near the falls of James River. Not budging, Virginia called out its militia and employed the use of Pamunkey warriors (led by Totopotomoi, successor of Necatowance). The battle was a complete failure, and the foreign Indians, known as Rechehechrians (or Rickahockans) smashed the offensive and killed Totopotomoi. After the battle some trade relations with them were established before they went further south into South Carolina where they were known as the Westos and became some of the most successful and terrifying slaving nation in the area, taking a large amount of captives for South Carolina export merchants. Some have said they were Cherokee, others that they were Erie, or even Souians. No one knows, but had the Powhatan Empire still been in place, it is doubtful that they would have chosen to settle on James River.

As for Opechancano, I could not help but be torn regarding his iron-clad resolve. Was it a good thing for his people or bad? And resolve he surely had. There were many Indian leaders who made war against white encroachment in their younger days, but as older men had seen enough and sued for peace. Opechancano was different. Nearly one hundred years old, he still had a spirit of resistance and literally went down fighting. His life was tumultuous. If only some discourse in his own words had survived, we would have been treated to a fascinating story. As it stands his life can only be reconstructed by interrupted snippets of information through the decades written by biased English observers, but even so, what a story they tell. Born somewhere around 1560, he would have heard of the Spanish incursions, heard of the Roanoke Colony, and was side by side with his brother as they forged the chiefdom together. After personally capturing John Smith, (who later held a pistol against Opechancano's chest) he waged three wars against the English, all the while defending the western boundary from his Siouan and Iroquoian neighbors. Only a man exceedingly capable and respected by his people could have maintained his position as *mamanatowick* for so long. This was a man who was fierce, independent, and resolved to defend his sovereignty. The question is, at what cost? Rountree has stated that it is possible his people, in a way, disowned him after his death because of the predicament they found themselves in through his wars. Certainly this is what they told the English. But it is just as likely, perhaps more probable that he became privately a symbol of Powhatan resistance and independence for the Powhatan people; a story that was told around the fire with pride. Who knows? His wars, ultimately, broke the military strength of the Powhatan people. But were they really his wars? Or was the Powhatan populace calling out for him to make a strike, and in response he drew up plans on their behalf? Such things just cannot be known for sure. For today, Opechancano clearly deserves his place among the great chiefs so commonly known such as Sitting Bull, Crazy Horse, Tecumseh, Pontiac and Geronimo. There are few men who could achieve what he did.

His English counterpart, Sir William Berkeley, was a man admirable in many respects, but I find he was given far too much credit in the victory of this war. It is my opinion that he was altogether a poor military leader. In fact, I find him blundering in every military engagement he had ever been in. He was an excellent manager of people, often ruthless, but equally often just and fair. Eloquent and well-read, he was a gentleman's gentleman, but he was no war hero. In the Bishop's Wars in England, he was by the King's side as bodyguard and field officer, but disgraced himself when he passed along faulty intelligence that caused the King embarrassment. In Virginia, Berkeley was absent for the most critical phase of the war, the main assault against Menmend and the building of the frontier forts. He is often credited with the construction of these forts and waging the war on his own, but he wasn't even there. If any one person deserves the credit for turning the war around in England's favor, it is Richard Kemp. It was his idea presented to the assembly that built the ring of forts (perhaps inspired by advice from Leonard Calvert), and his orders that directed the main campaigns against Opechancano. When Berkeley returned (empty-handed), he swept in dramatically on horseback to capture Opechancano and thereby took the credit for winning the war himself, standing on the shoulders of others. Other than ordering a few Indian expeditions in later years, his next show of military leadership was during the Susquehanna War and Bacon's Rebellion. Attempting to repeat Kemp's success, he built new forts to counter the Susquehannas, but the Susquehanna bands easily subverted them. The Susquehannas ultimately kept up their raids until they tired of Virginia and returned north. Frustrated with his failure, a rebellion swept the frontier as his cousin, Nathaniel Bacon, led an army that burned Jamestown and sent Berkeley running to the eastern shore. Only Bacon's death and the coming of winter allowed Berkeley to counter-attack. Ultimately, Berkeley was a good manager of domestic issues but not the capable military leader many have been led to believe.

Of course, the greatest effect the war had was on the Powhatan people themselves. It cannot be emphasized strongly enough, however, that the dissolution of the Powhatan Chiefdom was not the end of the Powhatan people. Without a central polity, however, each small nation had to look to its own interests. Many shrank to virtually nothing, with the last few surviving members joining a larger Indian nation. This made many of the nations coalescent in nature, though they retained their original tribal names. For example, when the Chickahominies were defeated at Oranioc, they retreated to Pamunkey lands to the north along with the Mattaponi. Many of them would intermarry there and tribal lines would be blurred for a time. The same is true for the Powhites, formerly Powhatan town near the falls of the James. As a very small nation, they survived longer than could be reasonably expected, but when their numbers became genetically unviable, it appears that they joined the Pamunkeys.

One of the most interesting examples is the Nottoways, who while Iroquoian, took in many Algonquian people to become one with them. Thus, in the waning years, the last Weyanokes and the one segment of the Nansemonds were absorbed by them.

These islands of Indian people appear to have maintained contact with each other for a long time, for when anthropologist James Mooney visited the Pamunkeys in the late 1800s, they still knew of many Indian communities in the region and pointed out to Mooney where to find them. It was through them, in fact, that he "discovered" the Nansemonds, without a reservation, still living in southern Virginia around Portsmouth on privately held land, as well as the Rappahannocks and Chickahominies. As for those who lived on reservations, the very continuance of these reservations is something worthy of note. It should be remarked upon that the Pamunkey and Mattaponi reservations are still in existence today and are the oldest active reservations in America. Established in 1649 after the end of the war, they continue to operate today as the longest established American Indian reservations in continual existence in the United States, and one of the oldest in all of the Americas. They continue to pay tribute to the governor of Virginia as stipulated in the 1646 Necatowance Treaty, making the end of the war something that still touches the lives of people 350 years after peace was declared. The Powhatans, after the war, had to change much to survive, most notably their culture, but survive they did, and today continue to live and enjoy greater political power than at any time since 1646.

“We’re Still Here”

In 1649, when Necatowance made his final appearance, several other Powhatan nations came forth and received the first Indian reservations known to American History that have been in continual existence. Interestingly, following this last meeting, Berkeley felt in danger of his life by Indian and English assassins and kept a bodyguard from there on out.[374] The Pamunkey and Mattaponi lived together on the Pamunkey River under the new leadership of Totopotomoi and his wife and cousin Cockaqueske, relatives of Opechancano. According to modern Mattaponi oral history, the main *quiakros* (priests) operated under stealth within the Mattaponi nation from then on, preserving an oral history that is still told today while the Pamunkeys maintained martial relations with Virginia.[375] Ascomowet of the Weyanokes came forth and received a reservation for his people south of James River, but quickly abandoned it, choosing to move back into Carolina country again. Ossakican represented the Chiskiacs who also received land for his people. No others came forward to officially receive land, so the Assembly allowed that each Indian *weroance* would be allotted land to the amount of fifty acres per bowman in his nation.[376]

In order to enforce Indian-free zones, boost defense and encourage trade, Virginia did not wish to dismantle the forts erected during the war, but at the same time found the costs of maintaining them impossible to sustain at public charge. In an

---

[374] Morton, *Colonial Virginia,* 165.

[375] Custalow and Daniel, *The True Story of Pocahontas,* xxiii. This oral history is highly questioned by modern historians and anthropologists, but is included here for the sake of balance of perspectives.

[376] Rountree, *Pocahontas's People,* 89-92.

innovative solution, they made deals with enterprising individuals who would receive the forts and lands surrounding them for free, provided they maintained and manned the forts at their own charge.[377] Abraham Wood, who had been promoted to Major, laid claim to Fort Henry on the Appomattox River, and, interestingly, Thomas Rolfe, the son of Pocahontas and great-nephew of Opechancano, became commander of Fort Royal. In this way, these forts became valued not only for defensive measures but also in the growing Indian trade as some of the first trading posts in Colonial America. Abraham Wood would increase in prominence, becoming a key contact person between the Indians and Virginia, as well as commander of the militia of Henrico and Charles City Counties. Rolfe became less active and dropped off the map. He remains an interesting point of speculation as to how exactly he felt as a multi-ethnic person, but it cannot be denied that he remained within Virginian society, and did not join the Powhatans. His claimed descendants are many and rose to prominence among Virginia's elite.[378]

In the Powhatan core area, where the biggest campaigns of the war occurred against the Pamunkeys, Chickahominies and Mattaponis, multiple refugee nations converged together for a long while. The Chickahominies took refuge with the Pamunkey in the upper waters of the river where they remained for some time and intermarried to an extent with them. The Mattaponis on the other hand, fled further north at first, where they lived near the Rappahannocks until they were pushed out in the 1660s and returned to the Mattaponi River. There the Chickahominies left the Pamunkeys but still lived near them, and all three tribes have

---

[377] Ibid., 86

[378] McCartney, *Virginia Immigrants and Adventurers,* 608, 759.

lived in the same region with each other ever since, with intermarriage between them commonplace.[379]

South of the James River, the Nansemonds were able to retain a town on the Nansemond River despite it being technically illegal according to the Necotowance Treaty. This certainly had much to do with the intermarriage that occurred with the Bass family, particularly Rev. John Basse. John was a home grown preacher within the Anglican Church, though he probably had Puritan tendencies.[380] He took in marriage an Indian woman known to us only as Elizabeth who was the daughter of the Nansemond *weroance.* Had he married a commoner this probably wouldn't have had as much of an impact, but being a part of the "royal" family gave him and his descendants' considerable influence, leading ultimately to what Helen Rountree refers to as the "Christianized" segment of Nansemond, who survive to the present day around Portsmouth. Naturally, a smaller traditional core apparently didn't like the direction things were heading within the nation and moved into the Blackwater region of southern Virginia in Surry County, called by the English Pochicks. Interestingly, a 1669 census shows that the traditionalists had thirty bowmen, while the Christianized Nansemonds had forty-five. That many young men, not including women, children and the elderly, suggest a population of about 200 people. The Christianized Nansemond was therefore not just the multi-ethnic descendants of John Bass

---

[379] Rountree, *Pocahontas's People,* 110-116.

[380] John Basse seems nominally to have been within the Anglican Church by the time his family's prayer book records were written, but his father, Captain Nathaniel Basse first settled the land with Christopher Lawn in what was has been positively identified as a Puritan settlement. Many Puritans were nominally Anglicans but who accepted Puritan theology. At the time of the Third Powhatan War, most people south of James River had Puritan tendancies.

and Elizabeth, but was actually the majority of the Nansemonds, most of whom would have been in fact "full-bloods."[381]

Others, like the Appamattocks and Powhites remained on their own lands for a time near the falls of the James River. The Appamattocks gave up their land on Swift Creek during the war and moved just above the falls as per treaty stipulations, having, by 1669, about fifty bowmen. The Powhites, by contrast, were much smaller having only ten bowmen by that time. Both groups struggled through the rest of the 1600s, and cease from the historical records shortly after the turn of the century. This does not mean that they all died out, but that the survivors joined larger groups like the Pamunkeys in their waning days, meaning that today's Powhatan groups are descendants of many of the original Powhatan tribes other than just their namesakes. For example, in 1708, a Pamunkey petition shows a "Mister Powhite" among them, indicating where the last of the Powhites went.[382] Additionally, several seemingly new groups appeared in Northern Virginia and Maryland with strikingly similar names to Powhatan groups, such as Appomataux and Nanzemond. This may suggest that splinter groups of their southern counterparts fled north following the war, but not enough is known to determine this beyond doubt.[383]

The Weyanokes continued an interesting history of moving from place to place between southern Virginia and Northern Carolina. They made few friends. Living in Carolina meant living for much of the time within Tuscarora territory, to whom they had to pay rent. They came into violent conflict with

---

[381] *Pocahontas's People,* 105-108; Rountree "Ethnicity Among the 'Citizen' Indians of Tidewater Virginia," 175-176

[382] Rountree, *Pocahontas's People,* 109-110.

[383] Ibid., 95, 96, 120

them and also some of their former allies among the Powhatan. They and the Pochick (traditionalist) segment of Nansemond raided each other several times, ultimately resulting in the death of the *weroance* and other leading men of the Pochicks. The Weyanokes also held a boy from the Powhites as a slave and sold him to the English, who later released him. Ultimately warfare and disease took its toll and they were reduced to ten bowmen by 1685. By the early 1700s they were further reduced, forcing them to join the Nottoways, who themselves continue to persist in southern Virginia.[384]

[384] Ibid., 92, 94, 108-109.

Figure 26. Official medals, "Ye Kinge of Pamunkie"
Medals like those pictured above, were distributed to tributary Indigenous nations by the Virginian colonial government in the 1660s. Their intent was to serve as an official badge of office approved by the colony and secure loyalty from native leaders. Courtesy of the artifact collection of Dr. J. Frederick Fausz of St. Louis.

Those who were allies of the English during the war probably expected preferential treatment following their service to Virginia, but this turned out not to be the case. English settlers poured into Rappahannock territory following the war, and the Rappahannocks retaliated frequently. Calling out the militia, a brawl ensued in which the *weroance* Taweeren was killed. Shortly thereafter they all moved to the ridge between the Rappahannock and Mattaponi Rivers, near the Mattaponi who had been their neighbors previously. After several decades they moved away again, and moved as tenants on a region of English plantations, though as an ethnic group they continued to intermarry with each other throughout history and reestablished themselves politically in the twentieth century.[385] The Accomacs had previously been extremely friendly with the English and were ever their allies, but they finally reached the breaking point when settlers crowded them out of their lands. The militias were called up again, and in a campaign that is poorly recorded, they were reduced to subjugation along with their neighbors. [386]

Overall, the Third Anglo-Powhatan War had a far greater impact than the previous Powhatan Wars, for while the past conflicts could not destroy the governing chiefdom; this one ultimately did, opening up a wide area for settlement. Nothing could be done to stop the Virginian land grab after that. The Powhatan nations became increasingly isolated from each other as they were surrounded by English claims and their land bases shrank further and further. Some, such as the Appamattocks, Weyanokes, Chiskiacs and Powhites, didn't make it, disappearing from records as independent nations as they were absorbed by larger ones. Others, notably the Pamunkey and Mattaponi, retained their reservations and became the largest and most obvious Indian nations to Virginian eyes. Those who could not retain their lands did not disappear either, however, as they became private land owners or employees on Virginian

---

[385] Ibid., 92-93,

[386] Ibid., 95; Rountree, Helen C. and Davidson, Thomas E., *Eastern Shore Indians of Virginia and Maryland*, 59-68.

plantations. In these cases, such as with the Nansemonds, Rappahannocks and Chickahominies, they kept in social contact with each other, continuing to marry each other and pass on oral histories. [387]

The power vacuum that was left by the absence of Opechancano's once powerful chiefdom became apparent as a mysterious nation of Indians called Rechehechrians, 500 warriors strong, soon settled at the falls of the James. As tributary nations, the Powhatans were oblidged to assist Virginia in dislodging them. Totopotomoi, Necotowance's successor, led his Pamunkey warriors along with English forces in a vicious fight known as the Battle of Bloody Run. It was a disastrous defeat for the Virginian and Indian allies as Totopotomoi was killed along with many warriors. Cockaqueske, his wife, became the next *weroansqua,* and was a very cunning and ambitious one at that.[388]

In 1676, the final acts of warfare against Powhatan people were fought as a rebel army under the command of Nathaniel Bacon and Lawrence Ingram ravaged the native landscape. Reservations were razed and women and children carried off as slaves. The Powhatans did nothing to provoke these attacks, but were used as a scapegoat for attacks carried out by invading Susquehannas from Maryland. During the Susquehanna attacks, Cockaqueske was brought before the Virginian assembly to demand the use of her warriors as scouts. After remaining silent for a time she gave a long oration in the Powhatan language, culminating with "Totopotomoi is dead! Totopotomoi is dead!" This showed her distain for the English

---

[387] Ibid., 269-277.

[388] Ibid., 93; McCartney, "Cockacoeske, Queen of Pamunkey," 245-249

use of her people as if they were pawns. In this war Cockaqueske was cut off from her people and lived in the swamps for several days as the reservation was ravaged, and many other Indians had similar experiences. Finally, Bacon was subdued by Berkeley, who had since regained his position as governor after the fall of Parliament to Charles II, and the Treaty of Middle Plantation was signed giving rights to Indian people who had obviously been wronged. This treaty is still in force today between the Mattaponis and Pamunkeys and the Commonwealth of Virginia, who continue to pay symbolic tribute to the Virginian governor every year.[389]

Figure 27. Chickahominy drummer and singer group Turtle Clan preforms at a tribal event for the Chowanoke Nation at Merchant's Millpond State Park in North Carolina, November 7, 2015. Drummers from left to right are Josh Stewart, Kennan Stewart, Bryan Whitehead and Chris Whitehead. Photo by the author.

---

389 Rountree, *Pocahontas's People,* 96-101; Everett, "'They shalbe slaves for their lives,'" 83-85; McCartney, "Cockacoeske, Queen of Pamunkey,"246-252.

Throughout the eighteenth and nineteenth centuries Powhatan struggles turned from military campaigns to battles of culture and ethnicity as the racial climate in antebellum Virginia became increasingly tense. As prejudices against African descended people became dangerous for non-whites, Powhatans began distancing themselves from them for the sake of safety. This didn't stop rampant accusation that they had extensively intermarried with blacks and weren't really "real" Indians anymore. Laws were continually passed restricting the rights of free non-whites. On the one hand, these laws were obviously unfair and insufferable, but on the other hand, it had the effect of hardening the resolve of the various Powhatan groups who continued to hold together.[390]

Following the Civil War and the freeing of the slaves, things did not get better, though for the first time since the early days of colonization, some people began to be interested in them again and began writing ethnographic accounts. Most notable was anthropologist James Mooney, who visited various groups of Pamunkeys, Chickahominies and Nansemonds. He was somewhat disappointed of finding culture surviving in the way it did in the old days, but still found much evidence of passed on traits, such as continued use of dugout canoes, cultivation of gourds, hunting and fishing techniques, and even some remembered Powhatan language from one Nansemond elder. At the turn of the century many groups began to reorganize, and by the 1920s several groups without a communal land base

---

[390] Rountree, *Pocahontas's People,* 189-207; Feller, *Constructing and Contesting Color Lines,* 28-65; Rountree, "Ethnicity Among the 'Citizen' Indians of Tidewater Virginia," 176-177, 179-180

incorporated with bylaws and chiefs as "citizen" Indians. As Helen Rountree stated:

> "The term "citizen" Indian is apt because today these Indian people live much as their non-Indian neighbors do. They own land in fee simple and pay taxes on it. Being no longer a treaty relationship with Virginia, they are subject to the jurisdiction of the counties in which they live. And they are modern-dressing, English-speaking, television-watching Baptists. Yet, they are a people apart. They are modern Indians: not Indians who happen to live the modern world, nor modern people who claim to be Indians."[391]

This resurgence of cultural and political organization ground to a near halt with the arrival of one man on the scene, Walter Plecker. As a physician and government official he began a personal war against any people of color whatsoever, and began a campaign of reclassifying anyone "passing" as white who had any trace of non-white ancestry as "colored," thus implementing the "one drop rule." The Indians of Virginia presented him with a problem since they were neither white nor black, the only two legal classifications according to him, and so he began to obliterate them with words, writing letters, changing birth certificates, doing everything possible to literally erase them as a people. Thus the Virginian Indians became victims of non-violent ethnic cleansing in what has been considered "documentary genocide."[392] The need for unity in the face of

---

[391] Rountree, "Ethnicity Among the 'Citizen' Indians of Tidewater Virginia," 173.

[392] Rountree, *Pocahontas's People,* 219-242; Moretti-Langholtz and Waugaman, *We're Still Here: Contemporary Virginia Indians Tell Their Stories,* 26-29; Moretti-Langholtz,

such obstacles was recognized by Chickahominy Chief Edward Bradby in 1940 when he wrote, "We need to get together and talk matters over and plan for the future. Indians are just like their brother pale face in the way of being hard headed, block headed, and sap headed when it comes to things for their own good. If we get that big "I" out of the way and place more emphasis on "we," then we will get somewhere."[393]

While Plecker failed in eliminating Powhatan people, there remained a stigma of being an Indian different than before. Often, what should have been a sense of pride was felt as shame of being Indian, and many parents stopped passing on oral history to their children in order to protect them from being Indian. Public proclamation of such things had brought humiliation and retribution for decades, and such things are not easy to overcome. However, by the time of the civil rights movement attitudes began to change and a resurgence of tribal activity brought about the reemergence of the Nansemonds, Pamunkeys, Mattaponis, Chickahominies, Rappahannocks, along with their Siouan neighbors the Monacans, as they regained political power, being officially recognized by the Commonwealth of Virginia. Since then, the Patawomeks and Nottoways have also been recognized, and others, such as the Chowanoke and Roanoke-Hatteras of North Carolina, continue their steadfast move toward federal recognition. All have moved steadily forward toward political empowerment, cultural revival and accurate telling of their history. Finally, in an event that has been anticipated for some time, the Pamunkey Indians were

---

Other Names I Have Been Called, 74-149; Feller, *Constructing and Contesting Color Lines,* 140-206; Elaine and Ray Adkins, *Chickahominy Indians- Eastern Division: A Brief Ethnohistory,* 108-110

[393] Ibid., 91.

recognized by the Bureau of Indian Affairs and established formal relations with the federal government in 2015, and many others may soon follow suit.[394]

[394] Rountree, *Pocahontas's People,* 243-268; Moretti-Langholtz, *Other Names I Have Been Called,* 150-289; Feller, *Constructing and Contesting Color Lines,* 275-357, Bureau of Indian Affairs, *Final Determination for Federal Acknowledgment of the Pamunkey Indian Tribe,* 1-22.

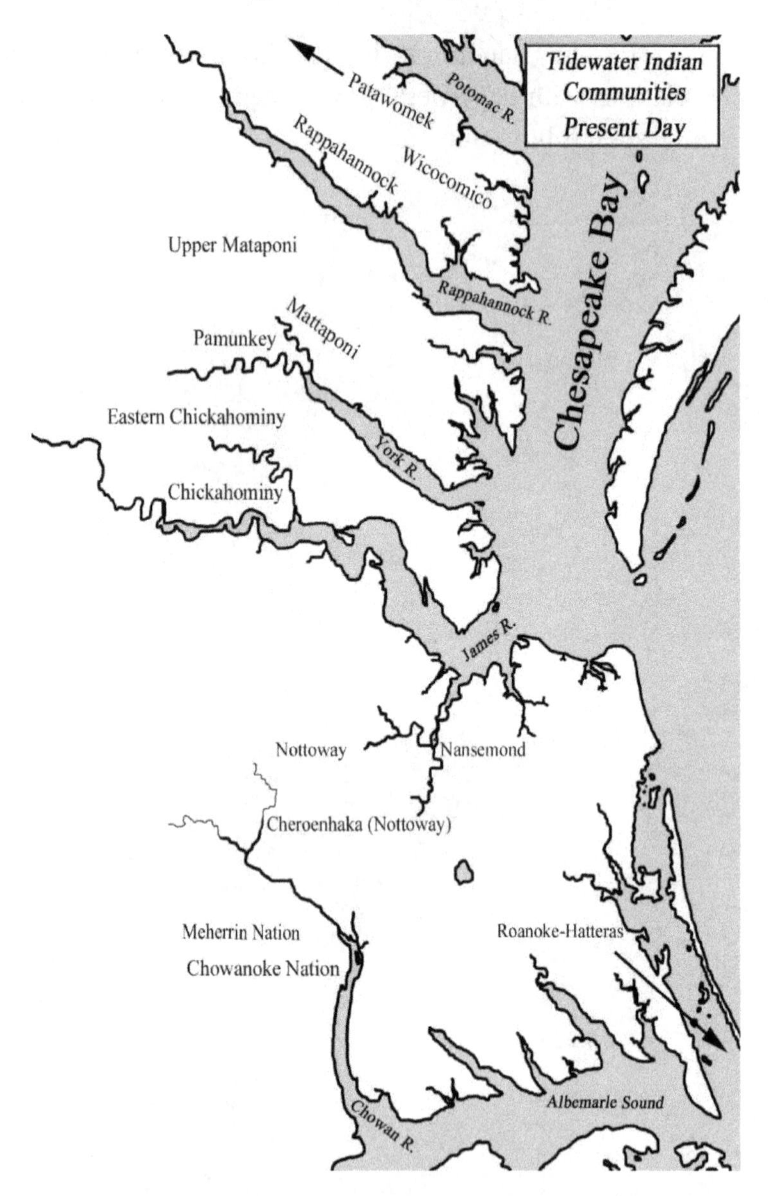

Figure 28. Present Location of Tidewater indigenous American groups in Virginia and northern North Carolina. Much of their present day location is a direct result of the Third Anglo-Powhatan War. This illustration shows both federal and state recognized tribes, as well as non-recognized but organized tribal communities. Map by the author

Appendix I:

Necatowance Treaty[395]

The following is the full text of the 1646 "Necatowance Treaty," verbatim, in keeping with the original spelling. Necatowance himself is a shadowy figure about whom little is known, other than that he took over leadership of the remaining Powhatan towns following the fall of Opechancano for only three years, after which, in 1649, no vestiges of the former polity remained and all of the small nations acted independently. This is among the earliest surviving treaties between American Indians and Anglo-Europeans in the Americas. It is unknown exactly how it was negotiated between Berkeley and Necatowance, although one does suspect that Henry Fleet was involved since he was the leading interpreter and participated in the capture of Opechancano. The following copy was entered into the Acts of the Assembly at the time when the articles of peace were presented to the burgesses for ratification, the first time, incidentally, that an Indian treaty was ever approved by a legislative body.

Att a Grand Assembly begunne at James Cittie ye 5th day of October 1646

Sir William Berkeley Liet Governor

Captains John West, Tho: Perkins, Tho: Willoughby, William Bernard, Hen: Brown, and Wm Brown. Mr(s) Richard Kemps Snr, Rich. Bennett and Geo. Ludlowe- Esquires

Be it enacted by this grand Assembly, That the Artes [articles] of peace foll [following] between the inhabitants of this Collony, And Necotowance King of the Indians bee duely & Inviolably observed upon the penaltie within mentioned as foll[follows].

---

395 National Archives, "The Thomas Jefferson Papers," Series 8. Virginia Records, Manuscripts: 1607-1737. Virginia Council and Assembly, 1643-62, Laws.

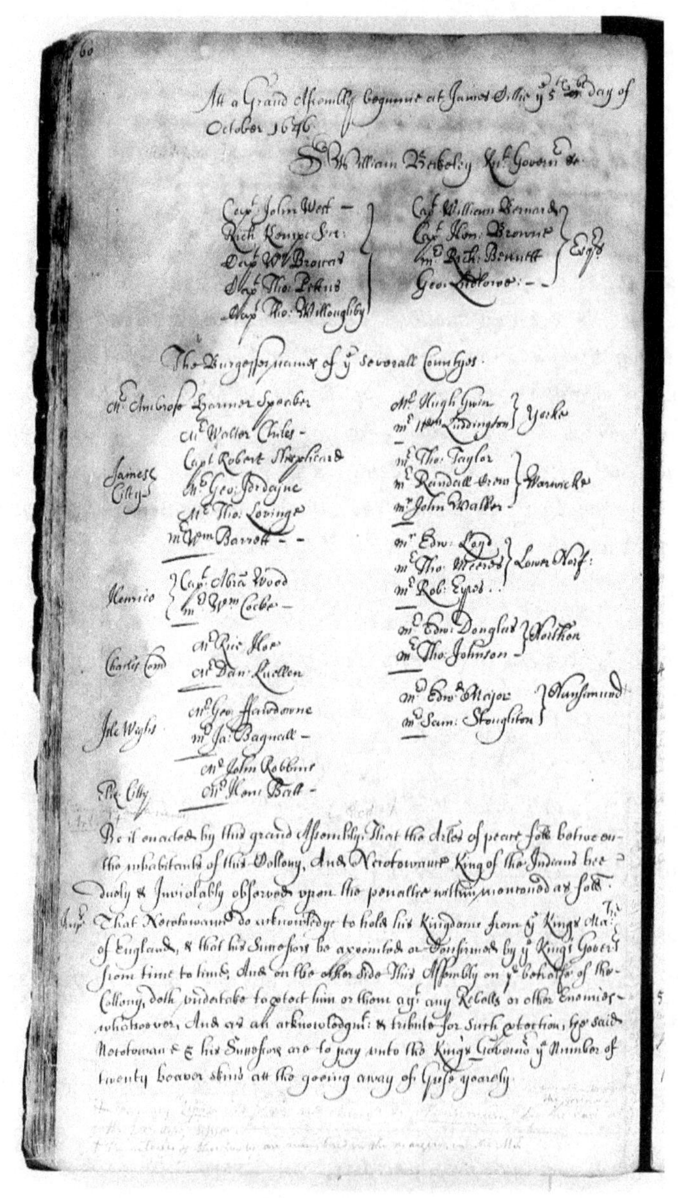

At a Grand Assembly begunne at James Cittie ye 5th day of October 1646.

Sr William Berkeley Knt Govern &c

Capt John West — Rich: Kempe Secr: Capt Wm Brocas Majr Tho: Pettus Majr Tho: Willoughby

Capt William Bernard Capt Hen: Browne Mr Rich: Bennett Geo: Ludlowe — Esqrs

The Burgesses names of ye severall Countyes.

James Citty: Mr Ambrose Harmer Speaker, Mr Walter Chiles, Capt Robert Shepheard, Mr Geo: Jordayne, Mr Tho: Loving, Mr Wm Barrett

Henrico: Capt Abra: Wood, Mr Wm Cocke

Charles Citty: Mr Ric: Hoe, Mr Dan: Lluellen

Isle Wight: Mr Geo: Hardy, Mr Ja: Bagnall

Eliz. Citty: Mr John Robbins, Mr Hen: Brett

Yorke: Mr Hugh Gwin, Mr Wm Luddington

Warwicke: Mr Tho: Taylor, Mr Randall Crew, Mr John Walker

Lower Norf: Mr Edw: Lloyd, Mr Tho: Meeres, Mr Rob: Eyres

Northton: Mr Edw: Douglas, Mr Tho: Johnson

Nansemund: Mr Edw: Major, Mr Sam: Stoughton

Be it enacted by this grand Assembly, That the articles of peace following betwene the inhabitants of this Collony, And Necotowance King of the Indians bee duely & inviolably observed upon the penaltie within mentioned as followeth.

Imp. That Necotowance do acknowledge to hold his Kingdome from ye Kings Matie of England, & that his Successors be appointed or confirmed by ye Kings Govrs from time to time, And on the other side This Assembly on ye behalfe of the Collony, doth undertake to protect him or them agt any Rebells or other Enemies whatsoever, And as an acknowledgmt & tribute for such protection, the said Necotowan & his Successors are to pay unto the Kings Governor ye Number of twenty beaver skins att the goeing away of Geese yearely.

Figure 29. 17th Century copy of the first page of the Necatowance Treaty. This version, approved by legislature following the actual peace talks, may have differed from the actual terms agreed to by Necatowance. Thomas Jefferson Papers. Courtesy of the National Archives.

Appendix I

Act I

That Necotowance do acknowledge to hold his Kingdome from ye Kings Maptie of England, & that his Successors be appointed or Confirmed by ye Kings GoverEs from time to time, And on the other side this Assembly on ye behalf of the Collony, doth undertake to ptect him or them from agt: any Rebells or other Enemies whatsoever, And as an acknowledgmt: & tribute for such ptection, the said Necotowance & his Successors are to pay unto the Kings GovernoE ye Numbers of twenty beaver skins att the goeing away of the Geese yearely.

Act II

That it shall be free for the said Necatowance & his people, to Inhabit & hunt on ye Northerner of Yorke River without any interruption from ye English pvided that if hereafter, It shall be thought fitt by the Governor & Council to grant any English to Inhabitt from Poropotank downwards that first Necotowance be acquainted therewith.

Act III

That Necotowance & his people, leave free that tract of land Between Yorke River and James River from ye falls of both ye Rivers to Kequotan to ye English to inhabit on, & neither be the said Necotowance no any Indians do repaire to or make any abode upon the said tract of land upon paine of Death & it shall be lawfull for any person to Kill any such Indian. And in Case any such Indian or Indians being seen upon ye said tract of Land shall make an escape, That the said Necotowance Shall upon Demand deliver ye sd Indian or Indians to the Englishmen, upon Knowledge had of him or them, unless such Indian or Indians be sent upon a Message from ye said Necotowance.

Act IV

And to ye intent to avoid all injury to such a messenger & that ignorance may be ptended to such as shall offer any Outrage, It is thought fit & hereby enacted That the badge worne by a messenger, Or is Case there shall be more than one by one of the company, be a Coate of Striped Stuffe which is to be left by the Messenger from time to time so Often as he shall return at the places appointed for their coming in.

Act V

And it is further enacted That in Case any English shall repaire contrary to the Articles agreed upon to ye said Northside of Yorke River, such psons soe offending being lawfully Convicted be adjudged as Felons; provided that this article shall not extend to such psons who by stresse of weather are forced upon the said Land, provided alsoe & if is agreed by ye sd Necotowance, that it may be lawfull for any Englishmen to goe over to ye sd Northside haveing occasion to fall timber Trees or Cut sedge, Soe as ye said psons have wart for theyre soe doing under the hand of ye GovE: Pvided alsoe Notwithstanding anything in this Act to ye Contrary That if it shall bee free & lawfull for any English whatsoever between the present day & the first of March next to kill & bring away any hogs yt they can by any means Kill or take upon the said Northside of the said River.

Act VI

And it is further enacted that neither for the said Necotowance nor any of his people, do frequent, come in to hunt or make any abode nearer to ye English plantations then the Lymits of Yapin ye blackwater & from ye head of the blackwater upon a Straite line to ye old Monakin Towne upon such paine & penaltie as aforesaid.

Act VII

And it is further Enacted that if any English do entertain any Indian or Indians or doe conceale any Indian or Indians that shall come within ye said Lymits, such psons being lawfully Commited thereof shall suffer Death in safe of Felony, without benefit of Clergy excepted such as shall be authorized thereto by virtue of this Act.

Appendix I

Act VIII

And it is further Enacted that the said Necotowance & his people upon all occasions of message to the GovE for trade, doe repaire unto ye ffort Royall onely on ye Northside, at which place they are to receive ye aforesaid Badges which shall shew them to be Messengers & therefore to be freed from all injury in their passage to the Governor upon payne of Death to any pson or psons wtsoever that shall kill them, the badge being worne by one of the Company, And in case ofany other affront, the offense to be prmissed according tp the quality thereof, & the trade admitted as aforesaid to ye said Necotowance & his people with the Comand of the Said ffort onely on ye Northside.

Act IX

And it is further thought fit & enacted that upon any occasion of Message to the GovernE or trade, The said Necotowance & his people ye Indians doe repair to fforte Henery als Appamattucke fforte, or to the house of Capt John ffloud & to no other places of ye Southside of the River, att which places the aforsd Badged of Striped Stuffe are to be remained.

Act X

And it is further thought fit & enacted That Necotowance doe with all convenience bring in ye English prisoners, And all such Negroes & Guns which are yet remaining either in possession of himself or any Indians and that he redeliver upon demand such Indian Servants as have been taken prisoners & shall hereafter run away, In case such Indian or Indians shall be found within the Lymitts of his Dominions pvided that Such Indian or Indians be under the age of twelve years at theire running away.

Act XI

And it is further enacted & Consented That such Indian children as shall or will freely & voluntarily come in & live with the English, may remain without breach of the Articles of peace, pvided they be not above twelve years old.

Act XII

And it is further thought fit & enacted That the Severall Commanders of the fforts & places as aforesaid unto which ye said Indians as aforesaid are admitted to repaire In case of trade or Message doe forthwith provide the said Coats In manner striped as aforesaid.

Appendix II:

Known Engagements of the Third Anglo Powhatan War and Partially Reconstructed Roster of English and Powhatan Forces

No full or partial roster or muster roll documents have survived for modern scrutiny. What is left is not nearly satisfactory for full reconstruction, but herein is as complete as possible a list of all known warriors, weroances, soldiers and officers associated with various commands, campaigns, forts and battles. While I would very much like to have a comparable list of Powhatan fighters and leaders to balance this list, the only individual Powhatans specifically named during the conflict are Opechancano and his successor, Necatowance. Nevertheless, following the list of English participants I have included a short list of Powhatan leaders metioned in records of the 1650s that I surmise were most likely involved most likely as *weroances*, or at least as warriors or war captains during the war.

Appendix II

Great Powhatan Assault of 1644 - April 18, 1644

Location: General engagement starting at the heads of the major rivers or fall line, particularly James and York Rivers, decreasing in intensity as they progressed toward the coast.
Action: By one estimate, about one thousand Powhatan warriors ambushed English targets throughout the Virginian frontier. Although the largest military action of the war, the only individual known is Opechancano himself. English casualties range from 4-600 in a two day attack. Powhatan losses occurred, but the number is unknown. Despite the number of people involved almost no people are individually listed in the action, as opposed to the 1622 assault, in which a careful list of persons killed was compiled in the aftermath.
Results: Powhatan victory
Associated persons: Opechancano

Initial Retaliatory Raids - May - June, 1644

Location: Unknown. Various points to protect frontier settlers.
Action: As commanded by Sir William Berkeley, initial orders for retaliation were given to militia commanders by April 30, but specifics of targets are unknown. Most likely these were forest patrols to protect groups of survivors until the colony could get better organized. No officers or soldiers listed. It appears that many Powhatans retreated in response to this action.
Results: English victory.
Associated persons: Unknown

Nansemond Raid - July 8, 1644

Location: Unknown. Somewhere in the Nansemond River system.
Action: The first specifically known retaliatory raid of the war, but the scope of the campaign and results and results are unknown. No officers or soldiers listed.
Results: Unknown.
Associated persons: Unknown

Weyanoke Raid - July 15, 1644

Location: Great Weyanoke Town.
Action: This raid destroyed the Weyanoke town on James River, and the survivors fled south into Carolina territory. No officers or soldiers listed.
Results: English Victory
Associated persons: Unknown

Pamunkey March/ Battle of Menmend, July 15 - August 5, 1644

Location: Campaign rendezvous in Kekotan. Battle of Menmend near moden day Manskind Creek. Further English sorties possible at unknown locations in York/Pamunkey River system.
Action: Under the command of General William Claiborne, the expedition left Kekotan in mid-July, splitting up into two groups: those transported by boat and an infantry column guarding the pack train. The boats transported the pack train across the river and attacked Menmend, possibly encountering an advanced Indian

fortified position. The remainder of the campaign lasted until early August.

Results: English Victory

Associated persons: Opechancano, General William Claiborne, and those on the following list. This is not a true roster, but a list of local militia officers nominated for command of the individual companies of soldiers during the expedition. Not all officers were necessarily involved, but at least two nominees from each county would be selected from this list for leadership. In all, three hundred soldiers were levied besides these officers, making this the largest assembled army in Virginia to this point. Taken from the June assembly meeting, 1644:

For James	(Capt. ffreeman)	
Citty	(Capt. Shepard)	or two
County	(Mr. Causey)	of them
	(Mr. Swann)	
	(Capt. Cheesman)	
For Yorke	(Capt. Popeley)	or two
County	(M. ffra. Morgan)	of them.
	(Mr. Tho Dobbs)	
	(Lt. Nich. Stilwell)	
For Warr:	(Capt. Tho: Harwood)	
County	(Capt. Tho: fflint)	or two
	(Thomas Davyes)	of them
	(WVim. Pawenett)	
	(Thomas Scurfeild)	
For Eliz:	(Capt. Tho Burbage)	
Citty	(Capt Nath Oldis)	or two
County	(Leift. Woolrich)	of them
	(Mr. Tho: Cheeley)	

	(Capt. Sibsey)	
For Lower Norff.	(Leift. Mason) or two (Leift. Sidney) of them (Mr. Woodhouse) (Capt. John Upton)	or two of them
Isle of Wight County.	(Mr. Antho. Jones) (Leift. Hackett) (Srgeant Stukeley) (Wn. Baldwin)	or two of them
North-ampton County.	(Capt. W. Stone) (Mr. Phill: Taylor) (Mr. Roger Marshall) (Mr. Edm. Scarborogh)	or two of them

Hen: Luellin: Allsoe it is ordered that Mr. Henry Luellin Chirurgeon bee entertayned as Chirurgeon Generall for for the Army and to contynue in that Imployment. and to have pay at the publique Charge. Allsoe that Doctor Wald-ron Mr. Dunnington. and Mountayne Row-land or some of them bee desired to goe along wth them.

Mr. Cleverio: And allsoe that Mr. Cleverio or some other to bee Minister bee entreated to bestowe his paynes with them.

Chicahominy March, August, 1644

Location: Chickahominy River, at the town of Oranioc near modern Diascund Creek.
Action: The last major assault of the summer of 1644, this action was meant to be a final blow in the English counter attack, in order to prevent further attacks on Henrico and Charles City Counties. In this attack naval support from a Maryland shallop was obtained, and it

appears that the town was destroyed, the Chickahominy refugees fleeing north to the Pamunkeys.
Results: English Victory
Associated persons: *Infantry:* Captain Ralph Wormely and Surgeon Thomas Ward. *Naval Support:* Maryland Governor Leonard Calvert.

Powhatan Autumn Offensive- October - December, 1644

Location: Unknown. Various points along the frontier.
Action: Following the Chickahominy March, English guns fell silent, which Opechancano correctly perceived to mean a shortage of ammunition. In a series of autumn raids, straggling and complacent Englishmen were picked off in ambushes and raids on frontier settlements.
Results: Powhatan Victories
Associated Persons: Unknown

English Autumn Raid, October 23, 1644

Location: Unknown
Action: A raid of unknown size was levied against an unknown target in response to Opechancano's counter-attack.
Results: Unknown
Associate persons: Unknown

Autumn Raids, November 26, 1644

Location: Unknown
Action: Several parties were given orders for attacking Indian targets to oppose Opechancano's counter-attack.
Results: Unknown
Associated persons: Unknown

Autumn Raid, December 3, 1644

Location: Unknown, but probably York County against a Pamunkey target.
Action: Raid commissioned to attack an unknown Indian target at the request of Lieutenant Nicholas Stillwell, a York county resident and veteran of the Battle of Menmend.
Results: Unknown
Associated persons: Lieutenant Nicholas Stillwell

Frontier Patrols from Middle Plantation, May-December, 1644

Location: Along the palisades between near Queen's Creek, Lower Penninsula.
Action: On April 30, 1644, Sir William Berkeley ordered sixty men to garrison Middle Plantation, the fortified central point of a palisade that cut off the eastern half of the Lower Peninsula from the rest of the interior. Specific operations conducted by these men are unknown, other than that the goal was to prevent Powhatan warriors from raiding the eastern side of the palisades. As such the guards and patrols were probably maintained along the length of the palisade throughout the year.
Results: While skirmishes were probably at a minimum in this area, it does appear that the soldiers of Middle Plantation were successful in keeping the eastern half of the Lower Peninsula free of hostile Powhatans, so in that it can be considered a successful English operation.
Associated persons: Unknown

Construction of Forts, February-May, 1645

Locations: Pamunkey River near former town site of Menmend on Manskind Creek, on a ridge near the head of the Chickahominy River, and the north side of James River near the falls.

Action: Since a group of carpenters could hardly be able to construct a fort without the protection of soldiers, the construction of the forts certainly had a guard to push back Powhatan defenders and provide protection to the work crews during the construction of the forts.
Results: English Victory
Associated Persons: Unknown

Southward March, April, 1645

Location: Beginning from Nansemond River south into Carolina, along east side of Chowan River to Yeopim Creek and back.
Action: In an effort to seek out the refugee Weyanoke group, and also to scout out Carolina territory for the prospect of future settlement, this was a scouting expedition to gather intelligence. No recorded skirmish or battle occurred.
Results: Intelligence gained that Carolina Algonquians were amicable toward the English and the new Weyanoke town was on the other side of the broad Chowan. Future expedition planned.
Associated persons: Commander: Mr. Richard Bennett; Soldiers: Henry Plumpton, George Rutland; Surgeon: Thomas Ward (veteran of the Chickahominy March).

Battle of Weyanoke Creek, Summer, 1645

Location: The forks of Wiccacon Creek, North Carolina.
Action: In one of, if not the, longest range attack against a specific Indian target in colonial history, eight river boats went from Nansemond River carried eighty soldiers into the Atlantic ocean briefly before entering the Albemarle Sound, camping at night on the northern bank until they sailed the last twenty miles up Chowan River to Wicaccon Creek, where a sharp skirmish with the Weyanokes left one Englishman dead and several more wounded. This was the second-largest English troop

movement of the war next to the Pamunkey March of 1644.
Results: Weyanoke Victory. Though the English would claim victory, it was in fact the Weyanokes who succeeded in their goal of turning back the English expedition and keeping them from their town. The location of the battle and creek would significantly contribute to the Virginia/North Caroling border dispute in the decades ahead.
Associated persons: Commander: Captain Thomas Dew, Soldier: Henry Plumpton (veteran of the Southward March), Abraham Pitts, John Skull (spelling of Skull uncertain), Surgeon: Christopher Ackeley.

Operations of Fort Royal, June-December, 1645

Location: Near Manskind Creek, York County.
Action: Specific actions of this summer are not mentioned. Orders to commanders stress continual marches to disrupt Powhatan subsistence and prevent attacks on English plantations. Sometimes joint expeditions were planned to combine forces with other forts to attack specific targets, with sufficient men to remain to guard the fort. At one point this year, a possible meeting took place between Sir William Berkeley and Opechancano's medium, using Henry Fleet as interpreter. Whether this meeting took place or not, the talks would fail and the war continues. By the end of the year fewer and fewer Indians were encountered as they retreated further inland. The garrison was approximately fifty soldiers.
Results: English Victory
Associated persons: Fort commander in 1645: Captain Ralph Wormeley. Commander by the end of the war: Captain Rogar Marshall.

Operations of Fort James, June-December, 1645

Location: Chickahominy River
Action: Specific actions of this summer are not mentioned. Orders to commanders stress continual marches to disrupt Powhatan subsistence and prevent attacks on English plantations. Sometimes joint expeditions were planned to combine forces with other forts to attack specific targets, with sufficient men to remain to guard the fort. By the end of the year fewer and fewer Indians were encountered as they retreated further inland. The garrison was approximately fifty soldiers.
Results: English victory
Associated persons: Fort commander in 1644: Captain Robert Higginson. Commander at end of war: Lieutenant Thomas Rolphe.

Operations of Fort Charles, June-December, 1645

Location: North side of James River at the falls, within modern Richmond.
Action: Specific actions of this summer are not mentioned. Orders to commanders stress continual marches to disrupt Powhatan subsistence and prevent attacks on English plantations. Sometimes joint expeditions were planned to combine forces with other forts to attack specific targets, with sufficient men to remain to guard the fort. By the end of the year fewer and fewer Indians were encountered as they retreat further inland. The garrison was approximately fifty soldiers.
Results: English victory.
Associated persons: Fort commander in 1645: Captain Francis Epps; commander at end of the war: Captain Thomas Harris.

Renewed Nansemond Campaign, June, 1646

Location: Unknown, but probably within the western branch of the Nansemond River.

Action: The associated counties of Upper and Lower Norfolk with Isle of Wight Counties were given orders to renew their assaults against the Nansemonds, "or any other Indians," near them, and erect a fort if need be. No evidence exists for the construction of a fort.
Results: Unknown
Associated persons: Unknown

Appomatoc Campaign/ Fort Henry Construction, June, 1646

Location: Swift Creek, Appomattox River system.
Action: After discovering a fishing weir constructed by the Appomatoc Indians, orders were given to destroy the weir and cut their growing corn. Following this the solders were to construct a new fort called Fort Henry for further attacks against the Appomatocs, which was done.
Results: English victory
Associated persons: Commander of Fort: Captain Abraham Wood.

Expedition to Intercept Opechancano, Spring/Summer, 1646

Location: Unknown, except that the route taken was via the northerly Rappahannock River.
Action: In the spring session of the Virginian Assembly, Captain Henry Fleet made a proposal to the burgesses for a diplomatic mission to make a peace with Opechancano. Once approved, a sixty man force was deployed and transported in his ships to the Rappahannock River to find Opechancano.
Results: Unclear
Associated persons: Captain Henry Fleet, Lieutenant Francis Poythers, in comand of sixty men: "*from Henrico 2 men, Charles Citty county 4, James Citty countye 13, Yorke county 16, Warwick county eight, Eliz. Citty county 8, and Northampton county 9.*"

Appendix II

Capture of Opechancano, Summer, 1646

Location: Unknown, but probably in association with Henry Fleet's expedition and within the York/Pamunkey River system.
Action: Most likely with intelligence gathered from friendly Rappahannoc and Accomac scouts, and also in association with Henry Fleet's voyage, Sir William Berkeley received information of Opechancano's whereabouts. With a force of horsemen, he stormed the camp, taking Opechancano and his followers prisoner.
Results: English victory
Associated persons: Sir William Berkeley, Opechancano.

Bibliography

Adkins, Elaine and Adkins, Ray, *Chickahominy Indians- Eastern Division: A Brief Ethnohistory,* (Elaine and Ray Adkins, 2007)

Anonymous, "A Perfect Description of Virginia [1649]," in Peter Force, ed., *Tracts and Other Papers, Relating Principally to the Origin, Settlement, and Progress of the Colonies in North America, from the Discovery of the Country to the Year 1776, Vol II* (New York, Reprinted Under the Auspices of the Out-of-Print Books Committee of New York, 1947)

Anonymous, "Northampton County Records in the 17th Century" Virginia Magazine of History and Biography No. 4 (April 1897) 4:401-410

Anonymous, "Surrender of Virginia to the Parliamentary Commissioners, March 1651-2" Virginia Magazine of History and Biography No. 1(Jul 1903) 11:32-41

Anonymous, "House of Commons Journal Volume 3: 16 October 1644", Journal of the House of Commons: volume 3: 1643-1644 (1802).

Great Britain House of Commons, *Journal of the House of Commons: volume 3: 1643-1644,* (1802).

- *Journal of the House of Commons: volume 7: 1651-1660,* (1802).

Barbour, Philip L. *Pocahontas and Her World,* (Boston, Houghton Miffin, 1969).

Jonathan E. Barth, "'The Sinke of America': Society in the Albemarle Borderlands of North Carolina, 1663-1729,"in *The North Carolina Historical Review* 87 (January 2010) 1-27

Bass Family Papers, *Book of John Basse, Norfolk County Virg*a *A.D. 1675,* with "Portluck Document," May 17, 1797, (photocopy from original, 8 leaves, call number 26371, Library of Virginia).

Bell, Albert D, *Bass Families of the South, vol. 1,* (Rocky Mount, North Carolina, 1961)

Beverly, Robert, *The History and Present State of Virginia* [1705], Louis B. Wright, ed., (Chapel Hill: University of North Carolina Press, 1947)

Billings, Warren M., ed., The Papers of Sir William Berkeley, 1605-1677, (Richmond, Library of Virginia, 2007)

- *Sir William Berkeley and the Forging of Colonial Virginia,* (Baton Rouge, Louisiana State University Press, 2004)

Binford, Lewis, *Cultural Diversity Among Aboriginal Cultures of Coastal Virginia and North Carolina,* (New York, Garland Publishing, 1991) originally published as PhD diss for U of Michigan, 1964.

Bland, Edward, "The Discovery of New Brittaine," in *Narratives of Early Carolina*, Alexander Salley, ed., (New York: Charles Scribner's Sons, 1911), 5-19

Bliss, Robert M., *Revolution and Empire: English Politics and the American Colonies in the Seventeenth Century, (*New York, Manchester University Press, 1990)

Boddie, John Bennett, *Seventeenth Century Isle of Wight County Virginia,* (Chicago, Chicago Law Printing Company, 1938)

Bond, Edward L., *Damned Souls in a Tobacco Colony: Religion in Seventeenth Century Virginia,* (Macon, GA: Mercer University Press, 2000)

Byrd, William, *William Byrd's Histories of the Dividing Line Betwixt Virginia and North Carolina,* William C. Boyd, ed., (New York, Dover Publications,Inc., 1967)

Cave, Alfred A., *The Pequot War,* (Boston: University of Massachusetts Press, 1996)

Claiborne, John Herbert, *William Claiborne of Virginia,* (New York, G.P. Putnam's Sons, 1917)

Bibliography

Coneiro, Robert L. "What Happened at the Flashpoint? Conjectures on Chiefdom Formation at the Very Moment of Conception," in Redmond, Elsa, ed, *Chiefdoms and Chieftaincy in the Americas,* (Gainesville, University of Florida Press, 1998) 18-42.

Cumming, William P., *North Carolina in Maps* (Raleigh, State Department of Archives and History, 1966)

Custalow Dr. Linwood "Little Bear" and Daniel, Angela L. "Silver Star," *The True Story of Pocahontas: The Other Side of History,* (Golden, Fulcrum Publishing, 2007)

Custer, Jay, "Late Woodland Cultural Diversity in the Middle Atlantic: An Evolutionary Perspective," in Custer, Jay, ed., *Late Woodland Cultures in the Middle Atlantic Region* (Newark, University of Delaware Press, 1986) 143-168.

Egloff, Keith, and Woodward, Deborah, *First People: The Early Indians of Virginia,* (Charlottesville, University of Virginia Press, 2006)

Ethridge, Robbie, *From Chicaza to Chickasaw: The European Invasion and the Transformation of the Mississippian World, 1540-1715*, (Chapel Hill, University of North Carolina Press, 2010)

Ehtridge, Robbie and Hudson, Charles, ed, *The Transformation of the Southeastern Indians, 1540-1760,* (Jackson, University of Mississippi Press, 2002)

Ethridge, Robbie, and Shuck-Hall, Sheri, ed, *Mapping the Mississippian Shatter Zone: The Colonial Indian Slave Trade and Regional Instability in the American South,* (Lincoln, University of Nebraska Press, 2009)

Coneiro, Robert L. "What Happened at the Flashpoint? Conjectures on Chiefdom Formation at the Very Moment of Conception," in Redmond, Elsa, ed, *Chiefdoms and Chieftaincy in the Americas,* (Gainesville, University of Florida Press, 1998)18-42.

Davidson, Thomas E., "Relations Between the Powhatans and the Eastern Shore," in Rountree, Helen, ed, *Powhatan Foreign Relations, 1500-1722,* (Charlottesville, University Press of Virginia, 1993) 136-153.

Dolin, Eric J, *Fur, Fortune and Empire: The Epic History of the Fur Trade in America,* (New York, W.W Norton & Company, 2010)

Dowd, Lea and Sylvestri, Patti, *Early Basses in Virginia, Including Captain Nathaniel Basse,* (Southern Bass and the Nansemond Tribal Asssociation, npublished manuscript, 1999)

- *Descendants of Edward Bass and Mary Tucker: Another Native American Family,* (unpublished manuscript, 1999)

Everett, C.S., "'They shalbe slaves for their lives,': Indian Slavery in Colonial Virginia," in Allan Galay, ed., *Indian Slavery in Colonial America,* (Lincoln, University of Nebraska Press, 2009) 67-108.

Fausz, John Frederick, *The Powhatan Uprising of 1622: A Historical Study of Ethnocentrism and Cultural Conflict,* (PhD. Diss., College of William and Mary in Virginia, 1977)

- "Opechancanough, Indian Resistance Leader," in David Sweet and Gary Nash, eds., *Struggle and Survival in Colonial America,* (Berkeley and Los Angeles, University of California Press, 1981) 21-37.

Feest, Christian F., *The Powhatan Tribes,* (New York, Chelsea House Publishers, 1990)

Feller, Laura Janet, *Constructing and Contesting Color Lines: Tidewater Native Peoples and Indianness in Jim Crow Virginia* (PhD Diss. The George Washington University, 2009)

Fleet, Beverley, *Virginia Colonial Abstracts Vol. III,* (Baltimore, Genalogical Publishing Company, 1988)

Foley, Louise Pledge Heath, *Early Virginia Families Along the James River, vol. 2,* (Baltimore: Genealogical Publishing Company, 1980)

Frank, Joseph, "News From Virginny, 1644," The Virginia Magazine of History and Biography, Vol. 65, No. 1 (Jan., 1957) 84-87

Galay, Alan, *The Indian Slave Trade: The Rise of the English Empire in the American South, 1670-1717,* (New Haven, Yale University Press, 2003)

Gallivan,M. D, *James River Chiefdoms: The Rise of Social Inequality in the Chesapeake,* (Lincoln, University of Nebraska Press, 2003)

- "Powhatan's Werowocomoco: Constructing Place, Polity, and Personhood in the Chesapeake, C.E. 1200 – C.E. 1609," in *American Anthropologist,* Vol. 109, Issue 1, 2007, pp. 85-100.

Gaunt, Peter, *The English Civil Wars, 1642-1651,* (Oxford, Osprey Publishing, 2003)

Gleach, F.W, Powhatan's *World and Colonial Virginia: A Conflict of Cultures,* (Lincoln, University of Nebraska Press, 1997)

Gradie, Charlotte M., "The Powhatans in the Context of the Spanish Empire," in Rountree, Helen ed., *Powhatan Foreign Relations, 1500-1772,* (Charlottesville, University Press of Virginia, 1993) 154-172.

Great Britain House of Commons, *Journal of the House of Commons: volume 3: 1643-1644,* (1802).

Bibliography

- *Journal of the House of Commons: volume 7: 1651-1660,* (1802).

Grizzard, Frank E., Smith, D. Boyd, *Jamestown Colony: a Political, Social, and Cultural History,* (Santa Barbara, ABC-CLIO, 2007)

Grose, S.E., *Appomattox County History and Events,* (Marceline, MO: Walsworth Publishing Company, 2001)

Hantman, Jeffrey L., "Powhatan's Relations With the Piedmont Monacans," in Rountree, Helen, ed, *Powhatan Foreign Relations, 1500-1722,* (Charlottesville, University Press of Virginia, 1993) 94-111.

- "Jamestown's 400th Anniversary: Old Themes, New Words, New Meanings for Virginia Indians," in Rubertone, Patricia, ed., *Archaeologies of Placemaking,* (Walnut Creek, Left Coast Press, 2008) 217-242.

Heath, Charles L. and. Phelps, David S., "Architecture of a Tuscarora Fortress: The Neoheroka Fort and the Tuscarora War (1711—1715)," (Paper Presented at the 63rd Annual Meeting of the Society for American Archaeology, January 1998, Seattle, Washington).

Heinegg, Paul, *Free African Americans of North Carolina, Virginia and South Carolina, fifth edition, two volumes,* (Baltimore, Genealogical Publishing Company, 2005). Digitized online at <http://www.freeafricanamericans.con>

Horn, James, *A Land as God Made it: Jamestown and the Birth of America,* (New York, Basic Books, 2008)

- "Servant Emigration to the Chesapeake in the Seventeenth Century," in Thad W. Tate and David L. Ammerman, eds., *The Chesapeake in the Seventeenth Century: Essays on Anglo-American Society,* (Chapel Hill, University of North Carolina Press, 1979) 51-95.

Johnson, Edward, *Wonder-working Providence of Sions Savior in New England* [1654], J. Franklin Jameson, ed., (New York: Charles Scribner's Sons, 1910)

Kelso, William M. *Jamestown: The Buried Truth (*Charlottesville, University of Virginia Press, 2006)

Kupperman, Karen Ordahl, *Indians and English: Facing Off in Early America,* (Ithaca, Cornell University Press, 2000)

Land, Aubrey C., *Colonial Maryland: A History,* (Millwood, KTO Press 1981)

Lewis, Clifford and Albert Loomie, *The Spanish Jesuit Mission in Virginia, 1570-1572,* (Chapel Hill,

University of North Carolina Press, 1953)

Mallios, Seth, *The Deadly Politics of Giving: Exchange and Violence at Ajacan, Roanoke and Jamestown,* (Tuscaloosa, University of Alabama Press, 2006)

Mathews, Samuel, "Mutiny in Virginia [1635]" in *Virginia Magazine of History and Biography* No. 4 (April 1894) 416-424

Mathews, Thomas, "The Beginning, Progress and Conclusion of Bacon's Rebellion in Virginia in the Years 1675 and 1676," in *Narratives of the Insurrections, 1675–1690*, ed. Charles McLean Andrews (New York: Charles Scribner's Sons, 1915)

McCartney, Martha W, "Cockacoeske, Queen of Pamunkey: Diplomat and Suzeraine," in Waselkov, G, Wood, P, and Hatley, T, ed, *Powhatan's Mantle: Indians in the Colonial Southeast,* (Lincoln, University of Nebraska Press, 2006) 243-266

- "Seventeenth Century Apartheid: The Suppression and Containment of Indians in Tidewater Virginia," in *Journal of Middle Atlantic Archealogy* I:51-81, 1985.
- "The Draft of York River in Virginia: An Artifact of the Seventeenth Century," in *Southeastern Archaeology* 3(2), (Winter, 1984)

McCary, Ben C., *Indians in Seventeenth Century Virginia,* (Williamsburg, Garret and Massie, Inc., Virginia 350th Anniversary Celebration Corporation, 1957)

McIlwaine, H.R., ed., *Minutes of the Council and General Court of Virginia, 1622-1632, 1670-1676,* (Richmond: Virginia State Library, 1979 [1924])

McSherry, James, *History of Maryland: From Its First Settlement in 1634, to the Year 1848,* (Baltimore, Published by John Murphy, 1849)

Meyers, Maureen "From Refugees to Slave Traders: The Transformation of the Westo Indians," in Ethridge and Shuck-Hall, *The Mississisppian Shatter Zone,* 81-103.

Milanich, Jerald, "Native Chiefdoms and the Exercise in Complexity in Sixteenth Century Florida," in Redmond, Elsa, ed, *Chiefdoms and Chieftaincy in the Americas,* (Gainesville, University of Florida Press, 1998)245-264.

Moretti-Langholtz, D, *Other Names I Have Been Called: Political Resurgence Among Virginia Indians in the Twentieth Century,* (PhD Disssertation, University of Oklahoma, 1998)

Moretti-Langholtz, Danielle, and Waugaman, Sandra, *We're Still Here: Contemporary Virginia Indians Tell*

Bibliography

Their Stories, (Richmond, Palari Publishing, 2000)

Morton, Richard L., *Colonial Virginia, Vol. 1,The Tidewater Period: 1607-1710* (Chapel Hill, University of North Carolina Press, 1960)

National Archives, "The Thomas Jefferson Papers," Series 8. Virginia Records, Manuscripts: 1607-1737. Virginia Council and Assembly, 1643-62, Laws.

Niell, Edward D., *Virginia Carolorum: The Colony Under the Rule of Charles the First and Second, A.D. 1625-A.D. 1685*, (Albany, N.Y.: John Munsell's Sons, 1886)

Nugent, Nell Marion, ed., *Cavaliers and Pioneers: Abstracts of Virginia Land Patents and Grants, 1623-1800,* vol. 1 (Richmond, Press of the Dietz Printing Company, 1934)

Oberg, Michael Leroy, *The Head in Edward Nugent's Hand,* (Philadelphia, University of Pennsylvania Press, 2008)

Pilkey, Orrin H., ed., *The North Carolina Shore and Its Barrier Islands: Restless Ribbons of Sand*, (Durham, N.C.: Duke University Press, 1998)

Plantagenet, Beauchamp, "A Description of the Province of New Albion (1648)," in *American Colonial Historical Tracts,* (Rochester, New York: George Humphrey) 1898.

Potter, Stephen R, "Early English Effects on Virginia Algonquian Exchange and Tribute in the Tidewater Potomac" in Waselkov, G, Wood, P, and Hatley, T, ed, *Powhatan's Mantle: Indians in the Colonial Southeast,* (Lincoln, University of Nebraska Press, 2006)

Potter, Stephen R., *Commoners, Tribute and Chiefs: The Development of Algonquian Culture in the Potomac Valley,* (Charlottesville, University Press of Virginia, 1993)

Powell, William, *John Pory: 1572-1636, The Life and Letters of a Man of Many Parts* (Chapel Hill, University of North Carolina Press, 1977)

Price, David A., *Love and Hate in Jamestown: John Smith, Pocahontas, and the Heart of a New Nation* (New York, Alfred A. Knopf, 2003)

Printz, Johan, "Report of Governor Johan Printz, 1644," in J. Franklin Jameson, Narratives of Early Pennsylvania, West New Jersey and Delaware, 1630-1707, (New York: Charles Scribner's Sons, 1912) 91-115.

Pryor, Francis, *The Making of the British Landscape: How We Have Transformed the Land, From Prehistory to Today,* (New York: Penguin Books, 2010).

Rackham, Oliver, *Trees and Woodland in the British Landscape: the Complete History of Britain's Trees, Woods &*

Hedgerows, (London: Phoenix Press, 2001)

Ready, Milton, *The Tar Heel State: A History of North Carolina* (Columbia, University of South Carolina Press, 2005)

Redmond, Elsa, ed, *Chiefdoms and Chieftaincy in the Americas,* (Gainesville, University of Florida Press, 1998)

Pilkey, Orrin H., ed., *The North Carolina Shore and Its Barrier Islands: Restless Ribbons of Sand,* (Durham, N.C.: Duke University Press, 1998)

Riordan, Timothy B., *The Plundering Time: Maryland and the English Civil War, 1645-1646,* (Baltimore: Maryland Historical Society, 2004)

Robinson, Conway, "Notes From the Council and General Court Records 1641-1659," VMHB No. 1(Jul 1900) 8:64-73.

Rountree, Helen, *The Powhatan Indians of Virginia: Their Traditional Culture*, (Norman, University of Oklahoma Press, 1989)

- *Pocahontas's People: The Powhatan Indians of Virginia Through Four Centuries,* (Norman, University of Oklahoma Press, 1990)

  Powhatan Foreign Relations: 1500-1722, (Charlottesville, University Press of Virginia, 1993)

- "Who Were the Powhatans and Did They Have a Foreign Policy?" in Rountree, Helen, ed., *Powhatan Foreign Relations, 1500-1722,* (Charlottesville, University Press of Virginia, 1993)1-19.
- "The Powhatans and Other Woodland Indians as Travellers," in Rountree, Helen, ed., *Powhatan Foreign Relations, 1500-1722,* (Charlottesville, University Press of Virginia, 1993) 21-52.
- Rountree, Helen C., "Powhatans and the English: A Case of Multiple Conflicting Agendas," in Rountree, Helen c., ed., *Powhatan Foreign Relations, 1500-1722,* (Charlottesville, University Press of Virginia, 1993) 173-205.

Rountree, Helen, and Turner, Randolph, *Before and After Jamestown: Virginia's Powhatans and their Predecessors,* (Gainesville, University of Florida, 2002)

- "The Evolution of the Powhatan Paramount Chiefdom in Virginia," Redmond, Elsa, ed, *Chiefdoms and Chieftaincy in the Americas,* (Gainesville, University of Florida Press, 1998)265-296.

Bibliography

- "On the Fringe of the Southeast: The Powhatan Paramount Chiefdom in Virginia," in Hudson, Charles, and Tesser, Carmen Chaves, eds., *The Forgotten Centuries: Indians and Europeans in the American South, 1521-1704,* (Athens, University of Georgia Press, 1994) 355-372.

Rountree, Helen C. and Clark, Wayne E., "The Powhatans and the Maryland Mainland," in Rountree, Helen, ed, *Powhatan Foreign Relations, 1500-1722,* (Charlottesville, University Press of Virginia, 1993) 112-135.

Sawyer, Roy, *America's Wetland: An Environmental and Cultural History of Tidewater Virginia and North Carolina,* (Charlottesville, University of Virginia Press, 2010)

Sainsbury, W. Noel , Calendar of State Papers Colonial, America and West Indies, Volume 1: 1574-1660 (1860)

Shea, William L., *The Virginia Militia in the Seventeenth Century,* (Baton Rouge, Louisiana State University Press, 1983)

- "Virginia At War, 1644-1646", in *Military Affairs*, Vol. 41, No. 3 (Oct., 1977), 142-147

Shultz, Eric B. and Tougias, Michael J., *King Philip's War: The History and Legacy of America's Forgotten Conflict,* (Woodstock, VM: The Countryman Press, 2000)

Smith, John, "The Generall Historie of Virginia...[1624]," in Philip Barbour, ed., *The Complete Works of John Smith,* (Chapel Hill, University of North Carolina Press, 1986)

Stanard, William G., "The Indians of Southern Virginia, 1650-1711. Depositions in the Virginia and North Carolina Boundary Case." Virginia Magazine of History and Biography 7-8. Virginia Historical Society, Richmond, 1900

Stanard, William G., and Stanard, Mary Newton, *The Colonial Virginia Register: A List of Governors, Councilors and Other Higher Officials, and Also Members of the House of Burgesses, and the Revolutionary Conventions of the Colony of Virginia* [1902], (Baltimore, Clearfield Company, 1989)

Strachey, William, *The Historie of Travell Into Virginia Britania* [1612], edited by Louis B. Wright and Virginia Freund (London, Printed for the Hakluyt Society, 1953)

Streeter, Sebastian Ferris, *Papers Relating to the Early History of Maryland,* (Baltimore: Maryland Historical Society, 1876)

Tate, Thad W. and Ammerman, David L., *The Chesapeake in the Seventeenth Century: Essays on Anglo-American*

Society, (Chapel Hill, University of North Carolina Press, 1979)

Thornton, Russell, *American Indian Holocaust and Survival: A Population History Since 1492,* (Norman, University of Oklahoma Press)

Tooker, William Wallace, "Meaning of Some Indian Names in Virginia," in *The William and Mary Quarterly* 14, No. 1, (June, 1905) 62-64.

Townsend, Camilla, *Pocahontas and the Powhatan Dilemma,* (New York, Macmillan, 2005).

Turner, E. Randolph III, "Native American Protohistoric Interactions in the Powhatan Core Area," in Rountree, Helen ed., *Powhatan Foreign Relations, 1500-1772,* (Charlottesville, University Press of Virginia, 1993) 76-93.

- Turner,E. Randolph, "Difficulties in the Archeological Identification of Chiefdoms as Seen in the Virginia Coastal Plain during the Late Woodland and Early Historic Periods," in Custer, Jay, ed., *Late Woodland Cultures of the Middle Atlantic Region,* (Newark, University of Delaware Press, 1986) 19-28.

Ubelaker, Douglas H., "Human Biology of Virginia Indians," in Rountree, Helen ed., *Powhatan Foreign Relations, 1500-1772,* (Charlottesville, University Press of Virginia, 1993) 53-75.

Walter, Alice Granbery, ed., *Lower Norfolk County, Virginia Court Records, Book "A" 1637-1646 & Book "B" 1646-1651/2,* (Clearfield Company Inc, Baltimore, 2002

Ward, H and Davis, S, ed, *Time Before History: The Archeology of North Carolina, (Chapel Hill, The University of North Carolina Press, 1999)*

Waselkov, Gregory A, "Indian Maps of the Colonial Southeast" in Waselkov, G, Wood, P, and Hatley, T, ed, *Powhatan's Mantle: Indians in the Colonial Southeast,* (Lincoln, University of Nebraska Press, 2006)

Waselkov, Gregory A., Wood, Peter H. and Hatley, Tom, eds., *Powhatan's Mantle: Indians in the Colonial Southeast,* (Lincoln: University of Nebraska Press, 1989)

Williamson, Margaret Holmes, *The Powhatan Lords of Life and Death: Command and Consent in Seventeenth-Century Virginia,* (Lincoln, University of Nebraska Press, 2003)

Winthrop, John, "History of New England [1649]" vol. 2, James Kendall Hosmer, ed., (New York: Charles Scribner's sons, 1908)

Index

Abraham Pitts, 167
Abraham Wood, 218, 246
Abraham Wood., 182
Accomac, 35
Accomac Indigenous Americans, 178, 210, 223
Accopatough, 35
African Americans, 145, 201, 212; Wormeley "servant" uprising, 136
Albemarle Sound, 165
Albermarle Sound, 200
Anglicans, 80
Anti-crown pamphlets, 120
Appamatock Indigenous Americans, 69, 146
Appamattock Indigenous Americans, 74, 75, 150
Appamattock Indigneous Americans, 220
Appomatock Indigenous Americans, 33, 182
Appomattock Indigenous Americans, 135
Appomattox River, 182
Argall Yeardley, 137, 140
Ascomowet (Weyanoke leader), 69, 131, 217
Bacon’s Rebellion, 40
Bacon's Rebellion, 225
Battle of Bloody Run, 212, 224
Battles: "Southward March" to North Carolina, 157; Assault, 237; Assault of April 18, 68, 86; Assault of Weyanoke Town, June 1644, 106; Associated with construction of forts, 160; Autumn and winter expeditions, 1644, 139; Battle of Menmend, 103, 112, 240; Battle of Oranioc, 113, 114, 241; Battle of Weyanoke Creek, 244; Capture of Opechancano, 193; Expeditions against Nansemond, 1645, 183; Expeditions on Swift Creek, 182; Expeditions sent from forts, 172; June 1644 expeditions, 237; List of known engagements, 247; livestock and corn slashing, 81; Nansemond Raid, 238; Powhatan counter-attack, 241; Raid against Nansemond, June 1644, 105; Southward March, 243; Weyanoke Raid, 238
Bridges Freeman, 203
Bristol, 100
Capture of Opechancano, 247
Carolina Algonquians, 153, 154, 157, 167
Casualty estimates, 82, 88
Charles City County, 75, 95, 103
Chickahominy Indigenous Americans, 32, 33, 69, 95, 96, 115, 127, 134, 145, 178, 218, *See*
Chickahominy Indigneous Americans, 218

Chickahomony Indigenous Americans, 74
Chicskiac Indigenous Americans, 42
Chiskiac Indigenous Americans, 69
Chounterounte (Nottoway Leader), 29
Chowan River, 133, 155, 166
Chowanoke Indigenous Americans, 154, 157, 210, 228, *See*; Powhatan Raids, 30
Christopher Ackeley, 168, 244
Christopher Ackely, 166
Civil Rights Movement, 228
Cockacoeske (Pamunkey female leader), 188
Cockaqueske (Pamunkey female leader), 172, 217, 225
Cornelius Loyd, 97
Corrowhaughcoheh (Tuscarora leader), 133
Currituck Inlet, 165
David DeVries, 59
Dutch merchant vessels, 140
Earl of Essex, 100
Edward Basse, 156
Edward Bradby (Chickahominy leader), 228
Edward Johnson, 84
Edward Wyndam, 153
Elizabeth (Nansemond woman), 34, 219
Elizabeth City County, 104
England: Overcrowded, 6, 11; Social Status, 6
English Civil War, 59, 96, 98, 99, 100, 163, 205; Civil Unrest, 2; Virginia schisms, 51; Virginian anti-crown pamphlets, 120; Virginian internal conflict, 38; Virginian Schisms, 53
Ervetsahekeh (Tuscarora female leader), 133
Fire, used in surprise attack, 72
First Anglo-Powhatan War, xviii, 2
Fort Charles, 147, 245
Fort Henry, 182, 218, 246
Fort James, 147, 160, 245
Fort Royal, 147, 160, 173, 174, 218, 244
Francis Epps, 147, 245
Francis Poythers, 246
Francis Yeardley, 137
Garrisons, 77, 82, 92
George Minifie, 148
George Rutland, 243
Governor Francis Wyatt, 38, 40, 41
Governor John Harvey, 40
Great Dismal Swamp, 152, 178, 183
Great Peter (Nansemond leader), 133
Henrico County, 75, 95, 103, 185
Henry Fleet, 174, 183, 187, 246
Henry Hill, 198
Henry Plumpton, 156, 167, 170, 243, 244
Herquapink (Chickahominy leader), 69
House of Commons, 137, 141
Interpretation of natural signs. *See* Premonitions
Isle of Wight County, 104, 145, 150, 151

Index

James City County, 104, 185
James Mooney, 226
Jamestown, 135, 173
Johan Printz, 205
John Bass, Nansemond marriage, 34
John Burton, 40
John Harvey, 98
John Rolfe (husband of Pocahontas), 36
John Skull, 168, 244
John Smith, 3
John Winthrop, 83, 161
John Woodson, 75
Kent Island, 116
King Charles, 100, 163; Orders to Leonard Calvert, 117
Lawne's Creek, 146
Leonard Calvert, 42, 113, 115, 198, 241; Hated by most Virginians, 116; Risk of assasination, 123
Ligon (Virginian shoemaker), 75
Lord Robert Rich, 56
Lower Norfolk County, 104, 145, 150, 151
Machumps (Powhatan informant), 1
Margaret Worleigh, 73, 173
Mary Tucker (Chowanoke indigenous woman), 156
Maryland, 113, 205
Mattaponi Indigenous Americans, 69, 135, 145, 178, 223; Oral history, xvi, 217
Mattaponi Indigneous Americans, 218
Meherrin Indigenous Americans, 31, 132, 167
Meherrin River, 133
Middle Plantation, 88, 174, 242
Miscegenation laws, 226
Monacan Indigenous Americans, 228
Nansemond Chief Emeritus Oliver Perry, xiii
Nansemond Indigenous Americans, 32, 34, 69, 77, 94, 114, 133, 135, 145, 150, 151, 219; Basse family, 34; Christianized band, 150; Pochick band, 76, 95, 114, 221; Pre-war conflicts, 36
Nansemond Indigneous Americans: Christianized band, 219; Pochick band, 219
Nansemond River, 164
Nansemonds Indigenous Americans, 96
Nanticoke Indigenous Americans, 43
Nathaniel Moore, 136
Naval Battles. *See* English Civil War
Necatowance, 202
Necatowance (Pamunkey leader), 198, 205
Necatowance Treaty, 159, 199, 200, 236
New Amsterdam, 205
New England, 84, 97; Indian warfare, 54
New Sweden, 205
Nicholas Stillwell, 139, 179, 242
Nick Major (Meherrin leader), 131, 133

Nicotaw Warr (Tuscarora leader), 133
Norfolk County, 97
North Carolina, 150, 153, 159, 165, 170, 220; Border dispute, 131
Northampton County, 105
Nottoway Indigenous Americans, 29, 131
Nottoway River, 131, 132
One drop rule, 227
Opechancano, xxi, 29, 33, 37, 39, 45, 56, 58, 111, 115, 132, 137, 173, 181, 187, 188, 190, 214, 218; "burial" mound, ix; 1644 War preparations, 2; Capture, 193; Early life, 21; First Anglo-Powhatan War Involvement, 21; Intent to win war, 62; Motives, 61; Murder attempt, 24; Prewar planning, 47; Second Anglo-Powhatan War involvement, 24; Tuscarora Raids, 31
Opitchapam (Powhatan leader), 21, 23
Oraniock Town (Chickahominy). *See* Chickahominy Indigenous Americans
Oraniok (Chickahominy town), 135
Ossakican (Chiskiac leader), 217
Pamunkey Indigenous Americans, 33, 69, 74, 95, 127, 134, 145, 178, 198, 218; Battle against Weyanoke refugees, 132; Federal Recognition, 229; Oral history, 197; Reservation, 197
Parliament, 56, 99, 136
Pasquotank Indigenous Americans, 165
Patawomek Indigenous Americans, 98
Pattanochus (Nansemond leader), 172
Pequot War (New England conflict), 32
Pocahontas, 3, 36, 218
Poteskeet Indigenous Americans, 165
Poverty, 171, 180
Powhatan Indigenous Americans: Use of palisades, 210
Powhatan Indigenous Americans, xvi, 103, 115, 138; 20th century reorganization, 228; Fishing during war, 181; Military tactics, 13, 16, 17, 19, 129; Origins, 4; Paramount chiefdom, 3; Population, 3; Post assault behavior, 92; Post-war coalescent communities, 216; Prisoners of war, 64, 85, 113, 135, 193, 201; Relationships with colonists, 39; Seasons, 7; Social Structure, 12; Subsistance, 4, 9; Territory, 3; Use of firearms, 74, 79; Warriors, 128; Wartime strategies, 68; Weapons, 15; Withdrawal following assault, 86
Powhatan Inigenous Americans: Spies, 59

Index

Powhite Indegenous Americans, 29
Powhite Indigenous Americans, 69, 146, 220
Premonitions, 67
Puritans, 57, 80, 84
Ralph Higginson, 147
Ralph Wormeley, 112, 244
Ralph Wormely, 147, 241
Rangers, 91
Rappahannock Indigenous Americans, 33, 98, 138, 178, 184, 187, 210, 218, 222
Reformation (privateer and merchant vessel), 137, 142
Richard Bennett, 123, 145, 148, 151, 152, 155, 200, 206
Richard Ingle, 51, 137
Richard Kemp, 34, 97, 98, 108, 112, 135, 140, 143, 148; Early life, 26; Response to royal orders, 117
Roanoke-Hatteras Indigenous Americans, 228
Robert Higginson, 245
Robin Tucker (Nansemond leader), 172
Rogar Marshall, 244
Roger Marshall, 173, 174
Royal orders to construct fortifications, 122
Sarah Woodson, 75
Seacocks, 95
Second Anglo-Powhatan War, xviii, 2
Secotan Indigenous Americans, 95
Severn River, 205
Sheriffs, 170
Sheriffs, embezzling public funds, 147
Sir John Berkeley, 148
Sir William Berkeley, 57, 79, 89, 92, 93, 96, 136, 148, 161, 163, 173, 184, 191, 195, 206, 215; Bodyguard, 217; Early life, 25, 87; Oath of allegiance, 101; Plans to put Opechancano on display, 194; Relationship with Virginian colonists, 25
Sir William Berkleley, 41
Slave (or servant) uprising, xix
Slavery, 204, 212, 221
Spanish incursions (1570s), 2
Susquehanna Indigenous Americans, 42
Swift Creek, 182
Taweeren (Rappahanock leader), 223
Third Anglo-Powhatan War: Powhatan assault, 3; Scope, 3
Thomas Deacon, 136, 141
Thomas Dewe, 164, 167, 244
Thomas Harris, 245
Thomas Ludwell, 202
Thomas Rolfe, 218
Thomas Rolfe (son of Pocahontas), 36
Thomas Rolphe, 245
Thomas Tuke, 170
Thomas Ward, 155, 241, 243
Tobbaco (as commodity), 38
Totopotomoi (Pamunkey leader), 172, 188, 212, 217, 225
Traders, 70
Travis Poythers, 183, 187
Tuscarora Indigenous Americans, 106, 132, 133, 153, 220

Upper Norfolk County, 94, 103, 145, 150, 151
Virginia: Ammunition shortage, 138; Ammunition shortages, 92, 96; Cavalry, 192; Consequences for trading with Powhatans, 49; Food shortages, 87; Forts, 145, 147, 163; Headright system, 6; Indentured servants, 92; Levies to fund war, 124; Low morale, 140, 179; Military structure, 12; Military tactics, 15, 16, 104, 135, 209; Militia organization, 107; Militia organziation, 103; Physical landscape, 7; Prisoners of war, 73, 173; Typical housing, 72; Use of horses, 210; Use of watercraft in warfare, 105; Virginian colonists, 9; Virginian Colonists, 7; Weapons, 14
Virginian General Assembly, 93
Virginian militia, xix
Wahunsenaca (Chief Powhatan), 3, 4, 21, 23
Walter Plecker, 227
Wareeks Creek, 152
Warrasquoyack Indigenous Americans, 95
Warreek Creek, 131
Warwick County, 105
Weapemeioc Indigenous Americans, 157
Weapemeioc Indigenous Americans, 155
Weyanoke Indigenous Americans, xix, 69, 74, 95, 96, 106, 114, 115, 146, 150, 152, 167, 200, 220; Battle against Pamunkey war party, 132
Weyanokes Indigenous Americans, 157
Wiccacon Creek, 131, 133, 167
Wiccocomico Indigenous Americans, 34
William Claiborne, 94, 95, 97, 103, 105, 107, 112, 138, 184, 206; abandons post as general, 142
William Harris, 136, 140
William Lenthall, 141
William Minifie, 123
William Strachey, 1
Williamsburg. *See* Middle Plantation
Yeopim Creek, 159, 200
Yeopim Indigenous Americans, 165
Yeopim River, 155
York County, 104, 185
York River, 104, 135

CPSIA information can be obtained
at www.ICGtesting.com
Printed in the USA
LVHW081053300622
722468LV00010B/269